Tal
Tales
&
Banter

Seán Óg O Ceallacháin

Costar Associates Ltd.

Other Books by The Author

Seán Óg - His Own Story
The Birth Of A Building
History Of Hermitage Golf Club (70 Minute Video)
Tall Tales & Banter

Radio Plays

An Braon Searbh
Aedín Agus An Chailleach

To Be Published

One Act Plays
A Scent Of Hawthorn
The Man From The Island

Tall Tales & Banter By Seán Óg O Ceallacháin.
Published by Costar Associates Ltd, 10 Burgh Quay, Dublin 2.
Tel: (01) 6798655 Fax: (01) 6792016
Printed by Kilkenny People.
November 1998.

Price £9.95
ISBN 0 9534527 0 0

This book is dedicated to my wife Ann, my son Finin, and daughters, Caitriona and Sinead.

"I think you must remember that a writer is a simple-minded person to begin with and to go on that basis. He is not a great thinker, he is not a great philosopher, he is a story teller." Erskine Caldwell 1958.

Réamhrá

Hugh O'Flaherty - Chief Justice

Hugh O'Flaherty

W hen I was in boarding school in St. Brendan's, Killarney, in the early 1950's I had the bright idea of purchasing an alley-cracker. This would really show up the others on the handball alley when I produced such a luxury item. In those days, Seán Óg had a sports shop here in Dublin and I duly dispatched my order and enclosed a postal order for what I reckoned would be the right amount. Back came a most apologetic letter from Seán Óg to say that while he had some alley-crackers in stock they were poor quality - so he would return my postal order for the time being but would keep me in mind when better stock arrived.

The scene shifts then to another aspect of Seán Óg's rich life. It is 1962. I think, and I am passing the sportdesk at the Evening Press office in Burgh Quay. Kerry have beaten Dublin earlier in the day despite Seán Óg's contrary predictions. Someone had rather mischievously left a green and gold cap at his place at the sportdesk. In comes Seán Óg, espies the cap and promptly puts it on declaring: "If the cap fits ..." True grit!

This book is a fine and comprehensive chronicle of an age whose customs and culture may be fast disappearing. When I admire from the outset, or walk carefully on its lush carpet with, the new Cusack Stand I think we have come a long way from the tale of "the Yank" recounted by Canón Sheehan in Sheehan in Glenanaar of a hurling tournament in the old days:-

" ... 'the Yank', throwing away a half burned cigar, and calmly divesting himself of coat and waistcoat, which he carefully rolled up and placed in the hands of a spectator, came forward, took up a caman, teased it, as if it were a Toledo blade, by leaning all his weight upon it, and said in an accent of cool indifference:

'Let me take a hand: I guess I can manage it."

Have we come too far in leaving the essential simplicity of these days? Is professionalism about to take over, is winning to be everything? Are we doing enough to preserve the essence of what Gaelic games should be about? It is too trite to blame the rules. My friend, Mick O'Connell, said that he never read the rules until he had given up playing and then could find nothing wrong with them. But if players do not obey the rules, can anyone do anything about it? There are, for example, only three things meant to do with your hands in Gaelic Football: catch (the ball that is), block and pass.

However, enough in the way of doubt and I suppose it is some consolation to reflect that in his own day in the earlier of the century Dick Fitzgerald in his book How to Play Gaelic Football thought there was too much pulling and dragging in the then "modern" game.

Now to Seán Óg's book: Tall Tales and banter, like the man himself, it is full of good humour in which nearly every one comes out well.

On reading through it, I was struck by the fact that my wife Kathleen (nee Brennan) had better credentials than I to write this foreword. After all, her father, Jack Brennan was a patron of the Sligo County Board - a position, in the past at least, generally reserved for the episcopate. As well, he was one of the umpires at that famous contest in the Polo grounds, New York, in 1947. Her sister, Christina Murphy, is a considerable GAA historian in her own right. Her cousin is Dr. Con Murphy whose warmth, kindness and many other human qualities are well captured here.

I recommend this book in a wholehearted way and I hope that we will continue to hear Seán Óg's dulcet tones calling out the names of those far flung towns and baronies for many years to come.

Of course, could it be any other way with the name that he bears because he cannot ever grow old. He must always be young. Neither can his wife Ann so I suppose we can adapt Keats's line from Ode on a Grecian Urn which also aptly enough speaks of "winning near the goal".

"For ever wilt thou love, and she be fair!"

By the way I never did get that Alley Cracker!

Hugh O'Flaherty
An Chúirt Uachtarach
Baile Átha Cliath.
The Supreme Court
Dublin.

Réamhrá

Joe McDonagh - President CLG

When I was asked to pen theses few words, my mind strayed back to my earliest memories of Seán Óg O Ceallacháin. I remember the many Sunday nights when, in the company of my father, we waited in anticipation for Seán Óg to enlighten us on the outcome of the Club games in Galway and from around the country. Then, Seán Óg provided the only link with the Club scene and while I was familiar with the names of the Galway Clubs, I often wondered at the seemingly exotic places he referred to from afar. Seán Óg also, of course, entertained us as a commentator with his own particular style and knowledge of the games adorning many an encounter.

It is only somebody with Seán's experience as a player and dedicated observer of our games could have compiled a work of "Tall Tales and Banter" such as this. We have always been regaled with stories and anecdotes on great players and Seán Óg has included many not heard of before in this wonderful refreshing and amusing book. They are all there, but my favourite is his cameo of Seán Purcell, a boyhood hero of mine and countless like me. Seán Óg has given selfless and trojan service to CLG and this represents another major contribution from a unique premise and not attempted before. It is a work that transcends the generations and will enthral its readers. I would commend it to anybody interested in the chronicle that is the colourful and unique history of the GAA and I am certain that it will prove as successful and popular as the author himself.

Seosamh Mac Donncha,
Uachtarán CLG.

Acknowledgements

The publication of this book would not have been possible without the great assistance of many friends and acquaintances. Michael Wright, former Offaly All- Ireland footballer and publisher of "Gaelic World" magazine and son Ken,were most enthusiastic about publishing the book.

Once again I had to avail of good friend and colleague Mick Dunne's comprehensive sports files and his knowledge of Gaelic games matters when I needed information checked. A special word of thanks also to Tom Woulfe, who read the manuscript and gave freely of his advice and supplied extra material. I would also like to thank my good friend, Michael Cronin, formerly of the "Irish Press Group" editorial staff for his careful scrutiny and corrections made prior to publication. This book would not have been published without the help of commercial sponsorship. I would like to pay a special word of thanks to Bank of Ireland head office for their immediate offer of sponsorship which cemented further my great friendship with the Bank stretching over a long period. I am extremely grateful to my other sponsors who rallied to my assistance and provided much needed sponsorship towards the book's publication. I would like to mention Cumann Luithchleas Gael; Leinster Council GAA; Church and General Insurance PLC; Irish Permenant PLC; RTE; TnaG; O'Neill's Sports International; Texaco; T&D Norton. I am endebted to John Gleeson whose book "Dictionary of Irish Sporting Greats" was an ideal reference source.

Again my grateful thanks to Michael Wright, his son Kenny for his typesetting, editorial and design expertise in producing this book. And my thanks also to all those friends of mine throughout the country, footballers, hurlers and officials, who gave me stories for inclusion in the book.

Mo Mhile Buiochas.

Contributors

I would like to acknowledge the great assistance I received from my journalistic friends who wracked their brains and produced some great strories which I was only too glad to include in this book. I am also indebted to Michael Wright of "Gaelic World" for the use of photographs from his library. I would like to thank all of those players and officials who were gracious enough to supply me with stories for inclusion in this book also. A special word of thanks to the following sports writers; Raymond Smith, Dave Guiney, John Guiton, Michael Dundon, Mick Dunne, Paddy Downey, Val Dorgan, Jimmy Magee, Mick Wright, Brian Carty, Miceal O Muirceartaigh, Eamon Young, Joe Lennon, Matt Fitzpatrick, Sean Murphy, Jack Mahon, Con Healy, Michael Commin, John Knox, Liam McDowell, Tim Horgan, Donal Carroll, John Roddy, J.J. Barrett, Tom Ryle, Owen McCann and may I be forgiven if I have omitted anybody.

PREFACE

It was Dinny Grey from the Na Fianna club, former Dublin minor football selector, who sowed the seed for this book. He suggested it to me at a club match at Parnell Park a couple of years ago. My good friend, Mick Dunne, the then editor of the "Gaelic World" GAA magazine, asked me to contribute a nostalgic piece for one of his productions and I submitted a few humorous stories about former great stars. It was following that publication that Dinny Grey's suggestion of a book resurrected itself and I proceeded to breathe life into the idea. So blame Dinny Grey for what now has emerged in the shape of this production. I have been involved with the Gaelic Athletic Association for over 60 years during which time I have travelled the 32 counties in the course of my work as a journalist in newspapers, radio and television. It has been my good fortune also to have played the game at top level, hurling and football, and have met virtually all of the players and county officials who will be encountered during the course of this book.

Naturally, the GAA has its own distinctive traditions, its characters both on and off the field, and its legendary figures, some of whom are still with us, some others who have passed to their eternal rewards.

The primary purpose of this book is to capture some of the great stories that make the rounds whenever a group of Gaels meet and relive past events, the scoring of a Christy Ring winning point: the Mickey "Rattler" Byrne shoulder which flattens: the cool defensive Pat Stakelum play: the Dinny Allen golf strategy: the Séamus O Riain's unusual New York cab driver: the Jimmy Keaveney pep talk: and many, many more which have gone into the making of this book.

Three former GAA Presidents make valuable and hilarious contributions as well as many other officials who have also shown us the sunny side of life.

This book is really a fun book with malice towards none. Some of the stories and events have passed into GAA folklore and belong to the counties from where they have stemmed. It is my hope that they will be accepted in the spirit in which they are being offered, and no offence is intended to anyone who may be mentioned. Some of the stories are lies, lies and more lies, and I believe every one of them.

I hope you, the gentle reader, will enjoy them too. The GAA is the largest sporting organisation in this country. Since its formation in 1884 it has produced leaders of great quality and renown, under whom the Association has flourished and continues to grow to this day. In 1968 I was involved in the promotion of the Cardinal Cushing Games in America, in which a London team was participating, and I had the good fortune to meet John P Collins, Assistant District Attorney for the Borough of Queens. He was Chairman of the American National Irish Immigration Committee. The committee was very much involved in pressuring political parties for support to increase Ireland's quota of visas to the United States. John P Collins was New York born, but his father was born in Ireland and took great pride in his Irish roots. John told me that when he was going through law school he had cited the rules of the GAA as the perfect example of democracy.

He was intrigued with the GAA set up, which his father had explained to him, where all the fundamental changes taking place in Ireland's largest sporting organisation came from the grass roots, the Club. He felt that true democracy was served when the smallest units could use their combined strength to make changes in the overall structures of the organisation, and change policy if such was needed. When I set out to gather material for this book I found that it was from the clubs that most of the stories emanated, be it about the characters in those clubs or about the clubs themselves. Naturally it was from the clubs that their legendary figures of later years emerged to take their places in GAA folk history. Sadly, the idea for this book wasn't thought about years ago, because some of the older club officials, great story tellers of past history, of big games, big named players and events, are no longer with us. I hope that this book will preserve some of the folk history of the past and encourage others to continue the good work.

Seán Óg O Ceallacháin.

CONTENTS

Brian Mullins ... of Dublin.

The Cassius Clay (Muhammad Ali) Saga

I n 1963 I got a call from RTE Sports Co-ordinator Oona Gormley, who asked me to travel to London to film commentaries on the Wembley Games, in hurling and football, an annual event promoted by the London GAA Board. The finals were played on a Saturday afternoon before big attendances at the famous stadium, where the FA final is staged. The tournament proceeds went to the London Board to pay off their running costs. It was a particularly busy weekend in London because Cassius Clay (Mohammed Ali), had arrived to prepare for his much publicised fight with British heavyweight champion, Henry Cooper, which was being staged the following weekend. The camera man on the trip was RTE staff man Sean Burke, with whom I had worked on many assignments for the Sports Department. The sound operator was Michael Francis. Sean Burke brought his Auricon camera which shot 1200 feet of film, and lasted 33 minutes. It was ideal for a Gaelic match at the time. It meant that he could film away without having to reload, using only two rolls to film an entire Gaelic match, but taking three rolls to film a soccer match.

The daily newspapers were covering the Wembley matches and most of the leading reporters were on the flight, including Peadar O'Brien of the Irish Press. Peadar told me he was hoping to get an interview with Cassius Clay before he left London. I confided to Peadar that I too, was hopeful of getting an interview with the great boxer, as I had a camera crew with me. Peadar and I contacted the Irish Press London editor Aidan

Cassius Clay (Muhammed Ali) talking to Jack Lynch (Taoiseach at the time) on the occasion of his fight with Al Blue Lewis at Croke Park in 1973.

Hennigan, who after a lot of phone calls pinpointed Cassius's whereabouts in London. He was staying with his entourage in the Piccadilly Hotel. My needs were more immediate than Peadar's, as I had to leave London shortly after the game on the Saturday, while he was staying on until the Monday. Sean Burke, Michael Francis and I checked into our hotel (booked for us by RTE, really a dreadful place, and we were not sorry to leave it when our job had been completed.)

I immediately phoned the Piccadilly Hotel and asked to be put through to the Cassius Clay's suite. The phone was answered by Angelo Dundee, the boxer's manager and trainer. I proceeded to give a spoof about being over from Ireland with a camera crew, hoping to get an interview with Cassius. I explained that a big boxing following would be travelling over from Ireland to watch the fight between Cooper and Clay, and an interview with Clay would help to boost the attendance from over the Irish Sea. I could sense he was impressed, but he would have to speak to Cassius. I said I would call around to the hotel later that evening and discuss matters with the star attraction. Angelo thought the suggestion made a lot of good sense and suggested we call around 8 o'clock. Sean Burke, Michael Francis and I duly presented ourselves at the Clay suite on the hour and were ushered in by Angelo Dundee.

After the usual exchange of greetings I again made my proposal about doing an interview with Cassius. Halfway through my preamble in swept the man of the hour himself, dressed in a ceremonial robe befitting an African king. He had in his entourage two striking Swedish blondes, one of them a masseuse, along with, I presumed, a couple of bodyguards. We got down to business after a brief exchange of identities (Seán Óg didn't ring a bell with him). I explained how a filmed interview with him would help to boost the fight takings enormously. He was very impressed. I asked him about doing the interview early on Saturday morning as we were booked to film the games at Wembley Stadium in the afternoon. Cassius said he worked out at 6 am if that was suitable. Sean Burke was doing his best to attract my attention. " Does that present any problems?" asked Cassius looking at Sean Burke. I shook my head and said no. I wasn't going to miss the chance of a lifetime getting an interview with Cassius. Sean Burke kept shaking his head and blurted out: "It can't be done." "What's the problem?" asked Cassius. " The problem is simple," said Burke, "we have no batteries for outdoor interviews." Sean was dead right. I hadn't thought about batteries for the camera. Cassius came up with the answer. " What about the gym?" The gym hadn't been mentioned up till then. " What gym?" I asked. " The gym in White City Stadium where I work out. I will be there at noon." Our problem was solved. We arrived in White City Stadium in plenty of time, and Sean set up his equipment. Cassius had a number of boxers helping out in his preparations for the big fight, including Jimmy Ellis, a little-known American, who was in later years to become a victim of Clay's punching power when Cassius knocked him out in a title defence. Exactly at noon, Cassius swept into the arena, ready to start his workout with Ellis. I explained to him that I had procured a punch ball and had tied it to a stand and placed it near us, at the ring side; When the interview was coming to an end, I wanted him to unleash one of his big punches, just to demonstrate his awesome power. On the signal from Sean Burke I started the interview with "The Greatest", who proceeded to use all the now famous asides: " I float like a butterfly and I sting like a bee" and "look at my face, smooth as a baby's bottom, I'm the prettiest boxer in the world." During the course of the interview I asked him had he heard of a great Irish battler called "Conn of the 100 fights". Back came the answer, " Yeah, but did he win them all?" I assured him he had. "You find him and I'll fight him" said the bould Cassius, even a small bit of Irish mythology failed to knock him off stride. It was really a great bit of fun, and Cassius entered into the swing of things. Coming to the end of the interview I motioned to him that we were ready to do the piece with the punch ball, our get-out-piece.

I set him up by asking him to demonstrate his punching power. In a completely unrehearsed action, he leapt over to where the punchball was, drew back his arm and unleashed a punch which sent the punchball soaring high into the air, missing Sean Burke's

World Champion Muhammad Ali knocks out Al Blue Lewis in Croke Park in July 1973.

camera by a mere inches. He then turned and roared; "What kind of a dump is this? Dundee, get me a new gym", and went storming off in a show of high dudgeon. It was the greatest piece of showmanship I had ever witnessed. Sean Burke had captured the whole performance on film, down to the punchball finale. A few minutes later Cassius returned and inquired: " Did you get all that?" We assured him we had. " Where did you guys say you're from?" he asked. I refreshed his memory. "See you at the fight" he said, and disappeared.

We had only time to pack up our gear and get a taxi to bring us to Wembley Stadium. We filmed both matches there before a big attendance, but quite honestly, I was thinking more about my Cassius piece and the reaction it would have when shown. Michael Francis, our sound man, intimated that he knew a friend in ITV who would pay handsomely for the Cassius interview. Sean Burke quickly put his mind at rest, emphasising that the film was RTE property, and that was that. When we arrived back in Dublin on Saturday evening, Sean Burke left the film for processing.

The following day I brought it to the editing room just to see it. It was, in my humble view, a classic, just as Sean Burke had described it. After a while more and more members of the staff began drifting into the small viewing room. The film editor, Danny Donoghue, kept showing it until Esther Byrne, the Sports Production Assistant, was alerted, and she arrived to take possession of the film on behalf of the Sports Department. A decision was taken to show the Cassius interview on the Thursday sports programme. Everybody in the Sports Department was delighted and amused with the filmed interview, but a slight snag loomed. Pope John XXIII was dying; if he passed away on the Wednesday, all TV programmes would have to be cancelled. It meant that the filmed interview would have no relevance, if it was not shown before the actual fight in the Wembley Stadium on the Friday. Pope John went into a coma on the Thursday and died peacefully on the Friday.

The Cassius interview went out as scheduled on Thursday's "Sport at Seven" programme and it made an instant impact. There was a barrage of phone calls from viewers requesting another showing, and overall the calls were very complimentary. The Sports Department received many calls over the following days asking that the Cassius interview be shown again; most of the requests came from people who hadn't seen the programme, but who had been told of its content. Unfortunately it was never shown again. The film disappeared a few days after its initial showing and was never found.

However, I felt a great sense of achievement having secured the interview with boxing's most colourful personality. The big fight at Wembley was a dramatic affair. Cassius was dumped on the canvas by a Henry Cooper left hook to the jaw in the third round, but two rounds later Cassius got his decision when Henry had to retire with a cut eye.

I played golf with Henry in the Clontarf club some years ago on the occasion of Shay Smith's "Press Radio & Television" Captain's prize. Henry told me that but for the cut eye, he would have beaten "The Greatest". It always reminded me of the old boxing story about the guy who staggers back to his corner in very poor shape, to be told by his trainer, " You're doing all right, he hasn't laid a glove on you." Three minutes later, the poor guy staggers back to his corner, this time with a black eye and a slight cut on his nose, to be told, "You're doing great, he hasn't laid a glove on you." To which the boxer replied, "Well, keep an eye on the bloody referee, because somebody is hitting me."

Driving off the 10th at Clontarf Colf club, from left, Henry Cooper, Sean Og and Bob McGregor.

Seán O Síocháin - *Former Director General of the G.A.A.*

**" If you can talk with crowds and keep your virtue
Or walk with kings - nor lose the common touch" - Rudyard Kipling.**

One thing that can be said of Seán, he never lost the common touch. His position as Ard Stiúrthóir of the GAA demanded many attributes which he measured up to fully. But patience was one of his greatest assets for such a demanding position. Sean had a marvellous sense of humour and he was never afraid to tell a story against himself. Indeed, it is to my regret, that I never chronicled all the stories he told me on holidays with him or on golf courses, playing with him. Sean always sat in on the Carrolls and Bank of Ireland All- Star Selection meetings in his capacity as Ard Stiúrthóir. During a break in one such meeting, Mick Dunne, Paddy Downey and myself tried to take a 'rise' out of Sean over the way the sports writers were treated in the allocation of All-Ireland tickets. It was all to no avail. But it did prompt him to tell us a true story about All- Ireland tickets. Jer O'Leary of High St Killarney was a great friend of Seán O Síocháin. He was also a treasure house as far as Mick Dunne and Paddy Downey were concerned. They would never pass his antique shop when visiting Kerry, on the occasion of an All- Ireland final, when both journalists were gathering information for their All Ireland previews. Jer was a mine of information. He had press cuttings going back many years, he had old photographs of Kerry teams, in fact, he was really a walking encyclopaedia on Kerry matters. He was a very kind man, most helpful, and was a great loss to the county and indeed to the press when he passed away. Seán O Síocháin always sent him tickets for the All-Irelands because of his great work for the Association in Kerry. A year after his death Seán received a letter from a daughter of Jer. It arrived three days before an All- Ireland football final. When Seán looked at the envelope, he saw it was addressed to "Seán O Síocháin, Oulton Road, Templeogue, Dublin." The postage date was two weeks before the actual All-Ireland football final. The letter writer wanted to know if the same arrangement for All-Ireland tickets was still in place, now that her father had departed this world, if so, would he send her the two tickets for the All-Ireland final. Seán, in his usual meticulous way, wrote back immediately to the O'Leary household explaining why no tickets wended their way to Kerry. He gently pointed out that the letter which had been sent to him had been addressed to Seán O Síocháin, Oulton Rd, Templeogue, Dublin. He explained that he lived on the North side, in Clontarf, consequently the postal authorities took a while to locate Seán, who was unlisted in the phone book.

A few days later Sean received a reply from Jer's daughter, acknowledging his letter. She accepted his explanation and apology........ but the last paragraph had the 'sting' in it. "Mr O Síocháin .... if a letter with just " Kerry" on it had been sent to Small Jer O'Leary it would have been delivered in Killarney the following morning ... maybe you're not as well known or as famous as you think."

I can recall a story relating to Seán and me concerning an All-Ireland ticket. I was returning from a match in the midlands, I had dispatched my match report for RTE Sport before leaving the venue. I got caught up in the crowd spilling out of the ground which delayed me but eventually I was on the road back to the capital. I was travelling a little faster than I normally would, trying to make up lost time, when I was caught in a Garda speed trap outside of a provincial town. The Garda quickly reminded me that I had exceeded the speed limit, in a 30 mph area, which I could not deny. I could see that my excuse for breaking the speed limit was having no effect on the guardian of the law. I then threw in the fact that I was genuinely hurrying back to Dublin to compile my Sunday night result programme but again to no avail. The Garda listened patiently to my tale of woe and handed me a speeding ticket, telling me to watch my speed limit the next time I was entering a town. A few days later I phoned my local GAA

Sean O Siochain, the late former Director General of the G.A.A.

correspondent in the town where I had got the speeding ticket and I asked him could he do anything about it for me. He rang me back a few days later, he had contacted the particular Garda and the story was, if I had a ticket to spare for the All-Ireland football final, he would see what he could do. I dropped into Seán O Síocháin in his office at Croke Park and explained my dilemma. He was most sympathetic after hearing my story. My heart gave a start when he next said " although all the tickets for the final have been disposed of, I have one ticket that might fill the bill." I never give it out because it is on the Cusack Stand, but you can have it with pleasure. " But" said Seán, holding up his finger, " I would advise you, never to exceed the speed limit in that particular town again or you may be in bigger trouble." Naturally that warning aroused my curiosity and I prevailed on the genial Seán to explain the warning. "Well, I don't give that particular ticket out for the simple reason, that it is behind a large pillar and the occupant of the seat will spend the whole of the match dodging from side to side trying to follow the play." said Seán. I took the ticket and quickly dispatched it to my contact. I always made sure to stick to the speed limit passing through towns afterwards.

The former Director-General of the GAA and I played a lot of golf together, be it on my home turf at Hermitage Golf club, where Seán was a five day member, or at his club Royal Dublin. We played in a number of charity outings and a third member of that team was well-known auctioneer and Insurance broker Shane Redmond. I got a call from Sean asking me to play in a charity outing at a North Dublin golf club. Both of us had engagements later that day so it had to be an early start, and that also suited Shane Redmond.

Our teeing time was 9 am and we were the first team of the many supporting the deserving charity outing to drive off. I had already driven off when a car swept into the car park beside the first tee. A figure emerged dressed in a club blazer and he headed in our direction. He quickly introduced himself as the captain of the club and thanked us for supporting the outing. Sean O Siochain introduced us to the club captain, first Shane Redmond and turning to me, said to the captain, " and you know Seán Óg."

The captain exchanged another few words with us, wished us well and allowed us to go on our merry way. We enjoyed the game of golf and the good natured banter which Corkonian O Síocháin invariably indulged in with Shane and myself. Unfortunately Seán and I were unable to attend the dinner and prizegiving that evening but we were represented by Shane, who did attend.

When speech time arrived at the dinner that evening, the club captain began by thanking all the players who had turned out in support of the charity which had raised a lot of money for a very good cause. " Indeed " said the captain " I was here early this morning to wish the first team comprised of Shane Redmond, Seán O Síocháin and his son Seán Óg the best of luck"

It brought the house down but the unfortunate captain didn't realise his error until it was pointed out to him later but he took the ensuing ribbing in the best of spirits. But I didn't let Mr. O Síocháin off the hook either, and for a good while afterwards, when I would phone him for a game of golf, I would preface my remarks by saying, " this is your son, Dad, are we playing golf today?"

Jimmy Magee - The Memory Man

My good friend Jimmy and I have been in the communication business for many years now and during all that time I never cease to marvel at his great capacity to remember teams, players, title winners, not alone in my own Gaelic Games sphere but in other codes as well. He has a phenomenal memory of events and incidents and well merited the name of "The Memory Man". He is very much in demand on sporting programmes, be it radio or television, and is held in high esteem by former and present day players, especially in soccer circles. We shared many great laughs playing on the Jimmy Magee "All Stars" team. I had the distinction of playing on the first team, along with my old pal, Frankie Byrne of Meath, to launch the Jimmy Magee "All Stars" charity games away back in 1965 in Ballyjamesduff, County Cavan. I recall Jack Mahon of Galway telling me a story about Jimmy. Jack, incidentally, also savoured the thrill of playing either with or against the "Magee All Stars" but Jimmy insisted that the great Galway centre back really made his name when playing with his "All Stars" selection. Jack's story goes like this. Jimmy Magee was working for RTE radio many years ago covering the World Cup in soccer in Mexico City. He set off for a meal after finishing work one evening and in his search for a place to eat, with some of the other reporters covering the game, he saw a huge sign which caught his eye, "Hiawatha", the Memory Man. Jimmy and his friends entered this saloon type bar, and there sitting on a stool was a Red Indian, named Hiawatha. A notice beside him stated; that Hiawatha would answer any question on the payment of $5, and if he failed to answer a question posed, the questioner would receive $5 and his original $5 back. Naturally Jimmy was coerced into taking up the challenge with Hiawatha. Without hesitation Jimmy stepped up to Hiawatha and said: "Hello" and Hiawatha replied "How, what is your question?" Jimmy said: "Who won the 1947 All Ireland Senior Hurling final?" Quick as a flash Hiawatha said: "Kilkenny won that match." Jimmy had lost his $5. Ten years later Jimmy was back again in Mexico City for a World Cup series and this time he decided to visit "Hiawatha" who was still in business. Jimmy had, what he thought, was a question which would really stump his Mexican opposite. Jimmy walked up to "Hiawatha" and held up his hand by way of greeting and said "How". Hiawatha quickly replied: "Terry Leahy, with a last minute point."

The "Jimmy Magee All Stars" played matches all over the country raising money for needy charities. Famous show band stars, great players, present and past, from various codes, all contributed to making the charity matches a great success. The "Magee All Stars" were invited to Ardee, Co. Louth to play a Louth team comprised of former great players, and it too was an outstanding success. Newcomer to the "Magee" bunch was a young Tony O'Hehir, son of the renowned, Michael. Now Tony, and he was the first to admit it, is a racing man out and out, and playing football was never his forte. But he was persuaded to play with the "Magee All Stars" against a very formidable Louth team, who included the famous defender Jim "Red" Meehan.

The "Red" Meehan in his day was undoubtedly one of the great half backs in football. He was fearless. He never believed in going around an opponent with the ball but invariably opted for the direct method, scattering friend and foe alike. And Tony

O'Hehir was soon to learn what it was like playing against one of the toughest defenders of his day, now facing him on the green sward of the Ardee pitch. There are ways of tackling a defender, if you are a forward, and there are ways you should not even try. It will never be known how he accomplished it, but Tony chased after a loose ball with the "Red" Meehan bearing down on him. Tony stuck his boot in to get at the ball, the "Red" Meehan went over Tony's outstretched foot and crashed to the ground.

He needed attention immediately and eventually had to be assisted off the pitch. Tony was very put out about the incident but he was assured by all and sundry that it just one of those things that often cropped up even in the most important of matches. The match itself ended, as usual, in a draw, the "All Stars" never lost a game. Later on in the "All Stars" dressing room the wags on the team, including Mr. Magee himself, didn't spare the gentle and the innocent Tony O'Hehir. Magee, the chief collaborator of the villany, said to Tony: "Do you realise what you are after doing? "Do you realise that hundreds of guys for years tried it and failed, and you came down here to Ardee, the gentle, meek son of the great Michael O'Hehir and you 'did' the great Jim Meehan."

An anxious Tony simply asked: "Who is he?" Magee replied: " When you go home, ask your father."

Jimmy McGee seen here collecting an Award from the Ulster Writers Asssociation.

Former GAA President Peter Quinn attended one of the Jimmy Magee All Stars matches. It took place in Lisnaskea, in his native Fermanagh. He enjoyed the game and the social function which followed. Jimmy remembered him telling a story about a great character in the county who used to live and breathe football. He could always be found telling willing listeners about his prowess as a footballer in the good old days. Naturally, the stories got better in the telling, and he was egged on by guys who had heard the stories time and again. Describing football in his day, the old character would say: "When I'd gupped for the ball, and when I got her, and I'd nearly always get her, I would kick her, right or left foot, over the bar, oh, from about ninety or a hundred yards, no bother. If you don't believe me, ask the late John Joe O'Reilly."

I remember playing with the "Magee All Stars" in Carrick-on-Suir against a Munster All Star selection, which included Christy Ring, Pat Stakelum, John Doyle, Babs Keating Liam Donnelly (Dublin) and a host of other great hurling and football stars. Our chauffeur that day for the trip to Carrick was Fr. Mick Cleary, and Frankie Byrne, Tommy Farrell, of Shamrock Rovers fame, and yours truly, were the passengers. It was the usual great occasion and a big attendance turned out to see the Show band stars, Brendan Bowyer, Tom Dunphy, Dermot O Brien, Larry Cunningham, Connie Lynch, Joe Dolan and the rest pitting their talents against the Munster household names. As the final whistle sounded, a great hurling star, who must remain nameless, holder of many All Ireland medals, turned to Tom Dunphy of the Royal Show band and said, in all seriousness: " well done, and I hope you win it out now." He was still living his younger days.

I remember that Carrick match for one particular reason. Fr. Mick Cleary, sustained a dislocated shoulder in an accidental collision with one of the opposition.

I had to drive his car home, a very painful journey for Fr. Mick. He still said 7 o'clock Mass the following morning. He was the curate in the parish and always celebrated the early Mass. Jimmy Magee, tells a story about a character in his native Cooley, in County Louth, away back, as he puts it, in the old days when a radio could only work on a "wet" battery. The battery had to be charged from time to time, in order to listen to the big games on the Sunday. This character took the train to Dundalk so that he could leave the "wet" battery in for charging. Much to his horror, the battery, resting on his lap leaked, and the acid burned holes in the front of his trousers. When the train arrived in Dundalk the poor man had to go to the station master and borrow a raincoat which covered the essentials. The lads in Cooley cruelly named him as the original "Flasher" when the story got around, they also claimed, that he was a baritone in the church choir who now sang tenor.

Bobby Doyle & Kevin Moran of Dublin

"**I** want you to sign for Manchester United, and I would like to complete the formal signing before you leave Manchester Airport." said United team manager Dave Sexton as he drove Kevin Moran to the airport. Kevin looked at the Manchester supremo and said: " I will have to think about it, and I'll let you know." Sexton looked with amazement at Kevin and replied " Do you know what you have just said? You will think about signing for the biggest club in Britain. Nobody has ever had to think about signing for United, and you tell me that you will think about it." Sexton, one of the finest individuals one could possibly meet and a very successful manager, has repeated that story many, many times since. But one has to go back to the situation which prevailed at the time and the circumstances which led to an unknown Irishman being offered terms by one of the biggest clubs in Britain. Kevin Moran's soccer career in his native Dublin bore no relation to the events which were later to bring him international fame, when he subsequently joined Manchester United. Kevin, who graduated with a B.Comm degree from UCD, played with Pegasus and his most memorable game was against Dundalk in Oriel Park when he outclassed no less a figure than Jimmy Dainty, a former English international left winger. Present at that game was Manchester United talent scout Billy Behan, and Moran's name went into his book. Kevin continued to play with Pegasus and eventually he signed up for a season or two with Bohemians. Kevin, in the meantime was playing Gaelic football with Good Counsel, Crumlin , and was the driving force for them at midfield. When Dublin lost the 1975 All- Ireland to Kerry, manager Kevin Heffernan and his co- selectors Donal Colfer and Lorcan Redmond felt that the side needed strengthening in the half - back line. The three officials decided to have a look at potential players in the local senior League. Donal, being a southsider, took himself off to O'Toole Park to watch a St Vincent de Paul tournament match between Good Counsel and Civil Service, who sported a number of leading inter- county stars. Kevin Moran played in his usual mid -field position and he was opposed by one of Donegal's best players Anton Carroll. Donal Colfer couldn't take his eyes off Moran. Here was a young 20 year old or so playing his heart out against a very experienced inter- county star and more than holding his own. But what Donal particularly liked was Moran's courage and commitment even though his side was losing the match, Moran never relented, he kept battling away until the very end, his strength being a very important factor. Donal got in touch immediately with Kevin Heffernan and told him that he believed he had the man for centre- half- back. That was good enough for "Heffo" and Kevin Moran was called into the Dublin squad to prepare for the 1976 season.

Kevin Moran quickly settled into the tough training sessions which Dublin always embarked upon at the start of a new season. Kevin was quickly accepted and got used to the slagging when told where Croke Park was, and how to get there, but he was to face a different situation when he arrived at Croke Park for his first National League game. Kevin got there in plenty of time and headed for the Dublin dressing room. He took his time togging off, just chatted away to some of the subs who had arrived before him. Kevin sat at the end of the bench and placed his bag of playing gear underneath. Bobby Doyle breezed in to the dressing room and walked over to where Kevin was sitting. " Up you get , Moran, you are sitting in my seat." Moran, moved up to allow "Doyler" take his perch. Next in was Gay O'Driscoll, who sauntered over to where Kevin was sitting, and the newcomer to the squad, was again forced out of his seat at the behest of Gay, who also claimed that Kevin was sitting in his spot. And so it went on, as the dressing room filled with Dublin players, each in turn sat in his allotted place, a practice started after the team won the 1974 All- Ireland. No matter where Dublin played after that success, either at home or away each player sat in his designated place and that applied to training as well. Matters were smoothed for newcomer Moran when Brian Mullins grabbed him by the shirt front and said: "O K Kevin, I'm looking after you now, you sit there beside me" and from then on Kevin Moran had his own patch on the dressing room seat, and he made sure that nobody else sat on it.

No doubt about it, the advent of Kevin Moran, flanked by two other newcomers, Tommy Drumm and Pat O'Neill, solved the selectors problem. They were a brilliant half back line. Dublin defeated Kerry in the '76 All- Ireland final. and Kevin won his first All- Ireland senior medal. As he explained to me: " I was really caught up in the whole euphoria of the Dublin scene. The sight of the 'Hill' on match day was mind boggling, and the dedication of the Dublin fans was really unbelievable. I had never experienced anything like it, I would have died for those guys, with their banners, their colours, whole families were part of that scene and we played for them. We had the best supporters in the world and that's something I never forgot during my years with the Dubs." But Manchester United scout Billy Behan was still very keen that Kevin Moran would go to Manchester for a trial but the Dublin star told him that he was too involved with Dublin and he would have to think about it. It was back to training for the League and of course the 1977 championship. Dublin retained their Leinster crown and qualified for the All- Ireland semi final clash with great rivals Kerry. That 1977 All- Ireland semi final was hailed as being the best exhibition of football ever served up by the counties, and Dublin once again claimed the honours. The Dublin players really celebrated after that back to back success.

Beating Kerry, who epitomised all that was good in the game, equalled the feryour that manifested itself after the 1976 victory which bridged a gap of 54 years since Dublin's previous win in a final against the mighty Kingdom. Kevin Moran and Bobby Doyle and the rest of the team took off for their favourite watering hole. Celebrations ran late and Bobby, who was a particularly close friend of Kevin, enjoyed himself immensely.

But Bobby felt that Kevin had something on his mind. He became morose and started muttering under his breath. Bobby asked him was he feeling unwell. Kevin said he was very upset and kept repeating it. "What's wrong with you? asked Bobby. " Do you know what I have done? said Kevin, " I've turned down Manchester United. Bobby still wasn't clear what prompted Kevin's change of attitude and repeated the question, " But what's wrong with you". Kevin appeared to be near to tears. " Manchester United want me and I turned them down. They wanted me over for a trial last year but I wouldn't go because I was playing with the Dubs." Bobby assured him that Manchester United would get back again to him and to forget about it. Bobby said that once Kevin had got the pressing matter off his chest he brightened up and they returned to the victory celebrations. Dublin went on to win the 1977 All- Ireland final beating Armagh and Kevin Moran now had two Senior All- Ireland medals.

There was very little break between the All- Ireland final and the start of the League which had been changed to two divisions, North and South. Billy Behan had approached Kevin before the All-Ireland final and asked him would he again consider going to Manchester for a trial At that particular time Kevin was still luxuriating in the winning of his second All-Ireland medal, but Behan was persistent and said that Kevin would do well to re-appraise the situation. A place in the Manchester squad would earn him big money and all that went with it. Kevin was in a pickle, but rather than dismiss the suggestion, he told Billy Behan to give him more time to think about it. Billy Behan was a very nice, courteous gentleman and Kevin respected him very much especially since he had helped many other players to join the famed Manchester club. The National Football League commenced on October 23rd and Dublin won their five matches to win the section and qualify for the quarter finals. Their opening game was against Kerry and 25,000 saw them beat the Kingdom by one point in Croke Park. An attendance of 20,000 watched them take the points against Cork in Cork and big crowds watched them in their wins against Kildare, Offaly and Galway. Kevin Moran figured in all five matches at centre-half back when the series went into the winter break. It was only when Billy Behan again contacted him that Kevin sat down to think about his future. Behan asked him to go for a two weeks trial to Manchester but Kevin said two weeks was too long, that he would go for three days.

Arrangements were made for Kevin's three day trial. It meant a quick trip over and nobody, especially the press, would know anything about it. Kevin himself didn't believe that anything would come of the visit but he felt he owed it to Billy Behan who had worked so hard on his behalf. Kevin was taken in hand by Manchester United manager Dave Sexton, to put it in Kevin's words, a complete gentleman. Kevin played in a reserve match and everybody seemed pleased with his performance. Medically he was found to be physically fit so there was no worry on that score. Dave Sexton drove Kevin back to the airport and on the way the Manchester manager said that he was very pleased with his trial workout and that he would like to have him on his panel. He then made Kevin the fabulous offer quoted at the begining of this story and Kevin's initial reaction which left Dave Sexton shaking his head. However, everything was eventually resolved to Kevin's satisfaction. He signed on as a professional with Manchester United at the end of February 1978. Kevin wasn't called into the first team squad but spent most of his time learning his trade with the reserves. Ken Montgomery, a Scot, and a leading sports writer with a Manchester newspaper wasn't too impressed with the young Irishman when he first saw him in action.

"He hadn't absorbed the pace of English football but no one could deny his courage or his commitment. He went in with his head where others would hesitate. He was in fact fearless and that was a quality which Dave Sexton liked very much." Kevin Moran lived in Manchester and came back to Dublin when the soccer season ended.

Dublin were preparing for the Leinster Championship first round against Carlow in Dr Cullen Park, Carlow. Kevin asked Tony Hanahoe could he do a bit of pre-season training with the Dubs and 'Hano' agreed. There was great speculation in the Dublin newspapers when Kevin Moran wearing a Dublin track suit, took part in the pre-match warm up at Dr. Cullen Park. But the fans were disappointed, he just sat in the substitute bench and was not called into the action. When the match reporters asked Tony and his selectors, Donal Colfer and Lorcan Redmond after the win against Carlow about the presence of Moran, they told the truth, he was in mid-season training for his English club.

Bobby Doyle in action in his days with Dublin.

Dublin's next championship outing was against Offaly in Portlaoise but Kevin Moran was not chosen for that match. It turned out to be a very competitive game and there were slight tremors in the selectorial area as Offaly were more than holding their own with the title holders. Manager Tony Hanahoe, Donal Colfer and Lorcan Redmond were also on edge, and at half-time the decision was taken to bring on Kevin Moran to plug a weakness in the defence, which had been very apparent. Ten minutes into the second half, Dermot Maher, who had got a knock, was taken off and Kevin Moran was installed at centre half-back. Selector Donal Colfer told me after that game that the decision to introduce Moran was the move which swung the game Dublin's way, plus of course a great goal from John McCarthy. It was the day that the crossbar broke, and very nearly crowned Paddy Cullen. Offaly star Sean Lowry agreed after the match that the appearance of Moran transformed Dublin from a losing team to a winning one. The "Dubs" went on to retain their provincial crown beating Kildare convincingly in the final. Naturally the reappearance of Kevin Moran was the subject of much media speculation. He was a professional soccer player and some of the sports writers began questioning Moran's credentials and his involvement with the Dublin team. But Kevin Moran had already secured the permission of his Manchester club to play with the county so he ignored the media hype on the matter. Dublin met Down in the All-Ireland semi-final. Donal Colfer and Lorcan Redmond readily agreed to a request from manager Tony Hanahoe for Kevin Heffernan to give a hand out in the preparations for the Down match which Dublin won readily enough. Kevin Moran, who was the sheet anchor at centre half-back, bid farewell to his team colleagues and management body, as he had to report back for pre-season training with Manchester United. Kerry in the meantime, had secured their place in the All-Ireland final following a decisive win over Roscommon. So the scene was set for another Dublin-Kerry confrontation. The fact that Kevin Moran was now back in Manchester was already occupying the minds of the media. Would Kevin Moran be allowed to play in the All-Ireland final? Would the Dublin selectors seek the permission of the Manchester club for Moran's inclusion on the final team.? Unknown to the Dublin management team, colleague Mick Dunne was already making arrangements to travel to Manchester with an RTE camera crew to film an interview with Kevin Moran for his TV All-Ireland preview. Mick had contacted Kevin Moran, who informed him that if Dave Sexton gave his permission for him to play in the All-Ireland final, Mick could certainly travel to Manchester and do the interview.

Mick Dunne immediately contacted Dave Sexton and explained his mission. He was preparing a TV All-Ireland preview programme and there had been much speculation in the Irish papers concerning Kevin Moran. Would the Manchester club release him for the big game? Sexton said he had no objection and if Kevin wanted to play he could do so with his blessing. He was asked had he any objections to Mick filming an interview with Kevin Moran in Old Trafford, and perhaps with himself. Sexton gave his permission but mentioned that he might be otherwise engaged. A date and time was arranged and Mick asked him would he tell Moran about the TV interview arrangements.. Dave Sexton confessed that he had never been at an All-Ireland final but he had heard about the game from former Irish International Noel Cantwell. It was he who told Sexton that he need not worry about Kevin Moran playing before big crowds at Old Trafford. Moran, had been playing before capacity crowds of 75,000 at Croke Park Mick thanked the Manchester supremo for his kind assistance and started making arrangements for the Moran T V piece. Meanwhile, the back room team of Tony Hanahoe, Donal Colfer and

Lorcan Redmond, assisted by Kevin Heffernan, were discussing matters relating to the forthcoming All-Ireland final clash with Kerry. They could see no way that Dublin could beat Kerry without the services of Kevin Moran at centre half-back. The problem could only be solved in Manchester. Kevin Moran had been permitted to play with Dublin when he was back home but he was now domiciled in Manchester and was most likely to be offered a first team place. When Dublin Secretary Jim King contacted Kevin Moran, he was told by the player that he would be delighted to play but this time they would have to talk to manager Dave Sexton. Kevin had omitted saying to Jim King that Mick Dunne from RTE had been on asking the same question. The issue was so important that Tony Hanahoe and Kevin Heffernan were delegated to go to Old Trafford and place the request for Moran's services before Sexton. It was all very hush hush and news of the visit of the two Dublin team officials to Manchester was kept a closely guarded secret. When Tony and Kevin reached Old Trafford they were directed to United's training ground where Kevin Moran and the rest of the United squad were working out. Kevin Moran had been told by Sexton before he went out on the training ground that he had his permission to play with Dublin in the All-Ireland final if he wished to to do so. He also told him that an Irish (RTE) film crew would be at the United ground after the training workout to do some interviews with him. When Tony Hanahoe and Kevin Heffernan put their case to Sexton about Moran he readily agreed. But he did stress, jocosely, that he wanted him back all in one piece. .

Tony and Kevin were very much taken by Dave Sexton, whom they found to be most helpful and courteous. He insisted on showing them around Old Trafford and before leaving Tony invited him over for the All Ireland final as their guests. He was delighted and told them to keep in touch. (Dave Sexton never made the trip over for the All-Ireland final, fog closed the Manchester airport on the Saturday night.) Having bid farewell to Dave Sexton the two Dublin team officials came out to the car park as Mick Dunne and his RTE camera crew were arriving to do the arranged interview with Kevin Moran, and needless to say, both were taken aback at the RTE man's presence. Kevin Moran appeared and after a quick word with Tony and Kevin, was marched off to do interviews with Mick Dunne, which were shown on his All-Ireland Final Special the day before the match. Kevin Moran was named at centre half back on the Dublin team to play Kerry in that 1978 final and put an end to the media speculation over his inclusion. Kevin Moran, flew over from Manchester on the Monday of All-Ireland week and joined up with his colleagues for training at Parnell Park on Tuesday night. To everyone's horror, Kevin pulled a hamstring during the session and team colleague at wing back, Dr. Pat O'Neill, advised him to take no further part in training. Kevin Moran's injury was a well kept secret and when he appeared out on the field on All-Ireland day, he had a heavily strapped thigh. Under normal circumstances he would not have been allowed to play but Moran brushed aside all suggestions and insisted on playing against Kerry. He was to pay dearly for that decision later. It was obvious from the start that Moran's hamstring was restricting him but it didn't effect his all round play. He performed as fearlessly as ever and during the course of the game he went down to collect a ball in a ruck of players. A Kerry forward came sliding in and his knee caught Moran on the forehead, splitting it wide open. Dublin selector Lorcan Redmond attended to him immediately but he couldn't stop the flow of blood, so severe was the cut. David Hickey, later to qualify as a doctor, suggested

After match chat ... From left, Kevin Heffernan, Tony Hanahoe and Kevin Moran.

Vaseline ointment for the cut, and Lorcan successfully doctored the wound with the ointment before bandaging Kevin's forehead. When Lorcan finished his job he mentioned to Kevin that he should leave the field and allow a replacement in. Kevin gave him a stony glare and said: "no f...k..g way, I'm finishing this match" and he did. The story of the 1978 All-Ireland final is now part of the history of the game. Dublin were well beaten at the end despite dominating the first half in convincing fashion. Kevin Moran returned to Manchester a few days after the All-Ireland, having to get five stitches in his forehead and a badly torn hamstring ligament, which was to keep him out of football for two months.

It still didn't prevent Kevin Moran from achieving a unique record which may never be equalled by becoming the first player ever to win an All-Ireland senior football medal and an English FA Cup medal. Kevin won his two FA Cup medals in 1983 and 1985. He won his two All-Ireland senior football medals in 1976 and '77. He gained a Carrolls All-Star award in 1976.

Kevin Moran, affectionately known as "The Man of Iron" at the Manchester club got a lot of good natured slagging from the team members over appearing back from his sojourn in Dublin, with the hamstring and forehead injury. He was reminded that Joe Jordan, had played the whole season at centre-forward and never got a scratch. Moran goes over to Dublin to play in one Gaelic match and comes back a "wreck". "It must be some game", said Jordan to Kevin.

Sean Purcell of Tuam

They were know as the "Terrible Twins" and for very good reason. They wreaked havoc on opposing defences and their inter- passing and shrewd positional play made them the most feared and most formidable football partnership in the game. Sean Purcell and Frank Stockwell inspired Galway to win the 1956 All- Ireland senior title after a lapse of 18 years. The deeds of Purcell and Stockwell, the latter scored 2-5, the highest individual score in any sixty minute All- Ireland final, and goalkeeper Jack Mangan, all from the Tuam Stars club, are indelibly imprinted in the history of Galway 's greatest football achievements. Sean Purcell is perhaps one of the most revered , if not 'The' most revered footballer in Galway. His performances over a long span of years whether in defence, midfield or attack stand out like beacons. He was a commanding figure and allied to a shrewd footballing brain was his ability to make a success of any role he filled with either club or county. It goes without saying, he would have been an automatic choice for the game's highest awards irrespective of where he played. He epitomised all that was good in the game and he was a sportsman par excellence. Sean Purcell was academically brilliant and easily qualified as a school teacher, and became known as the "Master." There is a story told about a celebratory function to mark the winning of that All- Ireland victory over Cork in 1956. The function took place in Galway and it was a sellout. Sean, as usual, enjoyed the occasion and celebrated with the rest of his teammates. Later that evening Sean was seen standing at a bus stop near the hotel in great form and hoping to get a 'bus to Tuam, where he lived. A city 'bus going back to the depot, as it was now approaching midnight, suddenly screeched to a halt. The driver had recognised Sean Purcell so he opened the door of the single decker and asked: "Master, Is it yourself that's in it? , are you OK.?" To which Sean replied: "I want to go to Tuam." "No problem" said the driver, "step on board" and his grateful passenger acknowledged the gesture with a "fair play to you driver, I appreciate it". The 'bus was nearing Oranmore when a 'bus inspector, heading back to the depot after his last inspection, noticed the city 'bus travelling out of the city at twelve twenty and signalled the driver to stop. "Hold it, Hold it, Where do you think you are going at this time of night."? The driver replied, "Tuam" The inspector asked "What in blazes is bringing you to Tuam.? The reply was immediate, "Take a look inside and you'll know". The inspector stepped inside and espied the passenger and in reverential tones said "Master, is it yourself. I saw you in action last Sunday and you made me feel proud to be a Galway man. You were brilliant. You took them apart, it was one of the greatest displays of football that I have seen, fair play to you". Said Sean, in a sleepy voice, "I just want to get home to Tuam". The inspector didn't mince any more words, "No problem, Master, leave it to me" and turning to the bus driver he said."bring this bus back to the depot and take out a double decker, the Master might like to have a smoke on his way home to Tuam."

Sean Purcell

Micheal Ó Muirceartaigh of RTE

Miceal is a great greyhound lover and indeed is very much into the greyhound industry and at one time was Chairman of Bord na gCon. He also had a number of greyhounds in training and to this day has still an interest in several dogs currently doing well on Dublin tracks. But Miceal is a cute Kerry "Hoor" as his illustrious county man, J B Keane , the noted playwright and novelist would say, because he would never give his sporting colleagues a hint, should one of his dogs have more than a chance of picking up a win at one of the local tracks. When such an event happened, Miceal would dismiss his dogs victory by claiming that the favourite in that particular race got "bumped" at the first bend and that led to his own dog's success. Miceal had a dog running at the Mullingar track and he phoned an old friend, Brian Geraghty of Galway to say that he would pick him up at his Ranelagh flat before proceeding to the Mullingar track. When Miceal reached Geraghty's abode on Dublin's south side he was told by Brian that he was just after washing his socks, and he would have to wait until the socks were dry. But the cute Kerry man solved the problem instantly. He tied Brian's wet socks on to the radio aerial of his car, and long before they arrived at Mullingar, Brian's socks were dry The story ended on a sad note, Miceal's dog was beaten by a nose, and the money plunged on it was lost. Brian went off to a local dance in disgust, and Miceal had to drive home alone. As Miceal put it so succinctly afterwards," Brian wouldn't have been able to go to the dance only that I dried his socks on the way to Mullingar on the car aerial." Miceal was a great friend of former great Kerry and Dublin All Ireland star Murt Kelly, who died earlier this year. Murt was a very shrewd judge of football and many was the time he was approached for his opinion on a team's performance after a major game. The selectors would change a team on the advice given by Murt. He was very experienced in a selectorial capacity for many years, in different grades. He was handed the managership of the minor team on one occasion. He decided to hold trials in order to run a shrewd eye over the talent that was on show. After one trial game, he was stopped leaving the field by a young hopeful, who believed that he had had a very solid game. Murt had a little knack of turning his head away when listening to some one posing a question. The young Kerry hopeful asked Murt very quietly " Will I see Croke Park? Murt thought about the question deeply, he was a very good actor. He put his hand on the young lad's shoulder, " You will, but you'll pay going in". Miceal and Jack O'Shea became very close for the simple reason that Miceal trained the Kerry players domiciled in and near Dublin in the UCD complex in Belfield for major matches. They would have a general get together at weekends with the rest of the panel.

Jacko was the captain of the Kerry team   for the meeting with close rivals Cork in the 1983 Munster football final. Miceal, as well as putting the Kerry players through their paces at Belfield, had another chore which had to be attended to for that important engagement - the winning captain's speech. Miceal spent a good deal of time tutoring Jacko on how to deliver the winning speech, both in English and Irish. It is a fundamental principle in the Kingdom that all winning captains deliver the speech in Irish and English.

Miceal started his tutoring early and explained to Jacko that he would need to have the speech ready for July and later of course in September, for the All Ireland final. So, by the time the Munster final came around the captain had his winning speech well and truly prepared, in Irish and English. As the '83 Munster final progressed the Kerry men were in the driving seat despite a great recovery by Cork. The second half was equally tense. The Kerry supporters were wishing that the referee would blow up full time as Kerry led by two points 3-9 to 2-10. Jacko was happy enough, he had played a storming game, moving up in attack to pick off scores while falling back in defence to help out when it was needed. The game was now in injury time, but Cork had one more surge left. They broke upfield in a good movement, the Kerry defence appeared to have everything under control, the ball was lofted towards the Kerry goal area, up popped Tadgh Murphy to slip the ball past Charlie Nelligan. The Kerry followers were stunned. Pairc Ui Chaoimh erupted as the Cork following celebrated the greatest larceny ever perpetrated against their neighbouring rivals. Sadly, one of Kerry's greats, Jack O'Shea never captained another Kerry team, who went on to win three All Irelands in a row.

So a winning captain's speech, so well rehearsed and so well prepared was never delivered. The man who helped with the tutoring end of things, had to suffer the trauma of those closing seconds as he commentated on how Jack OShea's men lost the chance of provincial and All Ireland glory.

There were a couple of sequels to that Kerry disaster. Jack O'Shea's little daughter, Linda, had been convinced by her father that he would be collecting the Cup after the match. But when she saw Christy Ryan of Cork being handed the trophy she turned to her mother, Mary and said " Shouldn't that be daddy's Cup". It may not be of any great significance, but I must mention that Kerry forgot to bring the Munster trophy to the match. Cork Secretary Frank Murphy produced a Cup, which was in his office at the venue, and that was the one that Christy Ryan accepted. The real trophy was later sent on to Cork.

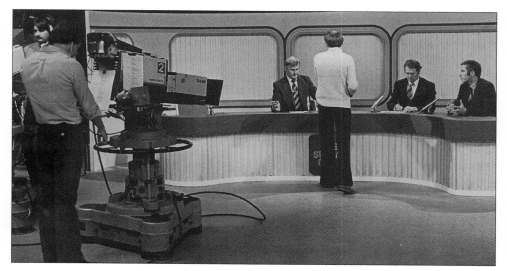

The "Sunday Game" 1980 from left Sean Og, Miceal O Muirceartaigh and Enda Colleran.

Kevin Mussen of Down

Kevin, from Hilltown, Co Down, was a product of St Colman's of Newry, and was a member of the Down senior football team which reached the county's 3rd Ulster football final in 1958 and was on the Down side which captured the first Ulster S.F.C. in 1959. But 1960 was the glory year for the county in the history of the Association, when Kevin, at the age of 26, captained Down to win the coveted All Ireland Senior football title beating Kerry in the final, the first county to carry the Sam Maguire Cup North of the Border. It was truly a historic occasion as thousands of Down fans, cheering, waving flags and buntings gathered at the border to witness the historic crossing The euphoria which followed that victory, and the celebrations, went on for many many weeks. Ironically, those people in the county who were not interested in Gaelic Games but who had watched the final on television or heard its progress on RTE radio were just as ecstatic as the committed GAA follower. None more so than Paddy the postman in Kevin's home town of Newry, a Protestant, who delivered letters to the Mussen household. The Sam Maguire Cup had done the usual tour of schools and colleges and it was awaiting another visit to a function one morning when Paddy the postman arrived with the Mussen post, swelled by many letters of congratulations from various parts of Ireland. Kevin answered the ring at his doorbell, to be greeted by Paddy, who commended him on his great win and the honour he had brought to the county. "Paddy, would you like to see the Sam Maguire Cup" asked Kevin. "Indeed, I would ." said Paddy " especially since the Cup is named after a good Protestant." Paddy was admiring the huge trophy and Kevin mentioned quietly to him that he was the first man from his part of the town to hold the Cup. Paddy quickly responded, " I suppose I am Kevin, but wasn't it a fine thing to take the Cup from those Fenian bastards." In 1969 when Down, the All Ireland champions, played Kerry at Wembley in the then annual Whit weekend games, the Down side contained many great characters... and none more so than goal keeper Danny Kelly, a brother of well known UTV personality Gerry Kelly, and that prince of corner backs Tom O'Hare. The Down party was collected at the hotel by coach and brought to the famous Wembley Stadium, where they were greeted by the stadium officials who proceeded to make them very welcome. The official in charge of the dressing rooms announced that Down would be occupying those used by England in their World Cup victory in 1966. The same official went to great pains to point out the different pegs and lockers used by the England team during that historic run. "This was the peg and locker used by Bobby Moore, No 6" announced the official. Danny Kelly, inquired of the official, who used peg No 1."That was Gordan Banks" said the official proudly, quick as a flash Kelly replied, "Tell him Danny Kelly was here".

Joe Lennon - Former Down captain

Joe has been acknowledged as being one of the game's finest wing backs and mid field player. He is the winner of three All- Ireland Senior football medals and captained the Down team which beat Kerry in the 1968 All -Ireland final . He won 7 Ulster Senior football championship medals; 3 National Football League titles and became the fourth Down player to captain a winning Railway Cup team in 1968, winning four provincial titles in all. He was a Physical Education teacher when he wrote a best seller about fitness in Gaelic Games. Since then he has become an authority on GAA playing rules and recently published a monumental volume "The Playing Rules of Football and Hurling 1884 - 1995."

Now retired as a teacher in Gormonston College, Joe is at present writing another major work on GAA Rules. He is a well known Gaelic Games analyst on radio and television and his services are very much in demand. He secured his degree in Physical Education in Loughborough Training College and played for John Mitchels of Birmingham.

On his return to his residence in Gormonstown he was invited to join St Patrick's of Stamullen in County Meath, his nearest club. Joe was a major addition and a powerful influence and the club achieved a great success when winning the Feis Cup trophy for the first time. One of the major attractions locally is Bellewstown Races, the oldest race meeting in Ireland. The Secretary of Bellewstown Racecourse, Joe Collins, told Joe Lennon that his records show that the racecourse is truly the oldest in the country, the earliest record of an advertisement for the races there is 1726.

There was, probably, a race course and athletics meeting there long before 1726. George Tandy, former Mayor of Drogheda and brother of the famous Napper Tandy, persuaded King George III to sponsor a race in Bellewstown in 1780. The king sponsored a race called "His Majesty's Plate" which had a prize value of £100. All subsequent English monarchs continued to sponsor a race in Bellewstown, Joe told me, until 1980 (i.e for 200 years) when the present Queen decided to discontinue the sponsorship of this Plate. However, Queen Elizabeth still sponsors a race at the Curragh - "The Royal Whip."

Joe's inquisitive nature also unearthed another gem unconnected with the sport of kings. George III's mistress was Lady Mountcharles of Slane Castle. That is why the road from Dublin to Slane is so straight- so King George III could get from the boat in Dublin to his paramour in Slane as quickly as possible. Joe innocently poses the comment (One wonders did George Tandy use a little blackmail on George III !!) However back to Joe's reflection on winning St Patrick's first Feis Cup trophy.

It was a marvellous occasion and as part of the celebration plans the St Patrick's team and supporters decided to attend the Bellewstown races, which they invariably did. The day was enhanced still further by reason of 'info' which enabled Joe and his team mates to build up a very tidy fund which was more than adequate to cover subsequent celebratory drinks. The decision was taken to return to Stamullen village after the races.

Stamullen is a quiet country village but it did sport a very fine hostelry, perhaps a little unique in fact. The public house was famous in its own right. It catered for all needs. It supplied farm machinery,drapery goods, hardware, groceries and everything from a needle to an anchor. Joe Lennon was a very familiar figure around the area and was very popular.

Joe Lennon... captained Down in 1964.

As the St Patrick's team and supporters headed for the pub, Joe spotted a well known local character sitting outside on a seat. Joe invited him in for a drink, explaining that the team was celebrating their great Feis Cup victory and an equally great day at the races.

The local character wasn't interested in the consumption of intoxicating liquor, explaining to Joe that he was a non drinker, never having broken his total abstinence pledge. " Come on in, anyway" said Joe " and you can join in the celebrations, it's not often we win a major competition on the football field." The reluctant hero entered the pub as the members of the team and friends started to order their drinks. Joe turned to the local character, Pat, and asked him to order what ever he wished. The local looked around the shelves of the pub and said quietly to Joe ; " Do you know what, I'll take that pair of woollen socks, if you don't mind."

Sitting in the back of the pub were two old brothers, Peter and Pat who farmed a bit of land at the back of the Stamullen playing pitch and they felt that all their birthdays had arrived together as they were plied with drinks by the successful local team members-all for free. Their piece of land wasn't great but they took corn and potatoes off it and the following year they would sow a bit of cabbage and Swede turnips. They were very hardworking and produced sufficient for their needs. The land they tilled wasn't great, Joe said, but at least it was theirs and that was important. They were preparing the land for sowing using a horse and plough when Peter stopped beside Pat one day and asked him: "Do stones grow, Pat, because we have an abundance of them." Pat took off his cap, scratched his head and replied : " I don't know, Peter, I never planted them."

Around the late 60's Down and Offaly were invited to play an exhibition football match in the famous Oxford University at the request of an Oxford don who was born in Offaly. Joe was a member of the visiting Down team which travelled on that occasion. It was a historic occasion as Gaelic football had never been played at the renowned University.

The two teams duly arrived and were greeted by the professor who had extended the invitations. The Oxford professor, a priest, showed them the beautiful set of medals which had been presented for the game. Both teams were impressed with the trophies , and as Joe feared, the battle to claim the valuable prizes took on a far different dimension later on in the day. The teams were taken on a grand tour of the famous seat of learning. Joe Lennon was particularly interested and accompanied seven other Down players on the grand tour. Bringing up the rear was Down corner forward John Purdy, a veterinary student, who was in the company of the priest but who eventually lagged behind the main party.

The Oxford don was very gratified with the reaction of the visitors to the many fine and noted architectural structures which were part and parcel of the famous college. He finally brought them to a field on the campus where the pride of his life, the deer were grazing. The party stopped at the gate to the field and the players saw the small herd in the distance. Beside a beautiful oak tree nearby stood a magnificent specimen of deer with a white tail. The priest gave the visitors a brief history of the animal, and they were impressed.

As the party was turning away from the gate, John Purdy arrived on the scene, the student vet. He walked over to the gate of the field, took one look at the animals, and with a big grin on his face, turned and in a loud voice said" Jasus, lads, them's some rabbits."

Outstanding Achievements.

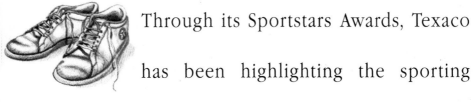

Through its Sportstars Awards, Texaco has been highlighting the sporting achievements of Irish men and women for thirty-eight years. Texaco pays tribute to the tremendous talent that exists across a vast arena of sports. This year has been no exception where achievement is concerned.  Texaco is proud to be associated with these people and will continue in the support of Irish sporting achievements in the coming years.

Approved Quality System

TEXACO

Eamon Young of Cork

In 1952 I was appointed to referee the National Football League semi final between Donegal and Cork on Palm Sunday in Croke Park. It was a red letter day for the Ulster county because they were creating history, being the first-ever team to represent Donegal in a major competition at GAA headquarters. The Cork team was captained by Eamon Young, one of the finest footballers I had the privilege to watch around that time, and he was one of of the stars of Cork's win on that occasion. The Cork trainer was an Army man, Corporal Jim Behan-O'Brien, who had prepared the side very well and they duly went on to beat Dublin in a very exciting League final, which earned them a trip to New York. When the party to travel to New York was announced, the only name missing was trainer Jim Behan-O'Brien. Team captain Eamon Young, who was an Army Captain informed the Cork County Board that if the team trainer was excluded from the trip, he would step down. The Cork County Board refused to budge and Eamon, a highly principled individual stuck to his guns and didn't travel with the team to the States.

He won a Munster football medal in 1943 and an All-Ireland medal in 1945. He won 2 Railway cup medals with Munster, in 1941 (the only Corkman playing with 14 Kerrymen in the side. Eamon Young is a gifted conversationalist, a prolific writer on the games and one of the most respected figures in GAA circles. He is also a Munster squash champion.

During the last war, Eamon, a Lieutenant with the Southern Command, was sent for special training to the North, along with three other officers. It was really a hush hush mission, but very crucial from a training viewpoint. The war at the time had reached a crisis point with the drive by the Allied Forces towards El Alamein The course which the Irish officers attended was at a training camp in Castlewellan, in County Down. It was a very important instructional operation, and a very strenuous one.

Eamon Young knew before he left for the North that his club Doheny would be playing Bantry in Drimoleague in a local football championship match, and Eamon Young's presence was vital to the hopes of Doheny. The game was on a Sunday and Eamon's course at Castlewellan finished on the Friday of that weekend.

A British Army car brought the Irish officers to the Border where they were collected and brought to the Curragh by Irish Army transport. Eamon got the night mail to Cork where he had arranged to pick up a bicycle. When the train got in about 2.30 a m. the parcel office was open, and he duly collected the bicycle and despite the fact that he had not slept for 24 hours, he cycled away with the objective of getting to Drimoleague for the match later that day. The distance between Cork and Drimoleague was 38 miles but that didn't bother the Cork star, he took it all in his stride.

The weather was very good, and more importantly, dry for the journey. But at 24 years of age, youth was on his side, and he sang songs on the journey in order to keep his mind on the trip. Naturally, he was also buoyed up by the burning desire of beating old rivals Bantry in the championship meeting that afternoon. He reached Bandon at 7a.m. without having eaten food for a considerable time He went to Mass in the local church at 7.30 a.m. After Mass, it was up on the bicycle again and off to Ballineen where he called in to see an old friend, Pete Mahony. where he knew he could get much needed food for the rest of the journey. Pete was amazed to see him and immediately prepared breakfast: "What in the name of God are you doing at this hour of the morning here in Ballineen?" asked Pete. Eamon explained that he had left an army camp on Friday, had been driven to the Border, collected and brought to the Curragh, to meet the night mail to Cork, and claim the bicycle which had brought him to his present destination. While Eamon was giving a blow by blow description of his journey, his host Pete was shaking his head.: " And 'twas all in vain, Eamon, did you not know, that match of yours with Bantry was called off on Friday because of a bereavement?."

My hurling club Eoghan Ruadh trained in the Phoenix Park beside the Hurling Ground, the other side of which, lies the Army Ground. Invariably around that time an Army match was played between local branches of the Defence forces, and I can safely say, having watched some of them, they were very competitive. Eamon Young recalled a football game between his Command and the Eastern Command at the Curragh, another venue where they took their football very seriously. Eamon was a very versatile performer, apart from being an excellent hurler, he could play in any position where his services were needed. Ten minutes into a football match at the Curragh, Eamon went up for a high ball but on coming down in possession he was tumbled and landed on his head on very hard ground, and couldn't remember any more.

He woke up on the ground with a bunch of players standing and staring down on him and then realised it must be half- time in the match. It was after the game that his colleagues told him that he had played out the remaining twenty minutes in an unconscious state, scored a point and laid on a pass for a very vital goal, and behaved impeccably. To put it in Eamon's own words: " I came to the conclusion then, that in an unconscious state I could play football at least as well as I could in the whole of my health. A fellow had to be a superb player to accomplish that feat, twenty minutes in another land during which I performed well enough for the lads to leave me on for the second half, can you beat that?"

In 1947 the GAA took the historic decision to play the All Ireland Senior Football Championship final in the Polo Grounds, New York. The winners of the Munster football final that year between Cork and Kerry, would naturally qualify for the All- Ireland semi-final but the real bonus lay in the fact that the All- Ireland semi final winners would earn the trip and the historical game of a life time in the Polo Grounds that year. It was only natural that the meeting of Cork and Kerry in that year's Munster football final was going to be one of the most competitive and vigorously contested Munster finals of all time. Adding further piquancy to that meeting was the fact that a record attendance turned up at the Cork venue to watch what turned out to be the most epic battle of all time between the great rivals. Weeks before the final it rained and rained and rained although on the day of the big game, the weather was fine. But the Athletic Grounds, which lay below the level of the Lee, began to show signs of wear and tear as the game progressed, a factor, according to Eamon Young that was to prove the greatest possible help to Joe Keohane- and the Kerryman's " roguery".

The exchanges were fierce and only a point or two separated the teams at any given time. With just five minutes remaining, Kerry were just ahead when their defenders conceded a penalty. If it was converted, Cork would be into the All- Ireland semi- final with every chance of capturing the Sam Maguire in the Polo Grounds. Referee Simon Deignan duly placed the ball in the centre of the fourteen yards line as Kerry defender

Bill Casey was receiving treatment for an injury. And according to Eamon Young, it was during those minutes that Joe Keohane perpetrated the most appalling "robbery" in the history of Gaelic football.

Said Youngie: "Lazily and with innocence written all over that honest face, Joe ambled out of the Kerry goalmouth, put his foot on the ball and got into a nice easy chat with Jim Ahern, who had been delegated to take the Cork penalty kick. " And why not " said Youngie, " they were the best of friends and knew each other well. I suppose Joe knew also that it was all over for Kerry because Jim Ahern had never missed a 'penno.' He had a kick like a mule and there was no way that a goalkeeper even of the calibre of "Danno" Keeffe would stop the ball. They chatted away there-Jim ready to take the kick and Joe standing happily there with his foot on the ball." Bill Casey was pronounced fit and Simon Deignan finally indicated that the kick should be taken. Jim Ahern, settled himself to take the kick, behind him most of the Cork team, including Eamon Young ready to charge in after the kick ... and only "Danno" Keeffe was there to stop them. Jim took off and kicked- and to the astonishment, dismay and utter fury of every Cork supporter in the vast crowd, and every Cork player on the pitch, there was a numbing shock.

Instead of the anticipated rocket that should have blasted the ball to the Kerry net, the ball trickled harmlessly along the ground and straight towards the welcoming hands of "Danno" Keeffe who, gathering safely, dispatched the ball gratefully down field- and that as it happened ended any hopes Cork had of making the historic Trans- Atlantic trip. To this day, and he laboured the point vehemently to me, Eamon Young swears that by the time that kick came to be taken, the ball had been pressed at least three inches into the mud by the strong and solid boot of Joe Keohane. While that chat was going on, Joe,he claimed,had been forcing the ball deeper and deeper into the mud: " Pure villainy" - says Eamon, though he did admit privately, that he would have done exactly the same, if the opportunity had presented itself to him. Naturally Joe Keohane, disclaimed all knowledge of the incident cited by the Cork star and was actually, visibly disturbed that he should be accused of such a foul act. He suggested that the ball had become sodden and mud encrusted and that the extra weight forced it into the heavy, yielding ground. " Jim Ahern, when he was taking the kick, most probably," he said, "dug his foot too deeply into the ground to compensate for the appalling conditions and that may have been the cause of his poor attempt." Continuing Joe said " I may have inadvertently placed my foot on the ball before the kick was taken but to suggest that the ball had been stamped into the ground is ridiculous. Had this been the case, how could I have got away with such a manoeuvre when all the Cork players, bar the goalkeeper, were crowded around the goal area? Remember these were intelligent men, very experienced footballers and most of them All- Ireland medal winners, who were wise to what one could or could not get away with on a football pitch. There was even a future Prime Minister of Ireland among them (Jack Lynch) I was also under the close scrutiny of 25,000 Cork supporters- and Cork people, deservedly, are credited with being a crafty,brainy breed. It Is difficult to pull the wool over their eyes. If my explanation is still unacceptable, will someone please tell me how a simple Kerryman like myself could fool the said 25,000 people, plus the Cork team, including the future Prime Minister -to- be in the broad daylight of a Sunday afternoon in an open field.?" And there you have it- who does one believe? But when Joe Keohane talked about the trip to the Polo Grounds in 1947, he always had a knowing smile on his face and said that it was quite an experience and a trip not to be missed—at any price.

Raymond Smith of Tipperary

There is no need to introduce Raymond Smith, perhaps Ireland's best known sporting writer. Every young journalist starting out in the trade acquires Raymond Smith's Gaelic Games handbook, which serves as a sports reporter's bible, giving facts and figures of every major competition launched by the GAA since its inception. I have been using Raymond's handbooks for the past 45 years and would not be without them. They are a marvellous source of information and they have helped to answer many a query that has arisen over the years. Naturally being a Tipperary man he has a deep love of hurling and when we meet at a GAA function or Leopardstown Race course, for a National Hunt meeting, he always has a new story. Somewhere else in this book he pops up in a story related to me by his kinsman Seamus O Riain. I happened to mention former Kilkenny hurling star Sim Walton of Tullaroan to Raymond. In 1967 I visited Tullaroan with a TV camera crew, Sean Burke was the camera man. The occasion was the 1967 All Ireland final between Kilkenny and Tipperary. My first port of call was to the then Kilkenny County Chairman Nicky Purcell, the local creamery manager and one of nature's gentlemen, whom I interviewed. I inquired of Nicky was it possible to get an interview with the famous Lory Meagher, who farmed in Tullaroan. Nicky gave me instructions on how to get to Lory's farm but he didn't rate my chances of getting an interview with him very highly. However, Lory's sister Rose, directed me to the area where Lory was saving hay. Sean Burke, the camera man opened the gate to the field and drove us to where Lory was busy, with a few others, stacking hay. Lory was a very shy person,and had no time for reporters seeking his views on major matches involving his native county. He always refused to be interviewed, but he was a great friend of my father, and I used that relationship to cajole him into doing an interview for me. I will always remember my closing words to camera, as Sean Burke focussed on Lory, "When the good man above made Lory Meagher, he threw away the mould." Yes Lory Meagher was really one of the greats. Lory, before we left him, suggested I drop in and have a word with Sim Walton, winner of seven All-Ireland titles.When we arrived at Sim's farm, his sister wasn't too happy about me doing an interview, especially for television. He had a two day growth of beard and was wearing an old jacket, she was trying to get him to shave before doing the interview, but he would have none of it. She insisted that he change his jacket, which he did. I placed him in front of a water pump in the middle of the farm yard, and began the interview . He had all his faculties about him even though he was perhaps the only survivor of the great Kilkenny teams 1904- 1913, and he was in his 80's. I asked him about Kilkenny's prospects against Tipperary in the All-Ireland final , which was coming up. He dismissed Kilkenny's chances with a snort " They wouldn't bate dust off a carpet".

I arrived back to Nicky Purcell at the creamery and he wouldn't believe me that I had the interviews with Lory and Sim. I assured him they would be going out on an

All-Ireland preview programme the following week. Kilkenny won that All Ireland beating great rivals Tipperary and Nicky Purcell told me some time later, that old Sim Walton's comments about the team " not able to beat dust off a carpet" was the catalyst which drove the Kilkenny players to glory to prove old Sim wrong, which they did. And that 's where Ray Smith comes into the story and my earlier reference to Sim Walton. Raymond said that Walton was one of Kilkenny's greatest hurlers in the period I mentioned 1904-1913. He captained the Marble City to All Ireland greatness and was equally at home in defence or attack. In Tipperary around that time was the famous Toomevara Greyhounds, who had a goalkeeper called Jack "Skinny O'Meara. In 1913 Kilkenny's Tullaroan played Tipperary's Toomevara in the Croke Memorial Tournament, in Dungarvan and both players figured in that match. The Greyhounds won the game 5-4 to 1- 1 and it led to a poem about that match game, which goes; " Then here's to Toomevara, May your Banner never Fall. You conquered Clare and Galway and you Shattered Cork's Stone wall. But I can Never forget the day when Kilkenny's Pride went Down, Before the skill of " Wedgers" men in old Dungarvan town." It came on to the All Ireland of that year, 1913, and Tipperay's Toomevara Greyhounds were roaring hot favourites to beat Kilkenny's Mooncoin. (The teams were reduced to 15 aside for the first time) Kilkenny had their revenge and won 2- 4 to 1- 2. Another famous poem emerged from that match. Tipperary goalkeeper " Skinny " O ' Meara was known as the" Barndoor"and he got his name because it was said of him, that he trained at home stopping swallows swooping down towards the barn door, the swallows flying in to eat the corn in the barn, and "Skinny" would be practising stopping the swallows. Sim Walton scored a famous goal against "Skinny" O'Meara in the '13 all Ireland final and it led to a ballad. "And there goes Walton the post is daunting. He is now attacking for the final score; Our cheers were heard on the hills of Clara, When he beat O'Meara, the "Barndoor", Raymond heard the ballad sung with gusto on visits to Kilkenny. Raymond also told me that Sim Walton pointed out to him, that Kilkenny won seven All Ireland's in a decade, but there was so much rivalry between Tullaroan and Mooncoin, that when Mooncoin won the county championship, they would leave some of the Tullaroan stars off the team in that era, and Tullaroan would do the same, when they had the selection. Sim was in no doubt that Kilkenny would have won ten All Ireland's in a row, but for the rivalry which denied the county team of players from both sides during that great era, and Raymond was convinced of it.

May I interrupt Raymond for a moment, to comment on a very important matter relating to communications at a time when telephonic link up country wide, was non existent for getting the results of matches from venues back to followers at home, who may not have travelled to a game. The popular way was to bring carrier pigeons to matches in a basket, and releasing some of them carrying the half time result, and the remainder bringing the full time result when the game had ended. We are really talking about the early years of the GAA when clubs represented counties in all the major championship matches. Perhaps the greatest blow the GAA suffered in the 1920's was the collapse of the" Freeman's Journal" which had devoted a lot of space to the Association's activities and events. In those days, the space devoted to sport in the national press was minimal by comparison with today's allotment. The GAA in particular got a significant injection with the coming of radio in 1926. In the early years of that medium relatively few houses had radio sets;

I'm told that the possession of one of them was quite a status symbol and neighbours gathered to hear broadcasts of big games in "radio" homes. That kind of community linkage of itself fermented interest in the GAA. I'm reliably informed that for the replay of the 1926 All Ireland football final between Kerry and Kildare, upwards of a thousand people assembled outside Benner's Hotel in Tralee 's main street to hear the broadcast of the game. At half time and with things looking blue for Kerry, every man, woman and child in the crowd marched into St. John's Church, nearby and said a rosary for a good result. They weren't let down, and so the perception that football is a para-religious ideology in Kerry is backed by a long tradition. In that year Kerry played Cavan in the All Ireland semi final in Tralee. At the conclusion of the game a group of Cavan supporters present were seen to release carrier pigeons to take the result of the game home to Breffni. So the use of carrier pigeons goes back a long time as Raymond Smith recalls in another story. This concerns The Tipperary " Thurles Blues" led by the mighty Tom Semple, after whom the stadium in Thurles is rightly named. The "Thurles Blues" were reckoned to be the greatest team ever to represent the county when they beat Dublin Kickhams in the 1908 All Ireland hurling final. The "Blues" were the precursors of the "Sarsfields" who followed but other club stars were included in the team representing the county at the time. "The Blues" met Cork's Dungourney in the Munster final in Tipperary Town the following year, and the Cork men were captained by the famous Jamsey Kelleher. At half time in the game, Dungourney were leading the "Blues" by 1- 6 to 1- 2 and the Cork supporters released the carrier pigeons with the news for the benifit of their supporters back home by the Banks of the Lee.

Of course, there was another little sting in the tale in sending the half time result back to Cork. Dungourney had disposed of their arch rivals the "Rockies" in the Cork County final so they news that they were going well against The "Blues" was bound to be heard by the "Rockies" supporters. Tom Semple, meanwhile gathered his men around him in the centre of the field at the Tipperary Town venue. There were no dressing rooms, the teams stripped by the ditch. One of the famous "Blues" players Pat Fitzgerald, recalled for Raymond, many years later, the team talk given by Tom Semple to his men during the half time break. Semple, the towering Thurles captain, pointed to the disappearing Cork pigeons, winging their way back home to Cork with the good news of Dungourney's very favourable position at half time. He said " there goes the pigeons, Cork think it is all over, these chaps cannot beat us if they don't get the ball in the second half, they must not get possession in this second half." Despite everything, Dungourney scored another goal early in the second half and led 2-6 to 1-2 but Semple's words were beginning to have an effect on his players. They mustered a huge effort. They denied Jamsey Kelleher's team possession of the ball, and slowly but surely they overhauled their great rivals to emerge victors by 2- 10 to 2- 6, holding the Cork men to just one goal in that pulsating second period. Naturally a ballad was penned shortly afterwards hailing the "Blues" marvellous success. " Why show fear boys while Semple is with you, That gallant old captain who leads in the fray, why should you doubt when you think of the past boys, That one word Dungourney all our trouble allayed" etc., Of course ballads predominated around that time, and great events, great victories were recalled in song and in stories to be repeated again and again. No matter where players congregate there is always an abundance of stories. On returning home from Mick Mackey's funeral Raymond Smith found himself in the company of a bunch of hurlers when they stopped off at Kinsella's in Castleconnell. Jim Devitt a great Tipperary hurler who played during Limerick's great glory spell in the early 40's, was also a very competent referee who was very much in demand and told this story. He was refereeing a junior football championship game in Tipperary and was applying the rules very strictly, but not to the satisfaction of one of the competing team's supporters. As he passed up along the line a voice rang out " Go home, Devitt, you are so blind, you wouldn't see a foul in a hen house." Suit length tournaments were very popular throughout the country long ago, and I remember playing with my club Eoghan Ruadh against Faughs on one occasion and collecting the suit length in Arnotts.

Suit lengths may have been unusual prizes for the winners of tournament, but at least they were very practical- the only snag was- you had to pay for having the suit made up. Of course, there were gold watch tournaments as well, and Raymond Smith went a little further with a tournament which was played in Tipperary, and the prizes were Bicycles for the winners. The two teams involved were fierce rivals, one of them came from a mountainy district and noted for their no " punches pulled" approach. Now the prizes offered to the winners of the tournament, 15 bicycles, was really unheard of and naturally the match generated great excitement and a very big attendance. Both teams were fired up for the battle for the very valuable prizes. It was inevitable that tempers would become frayed at some stage of the game, after all, very few of the combatants enjoyed the luxury of owning a bicycle. Entering the closing stages, a row developed in the middle of the field. The full back on one of the teams, a foxy haired lad, picked out his arch rival on the opposing side in the middle of the row. He raced up field and made straight for him, and gave the unfortunate man a fierce belt across the knees crying out, "You will never ride one of them bloody bicycles" Like most counties a great spirit of rivalry exists between certain clubs and in Dublin the situation was no different. In my days with the "Ruadhs" we had marvellous battles with Faughs, Young Irelands, U C D, New Irelands, Civil Service and Army Metro at senior level. "Ruadhs" were predominately a team made of Dublin born players and we were competing against the cream of inter county stars. The advent of St Vincent's, who were all Dublin born, helped to offer an additional dimension to the battle between the "city" men and the "country" men. Faughs, were always the team to beat because of the number of great inter county players they had, and invariably matches between Faughs and Eoghan Ruadh, packed Croke Park on a Sunday morning or afternoon. Faughs, were in the capable hands of Tommy Moore, who won two All Ireland medals with Dublin. He was also owner of a famous public house in Cathedral St. in Dublin. For a GAA man not to have visited that famous hostelry was like Muslim who hadn't visited Mecca. It- Tommy Moores's I mean- was the place to be seen during the week before and after an All Ireland. The story has been told many times about an Italian Cardinal who got disorientated in the vicinity of O'Connell St. during the Eucharistic Congress in 1932. In halting English, His Eminence asked a Kerryman, up for the Congress, for directions to the Pro-Cathedral. Quick as lightening came the response: "Sure,'tis up there opposite Tommy Moore's."

Raymond Smith prompted my mention of club rivalry in Dublin, when he referred to a similar situation in Tipperary between Thurles Sarsfield and Moyne - Templetouhy. There were times when both clubs met in football as well as hurling but the intense rivalry never diminished at any time. "Sarsfields" were travelling in a 'bus to play Moyne and everybody was very tense. Not a word was being spoken and a funereal atmosphere prevailed. But there was one man on the coach Mick "Rattler" Byrne, who was only too aware of the dreadful tension very evident all around him. He stood up and looked down the length of the coach and said " Jasus, lads, where's the funeral." That broke the ice and things returned to normal. "Sarsfields" won the match and beat their old rivals.

I had the privilege of playing against two famous Limerick stars who pop up in Raymond's Smith's next story, they are Mick Mackey and Jackie Power. I was promoted

Raymond Smith, Jack Boothman and Mick Dunne at the launch of Raymond Smith's book.

to the Eoghan Ruadh senior hurling team in 1943, and the club invited Ahane, billed as the "Wonder team from the South" to play against Ruadhs at Croke Park on Easter Sunday. The proceeds were in aid of the Merrion Church Building Fund, the parish priest was Eoghan Ruadh club founder, Fr Pat Flanagan. It was the first time that the Limerick champions had played as a team at GAA headquarters - and what a team they had, the Mackeys, Mick and John, the Herberts, Tony, Mick and Sean, Timmie Ryan and Jackie Power just to mention some. Both Timmie Ryan and Mick Mackey had captained Limerick to All Ireland victories. It was a further tribute to those great players that they had assisted Limerick to win five National hurling League titles in a row, 1934 -'38, an unprecedented feat. Ahane beat Eoghan Ruadh on that Easter Sunday in a thriller with Mick Mackey and Jackie Power, the two most influential figures. As Raymond Smith pointed out, Limerick helped to build more churches than any other county in Ireland. They were so much in demand at that time for challenge matches in aid of church building funds, that Jackie Power said to Mick Mackey after one such tournament " You know, Mick there must surely be a bed in heaven for us." And I'm sure they are now sharing it.

Laois had a famous hurler, Paddy Rustchitzko of Polish descent, a very polished player who played for the county against Tipperary in the 1934 All Ireland minor final, which Tipp won 4-3 to 3-5. I played against Paddy in the Leinster senior final in 1948 which Dublin won, and Paddy was a stylish wing back at the time, as good as any of his vintage. Raymond met Paddy, who worked in Portlaoise, and he told him of an incident which happened in the minor final. Ten minutes from the end of that match Laois were ahead and were on the verge of causing a major shock. Tipperary looked in deep trouble and drastic measures were needed to avert a catastrophe.

The rules governing the minor grade were rather lax around that time. Some counties indulged in the practise of playing over age players to attain their end. Laois were hanging on tenaciously to a narrow lead as the game entered the final stages. Tipperary introduced a substitute, a big lad, very well developed. Tipperary attacked the Laois goal and as the ball dropped around the square, Paddy Rustchitzko, caught it only to be buried, ball and all, in the back of the net by the big Tipperary substitute, who was whipped off by the Tipperary selectors a few minutes later. The Laois players protested but all to no avail and Tipperary won the game by one point. The Laois county Board objected to Tipperary getting the match but it was ruled out of order. Tipperary had a very strong voice at top level, they were one of the major counties in hurling, whereas opponent Laois were really a small fish in a very big pool. Four years later, Paddy Rustchitzko, was sitting in the local cinema one night watching a Western film and a big man sat down beside him. The newcomer tapped Paddy on the arm and inquired " Are you the fellow with the Russian name?" Paddy assured him that he was the same person. " Do you remember the 1934 All Ireland minor hurling final ?" " I'll never forget it " said Paddy " I lost my All Ireland medal." "Well" said the late comer "A lot of water has flown under the bridge since then but I was the big fellow that came in as a sub near the end and bundled you into the net for the winning goal, and I celebrated my twenty second birthday on the Saturday night."

Well known impresario and Fianna Fail Senator, Donie Cassidy, bought the famous GAA landmark Barry's Hotel, in Great Denmark St., where visiting GAA teams have stayed for many many years. The scene has changed dramatically with regards to the accommodation of teams in the capital for major matches.. While refurbishment was being carried out in Barry's Hotel, by new owner, Donie Cassidy, a bedroom was discovered, Room 14, where the walls were peppered with marks of sliotars, where on the eve of an All Ireland or Railway Cup final, players loosened up by smacking sliotars against the walls in that particular bedroom. Senator Donie Cassidy was only too pleased to preserve it, and it is named the "Christy Ring" room. The Cork legend, never socialised before matches He preferred to practice his striking while others were out enjoying themselves. The room is preserved, as it was when "Ringey" shared it.

Raymond's first All Ireland was 1951 when Tipperary beat Wexford. Train fare to Dublin cost fourteen shillings and sixpence. Reporters were allowed six shillings and sixpence for tea, and four shillings and sixpence for lunch.

When Raymond left Barry's for the trip to Croke Park he would stop and enjoy the luxury of a banana split in one of the ice cream parlours on O'Connell St. for the princely sum of two shillings. On a salary of two pounds a week this was really living it up.

The " Rattler" Byrne cannot be kept out of stories involving Tipperary teams and Raymond remembers one about the lion hearted Tommy Doyle who was making his first ever trip to New York by 'plane. Sitting beside him on the flight was "Rattler" Byrne. Tommy Doyle was very nervous and was only wishing for the trip to end. He turned to the "Rattler" and asked in a nervous voice, " What happens, if anything goes wrong with the plane? "Ah sure you have nothing to worry about, Tommy" said the "Rattler" there are two parachutes under the seat, you put one on, you jump out, you count to ten, you press the button, and you float down like a butterfly, it's as simple as that." Tommy looked at the "Rattler" and again in a timid voice asked "But what happens if the parachute doesn't open? " It's simple" said the "Rattler" you come back up and get the spare one." There was silence in the dressing room before the county final as the local curate began to address the team before taking the field for the big game against their arch rivals. " Now lads, more important today than victory is the honour of the little village. Don't sully the jersey. Let sportsmanship always prevail no matter how your patience is tested." And taking a little bottle of holy water from his pocket, he proceeded to splash it on the players sitting on the benches ending with the little prayer " And may the good man above preserve ye all from any little knocks." He got a round of applause from the players as he left the dressing room. The captain turned to his men and said " Well, ye have heard the holy man, now, who's going to knock out the goalkeeper? The Croke Memorial in Liberty Square in Thurles, opposite the chemist shop, was known as "the school around the corner". It was where the locals congregated on a Sunday evening to meet the players coming home from matches, to hear how they fared. Raymond was a school boy at the time and he loved listening to the ballyragging the players would get from the assembled gathering. In 1945. Tommy Doyle starred in the Munster senior hurling semi final against Paddy Donovan of Cork, although the great Cork man was in the autumn of his career at the time. Tommy was carried shoulder high from the pitch after giving a marvellous performance. Tommy arrived back to face the "school around the corner." "Well Tommy, how did you do? Tommy quickly put their mind at rest " Do ye know, my mother was listening to Michael O'Hehir's commentary, and there was nothing but my name on it, nothing at all but my name, it was unbelievable." But in the Munster final against Limerick he came up against Jackie Power, who was in his prime, and the story was completely different.

Jackie Power kept the wraps on Tommy, as Limerick hoped he would do, but all the damage was done on the opposite wing by "Mutt" Ryan, who was the" man of the match" from a Tipperary view point. When Tommy made his appearance later for the folks on the "corner" in Liberty Square, the usual question was put "Well, Tommy, what did your mother think? He wasn't going to let the side down and he replied " Do ye know something lads, there was so much interference on the wireless, she couldn't hear a thing."

Peter Donohoe of Cavan

My good friend and colleague, Mick Dunne, in his splendid commemorative book on the historic 1947 All- Ireland senior football final between Cavan and Kerry in the Polo Ground, New York, devotes a special chapter to the prowess of Peter Donohoe, one of the most talked about players who took part in that famous final, the only All- Ireland final played out side of this country. Peter Donohoe's personal contribution of 8 points played a significant part in the defeat of Kerry and won for him many accolades from all the local sports writers of the time. Arthur Daley of the "New York Times, " one of the more famous sports columnist of his day, dubbed Peter Donohoe, the "Babe Ruth of Gaelic Football, "a Dead Eye Dick with his kicking, which was the ultimate compliment that could be paid to Cavan's prolific scoretaker. Quoting further from Mick Dunne's excellent book, The "Herald Tribune" had their leading sports writer Harold Rosenthal state: "The name Donohoe, 23 years old publican's assistant rang last night, in recognition of his prodigious athletic feat- performed on a foreign shore, three thousand miles away from home. " There were others who went into raptures about the Cavan victory and the role played by one Peter Donohoe. In most cases , the American sports writers were viewing Gaelic football for the first time. They were visibly impressed with the physical fitness of the players, and the excitement which the football game engendered. The fact that the match was purely amateur was another factor which impressed the local scribes more used to writing about baseball and American style football, with all its protective gear. Peter Donohoe was born in Kilnaleck, in County Cavan, and was big for his age. He won a minor football title with Ballinagh and even then he was a very accurate sharpshooter both from frees and play. He won a county senior football title with Mountnugent, left the county and went to Dublin but came back at the end of his playing career to win another championship and league with Crosserlough. Peter, at 19 years of age, could handle himself very well and loved the game of football. It was during the war and petrol rationing was in force and there was little movement of cars or vans. Peter was prevailed upon to play, illegally of course, in a Westmeath junior football final in Mullingar. He left Kilnaleck by pony and trap early that Sunday morning, you were prohibited from travelling by car, because of the scarcity of petrol. Football matches were considered to be an unnecessary luxury for travelling to by car. He stopped in Finea where he was lucky to catch the eye of a van owner, who dropped him off, two miles from Mullingar. The van driver was unable to drive into the town for fear of being stopped by the Gardai, and asked to explain the use of the van on the Sunday.

So, Peter had to walk the two miles to Mullingar, where he met his contact, to learn the name of the team he was playing with, and also to be told of the big wagering which had been going on that week on the outcome of the game. Betting on matches was by no means a new phenomenon even around that time. It is just as prevalent in some counties to this very day. Peter's gear consisted of a pair of well worn football boots,knicks, and vivid green and white stockings, which he had picked up in his travels, all tied in a bundle by string. While the club or county provided the jersey, the onus was on the players to provide the rest of the playing gear. Peter could not afford to even buy new stockings, because the price would have bought two or three pints of stout which was more important for a growing lad. Peter's team won the match amidst great excitement and Peter's own performance was the subject of much favourable comment, in a match, where the standard of football was not particularly high.

After the celebrations Peter had to make the long journey back to his native Kilnaleck, helped undoubtedly, by several of the club members,through the use of various modes of transport. The following weeks were worrying, in case an objection was lodged against the illegal use of players in the Mullingar encounter. But he had been assured that such a contingency would not arise as the club he had played for, knew that the opposing club had also imported a few illegal players. The prime difference was that Peter Donohoe's marksmanship was the prime factor in his club winning the coveted title and medals. Naturally Peter played under an assumed name.

Six months later, Cavan played Westmeath in a senior football challenge in Mullingar, and to Peter's delight, he was chosen for his first senior trial. Peter had his boots, green and white stockings and knicks, the only article supplied by the county board was of course the county jersey. Peter enjoyed the experience immensely and was the recipient of much praise for his scoring expertise from frees and play in helping Cavan to a good win.

As the players were dressing, they had a visit from the Chairman of the Westmeath County Board, Dan Leavy, one of nature's gentlemen, whose house I visited years later in the course of my work on radio and "Evening Press." He thanked the Cavan Board officials for their visit, and hoped that his team could travel to Cavan at a future date for a return match. As he was leaving, he turned specially to Peter Donohoe and complimented him on his display, and leaning closer to Peter's ear said quietly: " I would recognise those green and white stockings anywhere," winked at him, and left the dressing room.

In the early stages of Peter's intercounty career he was chosen on a Cavan team for an Ulster championship game against Armagh at Breffni Park. At that time the old Breffni ground had sideline seating. The Park was reconstructed in 1952. A big attendance turned up for the Cavan - Armagh Ulster championship match long before any construction work was contemplated. It was the usual hard championship fare with neither side looking like potential title winners. Midway through the second half, only a few points separated the teams, and play was mainly confined to the other end where Cavan were under very strong pressure. One of Peter's colleagues in attack moved over to him and they were having a brief chat. "What do you think of that blonde sitting over there on the sideline" said the player, pointing to that area of the side line: " have you ever seen a better pair of legs.?" Peter surveyed the area in question, and the member of the fair sex, who was the subject of the player's scrutiny, admitted that he had never seen a more shapely pair of legs, a credit to the mother who brought her into the world. Play suddenly switched to Peter's end of the field, and his colleague, who had been so gracious in drawing his attention to the shapely damsel on the sideline, went bald headed for a high dropping ball, only to collide heavily with a bigger and a more physically endowed opponent. The Cavan forward had his shoulder dislocated. While Peter consoled his injured colleague after the game, both agreed, that an Ulster championship match was not the time or the place to be admiring the physical attributes of members of the opposite sex.

The Shamrocks

The " Shamrocks" were in dire trouble. They had waited patiently for this football championship match against keen neighbouring rivals from the "Lough" parish for over twelve months and things were not going too well. After only five minutes disaster had struck in a big way. The Shamrocks goalkeeper and full- back collided as both went for a high dropping ball, and both suffered a bad case of concussion, and had to be replaced.

More disaster followed a few minutes later when their freetaker and most reliable forward twisted his ankle badly in a fifty- fifty ball which resulted in the "Shamrock" player being carried off. The three substitutes were totally inadequate but that was the way it was in the club. The "Lough" grasped the situation very quickly and started to build up a very formidable lead, helped no doubt by a very porous "Shamrocks" defence. As the teams trooped off at half- time the "Lough", much to their own surprise, were leading 2- 15 to 0- 1, the lone "Shamrocks" point had been scored in the opening minute by their freetaker who incurred the ankle injury shortly afterwards. The "Shamrock" dressing room was like a morgue. Not a word was being said as the players mentally viewed their prospects for the second half. The thoughts were not very inspiring nor could any of the team visualise anything else but a repeat of the same. One of the team was the local schoolteacher and as he looked around the dressing room all that could be seen were drooping heads as players went through the motions of retying boot laces, pulling up socks or answering calls of nature. The half time break was rapidly coming to a close when the schoolteacher made a quick decision.

He slipped into the seat beside the team captain who was quietly pulling way on a cigarette: "Listen Tom, you are the longest serving member of the team and the players look up to you. I think you should say a few words of encouragement before we go out for the second half. Things are not looking good at present and you might give them a lift for the task that lies ahead". The team captain, who sat with his head down, drew a long drag on his cigarette and weighed up the comments of his friend the schoolteacher. He raised his head and looked at the teacher, who stood and said: "Ciúnas, Tom has a few words to say." The team captain stubbed his cigarette butt on the heel of his boot and stood up, as the rest of the players watched and waited for the captain's few words: "Well, lads, I have been asked to say a few words before we go out for the second half. All I can say is, the longer we stay in this dressing room, the longer we stay in the champioship."

Christy Ring of Cork

Enough has been written and said about "Ringy" to fill volumes and it is not my intention in this particular book to go into the life and times of one of hurling's greats. I had the privilege of playing against him and I make no apology for saying that he was, without doubt, a hurling genius with unrivalled skills. He generated countless stories which have now passed into the folklore of the game he adorned with such brillance. It is a tribute to the man that I have included some of the stories in this book. The legendary Mickey "Rattler" Byrne of Tipperary was only one of many great Tipp defenders who faced up to the challenge posed by Ring. Mickey remembered a particular National Hurling League game against Cork, which like all the other games against the Leesiders, was contested with championship fervour. Ring's accuracy was partly responsible for the closeness of the scoring and coming up to full- time the teams were level. Cork won a sideline cut about 45 yards out from the Tipperary goal area and the referee, Cathal McLoughlin(Dublin) told Ring, who had elected to take the cut, that it would be the last puck of the game. As Mickey explained: " Ring took two steps back, looked at the goal posts, and from the moment he hit it, the sliothar was on its way between the posts for the winning point." Later as the two teams sat down for a meal, Ring passed Mickey's table accompanied by trainer Jim Barry. Mickey turned to him and said: "By God, Christy, we'll have to shoot you," "Oh sure you might as well, Mickey" said Ring "Ye've tried everything else."

Two former Cork players were enthusing over a display given by the maestro in a local match between Glen Rovers and the "Barrs." One said: " Remember when Ring whipped the ball out of yer man's eye?" "Out on the sideline?" Yeh, yer man says to Ring " you could have killed me " " What did Ring say?" " If it was in your mouth, I'd drive it down your throat."

It was another one of those heart palpitating Munster hurling finals between Cork and Tipperary at Semple Stadium, Thurles. The atmosphere was electric and the exchanges flowed with frightening intensity. There was little between the teams. Tipperary held a slight edge mainly due to the performance of Tommy Doyle who had been holding the renowned Christy Ring scoreless from play. Ring was deadly from frees but he was being allowed little room due to the tenacious marking of the redoubtable Doyle. With minutes remaining Tipperary led by a solitary point as the Corkmen made one last burst. The ball was stroked out to Ring. He rounded Doyle and headed immediately for the Tipperary goal area. Beating off one or two tackles, Ring smashed the ball to the Tipperary net. Up jumped a highly excited Cork supporter on the sideline and proclaimed to all and sundry: "Toscanini for the music, Katie Barry for the crubeens, but it's "Ringey" boy for the gaols."

Learning the basic skills of hurling comes at an early stage of one's development. In my own boyhood days on Dublin's north side of Fairview we played and learned our hurling on Fairview Green, a walled patch of land, surrounded by houses built by Dublin Corporation. There was no such thing as coaching, we aped the big name players of those days who figured in big matches at Croke Park, and naturally no two boys could claim they were each that particular star, someone had to yield. We learned to pick and hit,

This life size bronze statue of legendary Cork hurler Christy Ring is on display at Cork Airport. Pictured from left are: Councillor, Joe O'Callaghan, the then Lord Mayor of Cork, Mrs Mary Ring, wife of the late Christy Ring, Mr. Barry Roche, Cork Airport, Bernard Allen T.D. and Sean McCarthy, Sculptor.

Tall Tales & Banter

both sides and improvise generally.

I can well believe that one young boy, Christy Ring, went through the same motions in his growing up days, as indeed did every other boy who truly loved the game. I remember Jimmy Smith, of Clare, telling me about his growing up days and he could well relate to some my own experiences. Jimmy remembered visiting Mary Ring, sister of Christy's, some years ago at her home in Cloyne, Co Cork and she recalled the hours the young Ringey spent practising. Mary also emphasised the great interest shown by an uncle of Christy who never stopped encouraging the young rising star in the making. He knew that Christy had exceptional talent, even as a small lad, and was always delighted to see him on the Cloyne pitch, which was directly behind his house.

There came a day when Mary and her uncle were sitting down at his home, Christy, as a young boy was as usual, in the field practising his skills when suddenly the ball came through the window in the room where they were sitting. Glass splintered all over the place and after a few seconds a very frightened Christy appeared in the doorway expecting the worst. There was dead silence which didn't help the mind of the young Ring boy expecting to feel the wrath of his uncle. Instead a smile appeared on the face of his uncle who asked: " Christy boy, how far out were you when you struck the ball?"

The 1954 Cork winning All- Ireland hurling side returned to a marvellous reception. The streets were packed with delirious supporters, the best reception ever accorded a winning Cork team for many years. At the meal for the teams at the Victoria Hotel in Patrick Street later, a learned friend, sitting beside Christy, was over the moon with the greatness of the occasion. Ring brought him down to earth with a bang: "Listen," he said, "we are still in Patrick St, where winning Cork teams and supporters have celebrated through the years, but we are a long way yet from the Mall". The Mall, was and is, the professional, financial and business apex of Cork. Little ever escaped the man from Cloyne, but you really needed to know him. He had a great sense of humour but he always appeared to be serious.

Tony O'Shaughnessy, one of the finest corner backs it has been my privilege to see, and to my mind, the real corner stone of Cork's three- in- a- row run of successes 1952, 1953 and 1954 always reminds me of an incident involving Ring, Tony and myself, on the morning of the 1952 All- Ireland final against Dublin. I dropped into Barry's hotel to have a chat with Christy and I bumped into Tony. He asked me to drive him to the Richmond Hospital in North Brunswick Street to see Paddy Downey of the "Irish Times", who was recuperating from an illness. Tony asked Ringey to go along too. The car I was driving at the time was a Fiat 600, a small two seater, but it had space at the back behind the front seats for another passenger. Ring insisted on sitting in the front seat, consigning Tony to the uncomfortable back seat, which was a tight squeeze, as Tony was no small man. As I drove towards the Richmond Hospital, Ring asked me: "Do they pay you much in Radio Eireann for that programme of yours on Sunday.?" (I hadn't taken over from my father at the time, but I did do an odd Sunday night, when my father was unavailable.)

I told him a lie, when I said the programme paid very well. Said Ringey: "Wouldn't you think a man of your standing would have a better car." I told him I couldn't afford a better car, but it got me around the city. Tony O'Shaughnessy poked Ring in the back and said quietly:"Shure, you haven't got a car yourself." Ringey gave him a look:

"That's not the point, I'm talking to your man here" pointing his finger in my direction. We drove along in silence until we reached the Richmond Hospital. The three of us walked up to reception and inquired about our patient. We were told that we could not possibly see Paddy as the doctor was on his rounds and there was no way the matron would allow us next or near the Ward. I asked a passing nurse to carry a message to Paddy, informing him that three visitors had called to see him; even the fame of one Christy Ring wasn't sufficient to persuade the nurse to allow us up to Paddy's ward.

Christy Ring

A few minutes later, as we were going down the hospital steps, we heard a shout from one of the Ward windows, and there was Paddy with his neck sticking out of the window, waving to us. We chatted for a while, he was only delighted to see us, but he was yanked back back into the Ward by the matron, who told us in no uncertain manner to clear off and not be giving the hospital a bad name. Even Paddy wasn't spared a tongue lashing from the same matron. Christy enjoyed the situation very much and as we were going out the gates of the Richmond, he looked back and chuckled: " She must be hell to live with."

The great Kerry footballer Paddy Kennedy, on a visit to New York, told me about meeting Christy in Gaelic Park on a warm Sunday afternoon. Ring and himself were chatting about football and hurling events back home, when they were interupted by a Cork-born exile, who cut in to greet Christy as an old friend. When Christy registered non- recognition the exile was taken back: " Don't you know me, surely you remember our meeting on the steps of Barry's Hotel after the 1942 All- Ireland hurling final?" was his naive response. Ring's response was equally naive: " I hardly remember the 1942 final at the moment" It ended that conversation. Ring was undoubtedly the master of the put down.

Christy and I were discussing a particular match one evening and an innocent bystander happened to throw in a comment. Ring looked at him and said: "What do you know about it, have you played the game?" The poor man admitted he hadn't. Ring said to him: "Well leave it to the men who did play, and listen" .Christy loved to talk about matches, but not too much about other players. I was reporting on a Cork v Wexford National League match in Wexford for RTE Sport. Christy was one of the Cork selectors. I approached him after the game, which Cork had lost, for a comment for my "Evening Press" column the following day. After posing some questions, Christy looked at me and said: "You know the game, you played it, you saw what happened out there today, why are you asking me?" It was typical Ringey reaction. After further pressure he gave me the comments I was seeking, but refused other reporters.

At a Munster Championship match in the 1940's in Thurles between Cork and Limerick, Ring was the victim of a lot of stick from his marker. Cork supporters were reacting with loud displeasure to the ill-treatment of their hero. A Limerick supporter nearby intervened and asked him to 'pipe down' and for good measure he added: " You're mouthing about robust but fair treatment that your man is getting out there. But it's mild by comparison with the treatment that he gets when he is playing for the "Glen" against the "Barrs, whereupon" one of the partisans whom he was lecturing, being a "Barrs" man, screamed " What we do to Ring in Cork is our f......k business."

Brian Geraghty of Galway

Brian was one of a number of very good Galway forwards, who operated on th county team around the late 50s and 60s. The problem was holding a place o the team because the competition at the time was cut throat stuff especially wit forwards of the calibre of Seamus Leydon, Cyril Dunne, Mattie McDonagh, Sea Cleary, Christie Tyrrell around. But Brian always seemed to make his mark when calle upon to perform, though missing out at times because of injury. Tuam and Dunmore playel dominated selections along with city club players. Brian's hero was, of course, Sean Purcel who was revered by Galway followers for years. Any time Brian visited his native heatl Uachtar Ard, he invariably called to see the Tuam star with whom he had a great friendshil Brian left Dublin on a Thursday and returned to the capital city on Saturday which wa a regular routine. On the week of the All Ireland senior football final between Down an Meath Brian was in touch with Sean and inquired if he was going to Dublin for th match. Sean hadn't made up his mind about his mode of transport, so Brian explained t him that he was going to Galway on the Thursday and returning on Saturday and tha he would collect him in Tuam on the Saturday. The arrangement was perfect and Sea gladly accepted the lift. On his way to collect Purcell that weekend, Brian responded to man who was thumbing a lift at Claregalway. The passenger explained that he was onl looking for a lift as far as Mountbellew or nearest point. Brian said that he was pickin up a friend in Tuam but he would drop the hitch hiker off on the way back near Mountbellev The passenger was good company and eventually turned to Brian and said: " I thin I know you, aren't you Geraghty?" Brian was chuffed at being recognised and nodde his head: " You played a bit of football in your day, shure I remember you well. Al you married or where are you now?" Brian explained that he was living in Dublin an was working for Bord Failte: "Ah, I knew that because I do a bit of work on local Galwa radio and heard you talking about football on it." Coming into Tuam Brian asked hi passenger to sit in the back seat to allow the friend he was collecting, who was physicall bigger, the freedom of the front passenger seat, especially for the long drive to Dublin, whic the passenger gladly agreed to. Sean Purcell was duly collected and Brian, assumin that the passenger would quickly recognise the famous personality who had joined then didn't want to insult his good friend by introducing the Tuam star by name. Sea immediately greeted the passenger and Brian explained that he was dropping the passenge off in Mountbellew. He also told Sean that the passenger in the back seat, had marrie the daughter of a school teacher who had taught in Tuam but had since passed away. Sai Sean: "I knew him well, he was a very fine teacher, God be good to him."

The conversation between Sean and Brian immediately turned to football and th impending game between Down and Meath that weekend. After a few minutes the intereste passenger leaned forward on the seat and tapped Sean on the shoulder and asked "Di you play a bit yourself, because I know your man did", pointing a thumb at Brian, wh turned and winked at his famous friend sitting beside him, "Stick with me, Purcel and you'll do all right."

Galway were very keen to atone for previous defeats at the hands of Kerry whe the two counties met in the 1963 All Ireland semi final in which Brian Geraghty playec

It was a comparatively young Galway team and extremely nervous and Kerry took command in the opening quarter. Eventually, thanks to great work by Sean Meade and Noel Tierney, the Galway men began to find their rhythm and the course of the game changed. In the end Galway got the verdict by a narrow margin of two points. In one of many attacks on the Kerry goal, Brian Geraghty went on a solo run, his favourite gambit, and quickly passed the ball to burly Mattie McDonagh in the centre, and Mattie proceeded to scatter opponents as they came out to challenge him. Geraghty, kept screaming at Mattie for the return pass but Mattie, his adrenaline flowing had only an eye for a crucial goal. The Galway man's charge was brought to an abrupt stop when he was grounded and the resultant free brought a point. But as Geraghty saw it, a great chance of a goal was lost because the ball wasn't fed back to him as the Kerry backs converged on Mattie.

As Brian and Mattie ran back for the kickout following the free, Brian quoted the first line of Pearses's poem, "The Wayfarer" to Mattie, "The beauty of the world hath made me sad this beauty that won't pass".

Down beat Galway in the National Football League semi final in 1962 at Croke Park, and it was a game contested with terrific fervour with no quarter given. A number of the Down players were attending College in Dublin, including Dan McCartan and Sean O'Neill, who were in a flat in Charlemont Road, Rathmines. Geraghty, who was a teacher at the time in Clongowes College, often stayed with the Down players when in Dublin. Dan McCartan was studying dentistry in the Dental College and Brian was a willing patient when it came to getting treatment for his molars. The Galway man made no secret of the fact that McCartan was an extremely efficient dentist, second to none, his fillings and general teeth care were exceptional. The League game against Down was no kid gloves affair.

Geraghty's tactic of running at defences didn't always pay off, often as not, he ended up on the flat of his back. He attempted his favourite gambit in this particular match against Down and had his front teeth loosened with an elbow and was about to suffer another wallop when Dan McCartan's voice was heard screaming "For Christ sake, don't hit him in the teeth, I'll have to put them back!"

A relation of Brian Geraghty's bought a well known hostelry down in Waterford, more on the Kilkenny side, between Slieve Rua and Glenmore, and he asked Brian would he prevail on Mícheál O Muirceartaigh to perform the official opening, to which Mícheál agreed. On the way down from Dublin, Mícheál and Brian, stopped off for a light meal, during which Brian posed the question to Mícheál: "In all your years of broadcasting matches, who was the toughest forward you ever saw?" Mícheál thought for a moment, and in his cultured Kerry accent proclaimed: "Brian, without any shadow of doubt I would say "Jock" Haughey of Dublin. Mícheál recalled a particular match between Dublin and Galway in Tullamore and "Jock" was marking Paddy Dunne, known as "The "Dunner", and a battle waged between the pair from the start, with "Jock" the more aggressive of the the two. Coming out after the match, Mícheál saw "Jock" leaning against a pillar and greeted him. "Jock" returned the greeting and inquired of Mícheál had he enjoyed the match. Mícheál informed him that he had, and added diplomatically: "And you had a good game yourself, "Jock?" The Dublin man told Mícheál that he was waiting for the "Dunner" and Mícheál, thinking that the battle between the two was about to be resumed, quietly suggested to "Jock" to let bygones be bygones and leave it for another day. "Jock" gave Mícheál an anguished look." What are you talking about, Mícheál, I'm waiting for the "Dunner" he promised he would buy me a jar after the match." At that moment the door of the Galway dressing room opened and out stepped "the Dunner", wearing a white jacket with a red rose, a black shirt opened to the navel and a gold chain He had black slacks tapered and black boots. He had a black Gucci bag and was wearing sun glasses. There was a brief exchange of hello's between the Galway man and Mícheál, as he watched the fierce rivals of a short time previous amble down the road on their way to having a 'jar'.

Tony Hanahoe of Dublin

T ony, acknowledged as one of the shrewdest centre forwards in football, had an added distinction of captaining Dublin to their All-Ireland successes in 1976 and 1977.

During those All-Ireland campaigns he was handed a role, which others might have disdained, drawing opposing centre backs away from their positions, to allow his Dublin colleagues to use the space to pick off scores. The gambit did not detract from Hanahoes's lethal presence as a roving forward when he helped to open up defences and lay on passes which brought crucial scores. He took over the Dublin team manager's job from Kevin Heffernan.

Tony spent a number of years managing the St Vincent's senior football team and enjoyed successes with them. One particular year he had as his assistant, colleague Jimmy Keaveney, another one of the heroes of the great Dublin teams of the '70s. Tony and Jimmy decided to assemble a panel for the senior football championship The panel included a number of young players who had come through the Under 21 team and looked to have plenty of potential. It was agreed that Jimmy would address the panel when it assembled for the first training session, which had been arranged for a Tuesday night. Jimmy always believed in calling a spade a spade. He pointed out to the players the importance of the training programme. Every player would have to toe the line, there would be heavy fitness exercises and every player would have to be present for the sessions, he wanted no slackers., he wanted no excuses, unless they were life threatening.

The players went away that night very impressed with Jimmy's pep talk and bursting at the seams as they waited for the Thursday night session. On the Wednesday night Jimmy was called to the phone at his home in Portmarnock. It was one of the newcomers to the panel. He explained to Jimmy that he would be unable to train on the following night: " Why can't you train?" said Jimmy in a very stern voice. "Because I have to do breathing exercises " said the young player. Jimmy's impatience got the better of him: " What f....k..g breathing exercises"? A very subdued voice answered: " Well, Jimmy, my wife is pregnant and the doctor is insisting that I go with her when she is doing the breathing exercises Jimmy exploded: "What's that to do with training, your not having the f....k..g thing."?

Playing illegally in counties other than your own, is not a new phenomenon. It has been going on in GAA ranks for many years, and I must confess, I was known to have broken the rules on occasions, but luckily I covered my tracks well. Many years ago I played with a Clare football club at the instigation of Clare born, Joe Power, with whom I played with on O'Tooles teams. Sean McDermotts, were at the time one of the major forces in Dublin football competitions.

Tony Hanahoe on the ball as Paddy Cogarty (Dublin) holds off Kerry's Pat Spillane.

They fielded very strong teams drawn from many counties, most of whom had won All-Ireland medals with their respective counties. "Birdie" Bradley was a well-known Clare footballer who also played with "Seans". He was a clever forward and used his guile to outwit opposing defences. He was well known to the other major clubs as a forward to be feared when ever he gained possession of the ball. Cyril Freaney, of St Vincent's bumped into "Birdie" at a game in Parnell Park and the Clareman asked him would he be interested in playing in a tournament match with a local Clare club. He could bring a few more with him from St.Vincent's. He told Cyril that he had invited a few other players from Dublin clubs to travel to for the game. Cyril roped in Jimmy Lavin, Denis Mahony, "Rah" Healy "Harrier" Roche of O'Tooles and a well known Offaly footballer who was only too pleased to travel. Jimmy Lavin was just out of minor ranks at the time and the trip to Clare was a first timer for him. "Birdie" omitted to tell Cyril and the lads, that the so called tournament match was actually a senior football championship final replay between Kilkee and Ennis Faughs. But fair dues to "Birdie" Bradley, he organised the trip well. The Dublin group was brought to Lahinch for Mass on the Sunday morning and then to Kilrush, the venue for the game, where they had a pre-match snack. Jimmy Lavin and the rest of the party strolled around Kilrush and could not help but notice all the posters in pubs and shop windows advertising the County Senior football championship final replay, taking place that afternoon. There was no mention of the tournament match in which they were involved. All was shortly to be revealed. "Birdie" Bradley was waiting for the Dublin contingent when they arrived early at the ground. He then explained that they were playing for Kilkee in the county final replay, they need not have any worries, the opposition had also packed their team with Dublin 'importees'. When the initial surprise had worn off, Cyril Freaney decided to make the most of it. All the Dublin players were virtual unknowns at the time, so it was a case of ' nothing ventured, nothing gained.' The Kilkee dressing room began to fill up with players and "Birdie Bradley was busy greeting each one. Eventually, the team was announced and all the Dublin players were included in positions they normally played in with their clubs. Jimmy Lavin, was chosen at full-back. Sitting beside him on the bench was a local player who informed him, that he was the goalkeeper. But, in fact, he was the full-back, now relegated to the goalkeeper's position, and he hoped Jimmy would maintain the high standard he had set in the drawn game in the No 3 jersey. Uunperturbable Lavin, assured the net minder that he could only do his best. Kilkee, won the game because of the quality players that were included, notably the Dublin contingent.

Jimmy Lavin had an experience of a different kind. Not alone did he maintain the high standard set by the previous occupant of the full-back berth, but he held the opposing full-forward scoreless from play. He was the man the opposition had being relying on for vital scores. Jimmy noticed that every time he soared up for a high ball, his goalkeeper came charging out to punch the ball, but Jimmy's neck seemed to suffer most. When it happened a second and then a third time, Jimmy decided to do something about it. During a lull in the play, Jimmy edged back to his goalkeeper and said: " Look, anytime you feel like taking over here at full back, just let me know, and I will take over in goal." Jimmy had no more problems for the remainder of the game.

Discipline, Tony Hanahoe told me, is to this present day, a very important factor in a player's approach to training. If a player adopts a complacent attitude on the training ground he will fall into that trap on the playing field. It was pre-requisite during Dublin's great run in the '70s that everybody had to be ready for training at 7.15 p m. It was a struggle for some, who lived on the South side of the city, having to brave traffic at its peak. There was usually a full panel when training commenced at Parnell Park but there were occasions when some fell by the wayside. One of the great characters on the 80s panel was corner back Mick Holden. On Saturday mornings Kevin Heffernan always had a match between the panellists. The game was in progress when Mick Holden arrived in his car. He immediately, went into the dressing room, got togged off and trotted on to the field and over to Kevin Heffernan. The manager gave him a stern look: " Well, Holden, what's your excuse this time, why are you late?" Mick's face was a study. "Well "Heff,I was driving across town this morning to training, and was stopped by the police. There was a bank robbery yesterday and apparently I looked like one of the guys that was involved. " "Heffo" kept staring at the Cuala man, trying to make up his mind about the authenticity of the excuse being offered: " Is that true, Mick?" asked the manager:. "No, but it sounds an awful lot better than saying I slept it out". The day before the 1983 All- Ireland final the Dublin players, after having a good workout, had a long pre-match talk- in, a normal practise. Heffernan, said to the players: "OK lads, is anyone having any problems sleeping? just put your hand up, we have a couple of sleeping pills here we can give you for tonight. You will have a good night's rest and you will play better tomorrow.." Nobody made a move as Kevin's eyes swept the room. But suddenly Mick Holden's hand was raised. " Heffo" was very much surprised, because he considered Holden to be the last player who would have had any trouble sleeping.

When most of the panel had dispersed Heffernan turned to Mick Holden and quietly said: " You know Mick, of all the guys on the team, you are the one guy that I thought would have no problem sleeping ". Mick had a big grin on his face and replied: " They're not for me at all, Kevin,they're for my mother, she can't sleep at all before any of these big games." Kevin Hefferan's language was unprintable.

Frankie Byrne of Meath

I had the privilage of playing with Frankie Byrne when both of us were members of the Clanna Gael club in Dublin. Frankie had qualified as a teacher and followed a long line of teaching colleagues who had worn the 'Clans' strip with distinction. They later went on to win glory on the inter county front with their respective counties. I followed a similar practice by joining 'Clans' as an ex pupil of Colaiste Mhuire, Parnell Square, an alma mater which had also supplied prominent players in time to the well- known Dublin club.

Frankie and I played along with Nick Rackard, "Weeshie" Murphy (Cork), Art O' Leary and Jim Morris of Carlow, Liam McAuliffe, Paddy Ferriter and goalkeeper Tim O'Keefe just to mention some. Frankie, may have been small in stature, but he was fearless in a chase for the ball and he possessed a spring, which enabled him challenge for high dropping balls against much taller opponents. Frankie had another talent. Unlike other freetakers that I have seen, he would stand back two or three paces and steer the ball accurately over the bar, and the same procedure was adopted for free kicks further out from goal.

Frankie, a qualified teacher of six months standing, played his first senior game for Meath (after graduating from St Patrick's Training College), in Drumcondra. In 1945 he was chosen on the Leinster football team to play Connacht, a team backboned by the dual All- Ireland stars from Roscommon, The Murrays, Jimmy and Phelim, Bill Carlos, Brendan Lynch, Donal Keenan. Frankie stayed in digs in Marino and was late getting to Croke Park because he had to collect his 14- year- old brother Sean, who was visiting the capital only for the first time, at Amiens St. Railway Station The train was late so Frankie, with his brother Sean in tow, headed immediately for Barry's Hotel to join up with the other Leinster players only to find that the team had already left for Croke Park . Frankie and brother Sean left the hotel and joined the crowds heading for Croke Park.

When they reached the ground Frankie went to the big gate beside the now Nally Stand and banged on the gate which was eventually opened by a fellow wearing a cloth cap. Frankie held up his bag and told him he wanted to gain admission as he was playing with Leinster that day. Frankie could tell that he wasn't impressed:. 'What's your name, son?' Frankie Byrne " he replied: "And I'm Eamon De Valera" said the fellow with the cap and promptly closed the gate.

Frankie, naturally began to get anxious, the inter provincial hurling match was on and he was keen to join up with the other Leinster footballers. He took his courage in his hands and headed over to the boys gate, pushed his brother Sean ahead of him, placed a shilling on the ledge and said "two please." Sean went through but when Frankie attempted to follow, the stile clicked to a halt and a voice from the darkened interior said " You're a hairy schoolboy "I'm still at school, ask my brother", said Frankie in what he imagined was a high, piping schoolboy voice. There was a moment hesitation, then he stepped on the pedal and Frankie was in and later won his coveted Railway Cup medal as Leinster beat the Connacht men easily enough. Frankie left his brother Sean to the train, and walked back to Barry's Hotel for a meal and later attended a Ceili in the Mansion House, where he was introduced to Christy Ring. Frankie felt he was walking on air. Sometime in the

Frankie Byrne

wee hours of the morning he left the Mansion House and walked home to his digs in Marino. With a teacher's salary of £3-6-8 per week you didn't travel by taxi. Besides, he was still walking on air. It had been quite a day. Incidently, Frankie's first major inter county match was against Longford in Longford, a League match. He also got his first taste of what some match writers deemed, 'uncompromising football.' In the early stages, Meath's corner forward, Paddy Meegan was the victim of a very bad tackle. Frankie turned to his marker and said of the perpertrator of the foul, "he's a right bastard". The defender looked at Frankie with a cold stare: "He is, he's my brother." Before the game was over Frankie knew there were two of them in it. It was the Friday afternoon before the All-Ireland football final of 1949. All the physical training and football practice had been completed and Frankie and the Meath squad were eagerly looking forward to the forthcoming clash with Cavan and the opportunity to bring the Sam Maguire Cup to the Royal County for the first time. Ten years previously one of the selectors, the great Mattie Gilsenan, had led Meath to its first All-Ireland final appearance against Kerry which ended in a two points victory for Kerry. In those days collective training was the norm for teams contesting All-Ireland finals in football and hurling. It simply meant that a squad of players came and lived together in a hotel, or hostel and trained every day- hence the term "collective training. It was banned in 1954 because Central Council saw it as being a move towards professionalism in what was an amateur sport." The Meath training camp was located in an Irish Hostel, Bru na Mi in Gibbstown, a few miles north- west of Navan. It consisted of a few wooden chalets grouped together to form a square and a large wooded hall which functioned at various times as an assembly hall, a refectory, a library, a games room and a chapel.

Apart from County Board officials and people making deliveries to the camp, visitors were few and far between, except perhaps for a few interested locals who would watch the training sessions from the sidelines Training was a private affair, so, when a large car, one usually associated with weddings and funerals, drove slowly through the gates and wound its way along the drive towards the front of the hall it occasioned more than a little interest. The car had two flags, one tied on either side of the front bumper, one the blue and white of Cavan and the other a tricolour. By the time the car came to a halt it was surrounded by Meath players. It disgorged four occupants- all male. Christo Hand pointed out that they were flying a Cavan flag in a Meath training camp, a gesture which could lead to a breach of the peace, and very nearly did. In fact, Christo grabbed the flag but was persuaded by the rest of the team to return it to its owners. The driver protested that they were also flying the Meath flag. He was left in no doubt that the players recognised it as a tricolour and that he, and his companions were not welcome.

He asked to see Kevin Smith and when Kevin stepped forward the driver took a package about the size of a shoe box from the car and presented it to Kevin as a token of his esteem for him and the rest of the team. Said Frankie:" Then the four of them wished us good luck for Sunday, piled into the car and drove out of the camp. We all turned to Kevin, and waited for an explanation. "I never saw any of those lads before" he protested, "but I'll bet you one thing, they're bloody Cavan men." With that he ripped the box open to reveal several dozen packets of chewing gum. A dozen hands reached for the contents. Kevin shielded the box as best he could and shouted: " They're going into the fire in the kitchen. I wouldn't trust those bastards as far as I could throw them." Kevin retrieved all of the packets and consigned them to the flames-all except one. Frankie persuaded Kevin to let him have one packet so that he could show it to a chemist in Navan the following day.

Frankie felt it was strange that four strangers should make such an odd gift to a football team. The following afternoon the local chemist told Frankie that the packet indeed contained chewing gum, but not one he would buy in a sweet shop. It was a laxative prescribed for people suffering from constipation. Obviously the visitors intended the Meath team should do some more running of a different kind over the weekend. Cavan were chasing their third All- Ireland title in a row having been crowned champions in the Polo Grounds in New York in 1947 and in Croke Park in 1948, and were hot favourites to record a treble. When Frankie conveyed the news to his colleagues, they were of the opinion, that the four visitors were gamblers who had bet heavily on Cavan winning and were doing their best to help the cause. Meath's historic win the following Sunday must have cost them "a packet"!

Seamus O Riain - Former G.A.A. President

Seamus was President of the GAA from 1967-1969 and proved to be one of the most popular figures to hold the Association's highest office. He placed great emphasis on the club and always stressed the importance of the club. He administered the affairs of the Association wisely and resolutely. He accompanied several Tipperary hurling teams to New York, apart from visits on official GAA business undertaken when he was President. He was held in very high esteem by John "Kerry" O'Donnell, at a time when relations between New York and the Central Council of the GAA were very much strained. During one of his visits to New York, Seamus was accompanied by that great character Ossie Bennett, trainer and masseur to the Tipperary team, and former great star "Sweeper" Ryan. All three decided to do a bit of sightseeing in the Big Apple. A visit to one of the major stores, Gimbels, which wasn't too far away from the team's hotel, was the first call, They reached the fifth floor of the store, where customers were invited to taste various brands of coffee, set out on a special table handled by two ladies. The purpose of the display was to get customer reaction to different brands of coffee. Three different cups of coffee were placed in front of the customers who had to decide which brand suited the customer's palate best. "Sweeper" Ryan, never tasted coffee in his life, being a life long tea drinker. He was persuaded by Seamus and Ossie to partake in the experiment, and they quickly brushed aside his attempts to opt out, assuring him of their support. The three men moved to the table where one of the ladies poured out a small cup of coffee for "Sweeper". The lady explained to him that they were asking customers about their preferences after they had sampled the three different brews. The second lady at the table held a clipboard and she was noting down details of the customers answers. "Sweeper" quickly downed the first sample, then proceeded to finish off the second cup and finally polished the third cup, all in very business like fashion. The lady holding the clipboard quietly asked: "Well, which of the three cups did you prefer?". "Sweeper" looked at his two colleagues but was getting no help from that quarter, only a shrug of shoulders, so he pointed to the cup in the middle of the three, and said: "I liked that one, it tastes more like coffee." The demonstrator looked pleased and turning to her clipboard, ticked off the answer to her first question. She then said to "Sweeper:" Now, how many cups of coffee would you drink in a day.?" To which "Sweeper" replied, without batting an eyelid "Oh, I'd say, 20 easily." The next question really threw "Sweeper", much to the delight of his two helpers, who were desperately trying to keep straight faces: " What brand of coffee do you generally drink, sir?" Sweeper" was stumped and turned appealingly for help to Ossie, who whispered from the side of his mouth: "Say Irel " "Sweeper" turned to his questioner, stuck out his chest and said: "Irel, " mam." That ended the coffee-tasting exercise for the Tipperaryman, who, getting icy stares from the two ladies, was dragged away by his two conspirators.

I must explain my presence in New York in 1968 to meet Seamus O Riain, the then GAA President and the Tipperary hurlers, who had arrived to play New York in the National Hurling League final. I had spent the previous three weeks with the London footballers who were playing in the Cardinal Cushing Charity Games. I was on my way home with the London team when I got a telephone call from Oona Gormley, Sports co-ordinator in RTE to say that I was to stay on in New York to do the commentary on the National League final between Tipp and New York, the first leg of which was to be played in Gaelic Park, in the Bronx, on that Sunday. The urgent request for my services was due to the fact that Michael O'Hehir had suffered a mild heart attack on his way back from the Epsom Derby, and he had been due to fly out to America the following day. Relations between John "Kerry" O'Donnell and the Central Council at the time were strained, although arrangements had been made to transport the team from the airport to the Manhattan hotel. I wasn't to know then that the Sunday match was going to be called off because of torrential rain, which had flooded Gaelic Park nor did I expect to be idle the following Sunday following the assassination of Robert Kennedy, when the games had to be called off, but that is another story.

On the Sunday morning, following the torrential rain the previous day, Tipperary had to make the journey to Gaelic Park in case the pitch was playable. No transport had been arranged for them so the Tipperarymens Association in New York immediately arranged for cars to transport the players to the ground, a considerable distance away from the hotel near 7th Avenue. Seamus O Riain, referee John Dowling and a couple of players were waiting for the last car . When it arrived Raymond Smith, of the" Irish Independent" who was covering the match for his paper, jumped into the waiting car with the players leaving no room for Seamus O Riain and John Dowling. However, Seamus decided to hail a cab for himself and John, for the trip to Gaelic Park.

Seamus sat in the front seat beside the cab driver, whose name, "O'Donoghue" and photo, were on an identity card on the glove compartment and Seamus said to him: " Begob, you have a great name." He replied: " I have it quite a long time". "I see" , said Seamus" how long have you got it.?" "72 years" said the driver. "And how come you are driving a cab at 72?" asked Seamus: " I only do Sunday work for a friend." was the reply. There was a brief pause in the conversation and the driver looked at Seamus: "Why did you say I had a great name?" "Because, " said Seamus: " I knew two people who had that name back home in Ireland who were in the War of Independence. One of them was Major Florence O'Donoghue, author of two books on the ' Troubles', he was a Cork man, whom I knew well, and indeed some of his family. The other O'Donoghue, was a Kerryman.

Seamus O Riain (centre of the front row)

"I didn't know very much about the Kerryman" Seamus told the driver," except that he was in the 'War of Independence' and took the anti Treaty side and then he went to America but I heard that he was a great footballer and played regularly in New York competitions." The cab driver turned to Seamus and said in a quiet voice: "I'm that guy." Seamus was taken back and said: " Well, isn't that extraordinary; isn't it a very small world." The conversation continued and Seamus was getting along great with his fellow Irishman, now a naturalised American citizen. Local elections were imminent and big placards of candidates faces were plastered all over the area, and Seamus remarked to the driver that there were two candidates he had heard mentioned, Bingham and Cunningham, and which of the two would he be voting for the House of Representatives. "I'll be voting for Cunningham, " said the cab driver. "That's strange," said Seamus " because moving around in Irish circles here I thought that most of the Irish that I met were going to vote for Bingham. Why are you voting for Cunningham.?" Back came the stunning reply: "Because he is my son- in- law." If Raymond Smith hadn't forced his way into the player's car originally, Seamus O Riain would never have made the acquaintance of an intriguing New York cabby with an equally intriguing Irish background.

Seamus remembers travelling to Walsh Park, Waterford, for a National Hurling League game against Waterford one Sunday afternoon and the game had attracted a very good attendance. Both counties were doing very well in the series at the time, so a win was vital to both sides. Sitting on the sideline with the Tipperary party was former great defender, Mickey Byrne who had long retired from the game. The Waterford supporters were giving the referee a lot of stick and were aggrieved at not getting what they considered their rightful share of frees. At times, Deise supporters vented their wrath on the Tipperary bench and Mickey Byrne replied to the comments in his own inimitable style. After a while he couldn't stick the jibes any longer and he roared at the Waterford fans " Heh, young fellows out there, we're in this business since 1884, so shut up." To which the reply came back: "What are you talking about, we didn't get a free since 1884."

Seamus recalls when growing up in Moneygall, a junior hurling championship match between Moneygall and a neighbouring parish team. In those days there were no dressing rooms, teams simply stripped beside the ditch. The local team had a particular character, a very small man who usually played in the goal. He never togged out, come hail or shine, because the togs were too long, so he compromised. He wore his long trousers and when putting on his boots and socks, he would pull the socks over the ends of the trousers, and pull the jersey over his shirt, and he wore a cap.

He was chosen to play in the forwards and was ready for action. He invariably dressed before everybody else and ran out on to the pitch and started hopping around, knocking heads off thistles growing around the field. On that particular occasion he was chosen at full- forward and an onlooker asked him " Where are you playing today, Neddy?" Without stopping his practising he replied: " Tippin them in", (meaning goals, which he never succeeded in scoring).

Dinny Allen of Cork

Dinny got his first taste of All-Ireland senior football final action when he played against Meath in the 1988 final when Meath won narrowly by a point, in a replay. But Dinny had his reward the following year when he led his county to All Ireland glory when they beat Mayo in a very exciting decider. Dinny was a proud captain when he accepted the Sam Maguire Cup from GAA president John Dowling. The gratifying aspect of the Cork win was the fact that they were regaining an All-Ireland title last held in 1973 under the captaincy of Billy Morgan, manager of the '89 winning team. Dinny was really chuffed to get his All-Ireland medal which he treasures very much. Six weeks after that epic experience Dinny got an invitation from Kerry's Mikey Sheehy to play golf in Killarney with two other Kerry players, Ger Power and John O'Keefe, which he duly accepted. The golf match was as keen as the great rivalry that normally exists between Kerry-Cork clashes and the 'craic' was equally as good. Arriving on to the 4th green it was Dinny's honour to putt first so he asked his playing partners to mark their respective balls as they were on his line of putt or thereabouts.

The three Kerrymen duly marked their balls as requested. As Dinny lined up his putt, he noticed that the markers appeared to be unusually large or at least bigger than the normal ballmarker. So he walked up to the one on his line of putt, to discover that it was the solid gold All-Ireland medal that winning teams get, and so too were the other two markers used by the other Kerry stars. Mikey Sheehy, a close friend of Dinny's, and the other two Kerry boyos pretended not to notice the look they were getting from the Cork-man, who was remembering that Mike and Ger had eight All-Ireland medals each and Johnno seven. Later in the clubhouse Dinny was prevailed upon to say a few words which he duly did, ending up with the comment: " and wasn't it great to be out there today on that beautiful course in a fourball that has won 24 All Ireland medals among us" The Kerry lads had no answer to that.! Cork played Kerry in a National Football League game In Killarney and Dinny had Jimmy Kerrigan and John "Kid" Cronin with him as passengers. A great character from the Glen Rovers club in Cork, "Langton" Mick McCarthy, asked to be taken with them to the game, so they put him sitting in the passenger seat in front. "Langton" sat into the seat and the car moved off for its destination. "Langton" had his head bent low under the glove compartment, which the lads thought was very unusual, but it didn't stop him from engaging in conversation with the other occupants. The car had passed through Ballincollig and Macroom and was now heading for the Kerry borders and "Langton" was still bending low under the glove compartment while still chatting away to the other occupants. "Kid" Cronin tapped him on the shoulder and said: "Mick, have you a sore back or what?" "No," said Mick," but my f...k...g coat is caught in the f..k..g door of the car".

Dinny didn't tell me of his venture into the race horse ownership business but my good friend Tim Horgan quickly put me in the picture. Dinny and a couple of affluent friends in the Glen Rovers club, decided to buy a race horse which they named "Molly Howe" Naturally, this was a very big step for the young entrepreneurs. They were given the usual assurance that this filly was something out of the ordinary, possibly a world beater. Her breeding lines were very encouraging and the Cork syndicate took an immediate fancy to what they regarded as a possible Oaks entry. Who could blame the young entrepreneurs from visualising the possibility of mingling with the rich and famous at Epsom or the Curragh in a matter of, perhaps, a couple of years. The syndicate watched her preparations very diligently, under the skilled hands of a wellknown trainer. After a period of time

Dinny Allen in action for Cork.

in which stabling and feeding costs appeared to be on the increase, the syndicate got a call from the trainer to say that "Molly Howe" had been entered for her first race. There was great excitement among the "The Glen" syndicate, a dream was about to come true.

The trainer explained that the race would provide very valuable information on her potential and he had chosen the particular race because of the quality of the entrants, which were really not of a high standard. The syndicate was warned by the trainer, not to indulge in any high stakes, as "Molly Howe" was really an unknown quantity. But human nature being what it is, the excited group had a minor plunge. Sadly, "Molly Howe" just didn't perform, she finished last of seven runners, a bad last at that. As it was "Molly Howe's" initial outing the syndicate was not too disappointed. There would always be another day. But there was no turning of the corner, race after race in the weeks and months which followed brought no great turn in the syndicate's fortunes. They rapidly came to the conclusion that "Molly Howe" was never going to make it. A year or so later the trainer rang Dinny Allen to tell him that "Molly Howe" had just produced a foal and Dinny said wistfully to him: "That's the first time she was ever in front of another horse."

Jack Mahon of Galway

Jack Mahon was keenly looking forward to seeing the 1965/'66 National Football League Final in which Galway would defend the title against Longford.... but disaster struck the former great Galway centre half-back the week before the game: he was rushed to hospital with a hernia complaint. It was a new experience for the Dunmore man who had never previously sampled hospital cuisine. Jack, All-Ireland winner with Galway in 1956, but on the losing side against Kerry in 1959, was eagerly looking forward to the League decider against surprise packet Longford. They had reached the Leinster Championship final for the first time ever the previous year. But Jack was now ensconced in the Galway Regional Hospital with no chance of seeing Galway win another National League title. His operation, under well known surgeon and former Cork footballer, Bernard Murphy, was set for Friday morning of the League final weekend. Jack had another experience which he hadn't bargained for on his first visit to a hospital and that was the preparatory procedure involved when an operation of that kind is carried out. A local barber visited Jack in the ward and informed him that he had to be shaved. Jack informed him that he had already shaved and his services weren't needed. The barber explained to Jack the kind of shaving that he had in mind:"Just pull down your pyjama bottoms, please " he said, and opened a bag he was carrying and took out the old fashion razor. Jack was extremely embarrassed as the barber sharpened his razor on a leather strap. He looked up at Jack and said: "Mr Mahon, isn't it ?" Jack gave him a nod: " But I know you, didn't you teach me in school?" Jack looked down at the man holding the razor and said in a weak, but hopeful voice: "Did I do alright with you?" to be greeted with an enthusiastic reply: " You were great, you were very nice indeed" as Jack sank back in the bed in relief. The news of Jack Mahon's ailment wasn't to remain a secret because the daily press sports writers from Dublin, Paddy Downey (Irish Times) Mick Dunne(Irish Press) and John D Hickey(Irish Independent) had arrived in the county early that week from Longord. The League final always got major coverage and the presence of newcomers Longford had generated major interest in the game. John D Hickey of the "Irish Independent" travelled out to Tuam to have a word about the match with the Galway Football Board Chairman Fr. Paddy Mahon, a brother of Jack. It was only then did John D hear about Jack's ailment which was to make him miss seeing the League final. The following day, which was a Friday, John D. went to the Regional Hospital in Galway with a photographer to visit Jack Mahon. When he visited the ward he was told by one of the nurses that Jack Mahon had just been wheeled down to the operating theatre. John D. asked the nurse about the possibility of getting a picture of Jack in the theatre. The nurse told him that she did not think it was possible but she would inquire. Jack, at the time, was being prepared for his hernia operation.

Well known Connacht rugby star Joe Costello was standing by to administer the anaesthetic while surgeon Bernard Murphy was being prepared when the phone in the theatre rang. Surgeon Murphy was called to the phone by one of the nurses. He came back to the operating table and said to Jack: "Do you know who that was, John D. Hickey and he wanted permission to take a photo of you on the operating table." "What did you tell him?" asked Jack. "I told him he was not going to have that privilege. He might be a big man up there in Dublin but there was no way was he coming down here to my holy of holies" said the good doctor. Jack listened to the National League final on the radio.

The Longford team lived up to their promise by pipping the then reigning All-Ireland champions by a single point. Naturally, Jack was very disappointed with the result, although full credit had to be given to Longford, who, on the day, were fully deserving of their one point success. The day wasn't over for Jack Mahon. He was dozing off to sleep around midnight when he felt his arm being shaken. He woke to see team captain John Donnellan standing by his bed. They were very close friends. John had dropped in to tell him all about the game that afternoon in Croke Park. It was 4 a m when he was ushered out of the ward to allow Jack Mahon have his well earned rest.

Any time Kerry great footballler Mick O'Connell visited Galway he invaribaly sought out Jack Mahon. Both would spend a lot of time discussing the game and various players. Mick was attending a skipper's course in a local Vocational school where Jack Mahon taught and he would drop up to Jack afterwards. Mick was well known for his fishing exploits in Valentia and the Skelligs. In the course of the conversation Mick asked Jack was there any football being played locally that he could have a look at or even get involved in. Jack suggested a nearby field where Army games were played and where people who felt so inclined could join in if numbers were short.

One evening Mick arrived up to the field wearing a beret, which he wore at times, and asked could he join in. Nobody recognised the Kerry star with the black beret. He was handed a jersey and proceeded to enjoy himself. There was no doubt that he was a cut above the rest Mick fielded impeccably and laid off passes and wasn't afraid to show off his scoring expertise. On one occasion in the game Mick called for a pass but when it was delivered it finished up yards behind the Kerryman, who had to scramble back for it. Mick called over the player who had sent him the pass and said: " Listen, when you are giving me a pass, will you make sure that it is four yards in front of me. That way I can run on to it and collect it without losing my stride."

Jack Mahon and former GAA President Mick Loftus.

The player gave Mick a scornful look and said:" Jasus, who the hell do you think I am, Mick O'Connell of Kerry." Dunmore, County Galway, has many claims to fame, indeed some might rightly say, it was the "Home of Football " but none greater than the number of star footballers who have graced the football scene with the county going, back many, many years. Mick Donnellan, father of John and Pateen, was the first Dunmore man to gain an All Ireland medal in 1925 and he captained Galway in the 1933 All Ireland final against winners, Cavan.

Brendan Nestor was, perhaps, one of the greatest players ever to wear the Dunmore and county strip, winning All- Irelands in 1934 and '38. That 1938 final was the first All- Ireland senior football final I attended and John Dunne, who captained the side I remember clearly at mid field, while Brendan Nestor stood out as one of Galway's best forwards. The other Dunmore man, Frank Fox, won his All-Ireland medal in 1934.

Jack Mahon, All Ireland winner in 1956, was followed by the great three in a row Galway side which boasted Dunmore's John and Pateen Donnellan, John Keenan and Seamus Leydon. Success at County final level, irrespective of the county, means a lot. The honour of the village is at stake and the build-up to the county final captures the same euphoria as if an All-Ireland were at stake. That scenario is enacted virtually in every county throughout the land come championship time during the year. The joy of victory means a week of celebrations and some individuals on the team, depending on their contributions, command even greater adulation. The loss of a county crown plunges the local team into depths of dispair, knowing they would have to account for their actions on their return home. Brendan Nestor was always conscious of that fact whenever he set out to achieve county glory and at times it acted like a spur, driving him to greater heights.

In Dunmore winners are always remembered, football is the beginning and end of all things there, and reputations are built on it, it's that important. Dunmore qualified to play a very good Ballinasloe team in the Galway championship final. It wasn't Dunmore's day, they were well beaten by the Ballinasloe men. Brendan Nestor knew only too well that he had now to face the people of Dunmore and explain where things had gone wrong. He was dropped off at the top of the square, carrying his football boots, with the socks and knicks wrapped around the boots, there were no fancy holdalls or cases around that time. Sitting in a window looking out on the street in Dunmore was a great character called "Whaler" Walsh. Naturally, the news of Dunmore's defeat had already reached him. Brendan knew he had to go through the routine of explaining how they had lost. He reached "Whaler's" house when the voice cried out: "Well, Brendan, how did ye do.?"

Brendan looked at "Whaler" and replied: "We were beaten, Tom, but you should have seen the pitch we were playing on." The "Whaler" butted in: "Was it bad, Brendan"? Brendan (knowing he had to keep up the charade) continued: " was it bad you ask, high grass, thistles, potholes, and would you believe it, a heap of rushes in one corner, impossible to play on it." Tom "Whaler" Walsh had the last say: " And tell me, Brendan, what kind of a field were the other crowd playing in?"

Jack Mahon is probably one of the best known GAA men in the county. A prolific writer on the game and author of books dealing with it, apart from Quiz books, which are very much in demand. His house is an 'open house' and well known players drop in for a chat. The Donnellans and the Mahons were always very close family friends, political friends, and of course sporting friends as well. Jack's grandmother taught old Mick Donnellan, and Jack's mother taught John, his son. Jack Mahon met Mick Donnellan one evening and the conversation turned to football. Mick told him he had won a Down senior football championship medal, illegally of course, many years back, a medal he treasured. Jack was very interested in the Down medal. The only other county medal Jack had seen was his own Galway county championship medal. Jack asked Mick would he loan him the medal that he would like to see it. Mick said he would give it to his son Pateen to drop it in to him.

Sean O'Neill, who was later to become a household name for his football exploits with his native Down, was attending an accountancy course in U CG and he dropped in to make Jack's acquaintance in Dunmore, where they discussed football. Sean, who was to become one of the finest forwards in Gaelic football, had never seen a Down County championship medal until Jack showed him Mick Donnellan's medal. He was intrigued with it. He held it in his hand, noted the date on it, the late '20's, and said: " I hope that will not be the nearest I will ever get to winning a Down senior football championship medal." Some years later, Sean won his county medal with his Newry club.

Meath and Sligo fulfilled a National Football league fixture in Pairc Tailteann, Navan, on a very cold and wet November day. There was a sparse attendance and naturally, the game suffered because of the conditions. Sligo had to bring a substitute in for one of their players who had got a bit of a knock. The substitute ran on to the pitch and took his place at full - forward and his marker was none other than Martin Quinn. The Sligo player was immaculately turned out, snow white togs, nice clean jersey and stockings to match. He looked up at the towering Martin Quinn and said: "I wonder do I need gloves"? Martin put his hand on his opponent's shoulder and said: " Well, for all the ball that you will get, I don't think it will matter."

Mick Higgins of Cavan

Not alone was Mick a forward of the highest calibre in his day, but he commanded a regular place on Ulster teams for years. Mick could be termed a striker, a forward who possessed wonderful anticipation and perception whenever a ball hovered around the opposing goal area, and he would strike, either finishing for a goal or taking a crucial point. In the historic 1947 All- Ireland final between Cavan and Kerry in the Polo Grounds, New York , Mick Higgins was actually returning to the land of his birth, as he was born in the Big Apple. In the 1947 final Mick gave one of the best displays of his career. And it was a Mick Higgins goal , scored at a crucial stage of the second half in the 1952 Ulster football final against Monaghan at Breffni Park, which I had the pleasure of refereeing, that won the day for the Breffni men. Mick is one of the most modest of persons, preferring to speak about others rather than about himself. Kerry star Joe Keohane told me that Higgins, Peter Donohue and Joe Stafford , were the key figures behind Cavan's Polo Ground win when we were involved many years later with the Cardinal Cushing Charity Games in New York. Mick remembers a League game against Longford in Longford. Cavan were being held to a low score, much to the annoyance of Donohue who felt that his side were getting little by way of frees from a very indulgent referee. Out of sheer frustration at the time, Peter roared at the referee: "Will you open your eyes ref, are you blind?." The overworked referee came trotting over to Peter, took out his note book looked at Peter, towering above him and asked: "Who is refereeing this game, you or I?" To which Peter replied: " neither of us." Then he got booked for his pains. Cavan County Secretary , Hughie Smith, was another one of those great GAA officials noted for his wit and put down ability. Hughie had responsibility for a Cavan Junior football team playing Meath in Navan and Mick Higgins happened to be sitting with the team officials at the time. Hughie, being the County Secretary, made several switches

Mick Higgins (Right) receives a Bank of Ireland "Hall of Fame" Award from Dr. Mick Loftus, then President of the GAA.

and changes but all to no avail, and the home team won the game with comparative ease. Walking across the pitch after the match, Hughie was accosted by the young Cavan full-back, who hadn't had a particularly good game, and he said to Hughie:" Why the hell didn't you move me out to the middle of the field.?" Hughie, without batting an eyelid quickly answered: " " I don't know why I didn't move you into the middle of the next field."

Perhaps the presence of Mick Higgins among the other team officials at that particular match prompted Hughie Smith to call on his services to act as manager of the Cavan team the following year when they were paired against Armagh in the Ulster championship. As Mick pointed out, being manager entailed many things unknown to him but he was soon to learn. But there were moments when he had wished that the choice of manager had fallen on someone else. In the Armagh match Mick's valiant lads were doing quite well but Armagh began whittling away at the Cavan lead and the main danger stemmed from the Armagh mid- field which had got completely on top. Mick, after a quick word with his selectors, decided that a change was necessary.

One of the substitutes was big Jim O'Donnell who had one great asset, he could catch high balls, and that was the most pressing need at that time to offset the Armagh dominance. Mick signalled to big Jim to get ready for the action and gave him his instructions. Big Jim ran onto the pitch only to return quickly seeking the slip of paper bearing his name for the referee.

Big Jim, hadn't moved twenty paces onto the pitch, when he was back and asked, " Have any of you lads a spare pair of gloves?" Mick roared at him:" will you for God's sake, take your place." But big Jim wasn't ready yet, he trotted back to Mick, and said: "Mick, would you ever mind the false teeth?" handing the exasperated manager the precious molars. Mick's reply was unprintable.

Scéalta Gearra

A major problem arose in a Kilkenny hurling league game in Freshford. Both teams were out on the field, pucking the ball around, awaiting the start but there was no sign of the referee, who, it transpired had not received notification of the fixture. Rather than abandon the match, a neutral spectator and a referee, offered his services but he had no whistle. A frantic search began but nobody could come up with a whistle. A very enterprising official from the home club slipped out of the ground and across the road to a sweet shop. He bought fifteen "Lucky Bags" before he found what he was looking for—a whistle. He dashed back to the playing pitch and gave the whistle to the referee, and he used it, and the game ended in a win for the home team. Naturally the club reimbursed the official for his outlay in quest of the whistle.

A Kilkenny football team travelled to Limerick to play the home county in a National Football League game and had to take the field with fourteen players because of the absence of a number of players on club football duty. In order to comply with the rule that a team must have a full complement starting the second half, the coach driver was handed a jersey and installed between the posts. Kilkenny lost the game but not through any great fault of the standby goalkeeper.

In a local Westmeath senior hurling league game, the father of the centre half - back of one of the competing sides always stationed himself at the half way line, the poor man suffered from weak eyesight, but he brought a younger son along to pinpoint where the action was taking place: " Where is the ball now, son?" he would ask: " It's been pucked out from the other goal," said the young lad. The father would then roar across to his son, playing at centre- back: " Start pulling, Johnny."

It was junior hurling championship final time. The two clubs who had reached the final were well known to each other. On previous occasions when they had met there was no love lost between them. Their meeting in the county final had attracted a very large audience who had come to see some 'fireworks', as one neutral put it. In one of the dressing rooms the team was getting final instructions from the manager: " I want ye to listen, and listen well. We are going out in a few minutes to play this county final, and I want ye to play as ye have never played before. We may have lost a few battles against them over the years but we never lost the war. My final word to ye is, if a row breaks out here today, don't drop your hurleys, they have too many good boxers on their side."

A Kerryman, during a chat about his forthcoming wedding with his Parish Priest, let slip that they intended to spend the honeymoon at home, as their parents did. "Now Joe" retorted the P.P.: "Those honeymoon at home days are out of date. Were you ever at the Spring Show in Ballsbridge? Any farmer who wants to keep abreast of progress should visit the Spring Show every 2/3 years." Joe admitted that he had never been to Dublin even for an All-Ireland. On being assured by Joe that he would take in the Spring Show during his honeymoon, the Parish Priest wished himself and Mary well and sent him on way. Joe tied the knot in the time honoured way the Saturday before the Dublin Spring Show. On the following Thursday the Parish Priest, who had been doing his annual trip to Ballsbridge, was sauntering up O'Connell Street when he spotted the bould Joe window shopping at Clery's. After exchanging the usual pleasantries the Parish Priest inquired - with no little apprehension - about Mary. In the absence of an immediate response he repeated the inquiry with some concern. However he was assured that there was no cause for concern, as Joe explained ... that having visited Dublin a couple of years before, Mary stayed at home this time!

Two Dublin boys sitting on the Railway End wall in Croke Park during a major game and one boy says to the other " Hey, Jemser dee yah remember last year when we were sitting on this wall and the gardai pulled us off it and made us look at the All Ireland football final"?

An Irish social worker and his wife were living in very primitive conditions as they tried to cope with their abode, a hut made from bamboo canes and leaves in Africa. The wife asked her husband to procure some food for the dinner. He arrived back after an hour and she asked " Well, how did you get on" ? He replied " It's like a bloody jungle out there."

Working on a building site in London was this great character called the "Mule" Deignan, a huge figure of a man, and his great boast to his fellow workers was, that he got a trial with the Leitrim minors . One of his cynical workers declared "If you could find a gorilla under the age 18 he too would get a trial for the Leitrim minors."

During the course of a minor football championship game in Castlebar, one of the teams was losing badly and in desperation they brought on an over age substitute a man who was in fact about 35 years of age. He was quickly spotted by one of the opposing officials, who said to a fellow selector," will you look at that fellow, he has hair on his arse," " He has more than that" said the other selector, " he has hair on the palm of his arse."

Antrim played Sligo in an Under-21 football tournament match in Casement Park which Antrim won. One of the linesmen on duty was from the home county, a fact, which became very clear during the course of the game. Every ball which crossed the line was given as an Antrim kick in, even though some decisions should have gone to the visitors.. The referee had to change the linesman's decision several times. The ball crossed the line beside the Sligo dug out but the linesman again flagged it as a kick in for Antrim and wrongly so. One of the Sligo substitutes roared at the linesman: "For God's sake, would you do your job fair.?" The linesman whipped around and countered: "Is Extradition fair?"

Long Paddy Hayes, 6'4," played with Drumcullen in County Offaly. He was a big gangly lad about 17 years of age, but every time he ran for a ball he would lose his balance and end up on his knees. The crowd would roar: "Go on Hayes, get up." He fell again chasing after a ball and even on his knees, he looked a fair stretch of a man. Again the crowd would roar, "Go on Hayes get up" until a wag in the crowd shouted: " Leave him be, isn't there enough of them up."

There was a man called Dan Tierney who got married in a town in the county, and about six months later he was in Birr doing a bit of shopping with the wife when he met an old friend, Willie Furey, who said: "Ah good man, Dan, and this must be the wife, I don't think I ever met her." And Dan turned to him and said quietly: "Ah Willie, I wish I had your story."

There was this conman who lived in a town in the midlands, who would do any turn, rightly or wrongly, to make a few extra shillings. He travelled around and conned a lot of people with his smooth talk, and never let his conscience trouble him. He went to confession in a local church one Saturday night to the parish priest, who was a very old man. The church wasn't heated so the good P. P. brought a hot water bottle with him and sat there with a rug around his feet for the night, listening to all the penitents. He removed his boots and placed them outside the confessional until he was ready to leave. Tommy the conman, arrived up to the confession box and saw the lovely boots and couldn't resist them, whipped them up and went outside and hid them. He went back into the confession box and confessed that he had stolen a pair of boots and would the priest take them: "Give them back to the owner," said the priest, "But I did offer them to him" said Tommy," but he wouldn't take them." "Well in that case" said the priest, " you should keep them."

Paddy Cullen of Dublin

Paddy was a great goalkeeper, one of the best to represent his county during Dublin's halcyon years under Kevin Heffernan. He won 3 All-Ireland senior football medals, 1974, '76 and '77, winning National League titles in 1976 and 1978, and 4 All Star Awards. He was appointed Dublin manager 1990-'92, helped them to win National League in 1991 and reach the All-Ireland final in 1992. In 1984 Paddy was negotiating the purchase of a pub in Ballsbridge. It developed into a long drawn out affair. Matters were eventually coming to a head and there were clear signs that the sale of the pub was imminent as the parties had agreed on the price and there were only minor details to be cleared up. The '84 Olympics were taking place in Los Angeles and Paddy and a few friends were persuaded to make up a party of eight to travel to LA for the Games. Included in the group was Gerry Duffy, a well known Irish international cricketer, and John Drumgoole of the St Vincent's club, together with friends of Paddy and John, who made up the travelling party. The flight to LA was leaving from Shannon, so Paddy arranged to ring his solicitor to inquire about progress on the pub negotiations on the way down to Shannon. Paddy had given no hint to his friends that he was pursuing a major business deal so he asked that he be allowed to get out and make a phone call to Dublin and they readily agreed. They stopped off at a well-known hostelry about ten miles from the Airport. Paddy made his call to his solicitor, to be told, that at that particular moment, he was the new owner of a famous watering hole in the fashionable Ballsbridge area. Paddy, naturally, was only delighted, and could not contain himself, and broke the news to his travelling companions. All hell broke loose. Bottles of champagne were ordered and the purchase of Cullen's pub in Dublin 4 was celebrated to the fullest. Paddy, realising that ' tempus fugit' and the party had still ten miles to travel to Shannon, called a halt to proceedings and the party took to the road, all in fine fettle. The Cullen party checked in at the departure area and in due course their flight time was called. A very spirited Irish party boarded the 'plane which took off for its destination. Hours into the flight, everybody was in great form, stories began to be told, and the 'craic' was mighty, laughter and good natured banter became the order of the day. The Cullen party seats were next to the First Class section and as the hilarity continued, a very beautiful damsel emerged from the First Class section and immediately spoke to John Drumgoole: " I had to come out and see what all this infectious laughter and jolity was all about." she said, explaining that she was the pilot's wife, making the trip to L A. She took a seat beside John Drumgoole, who in turn explained to her that the party was going to the Olympic Games, and he pointed to Paddy Cullen, nearby and said: " And that's Declan Hegarty, the Irish hammer thrower."

Paddy Cullen congratulates D.J. Carey as he prepares to accept another award.

Paddy nearly fell out of his seat. He succeeded in keeping a straight face, but with some difficulty, knowing that Drumgoole was capable of a lot worse. The pilot's wife gave Paddy a hard look and asked, rightly so: " But should you be drinking if you are one of the athletes." Into the breach stepped Drumgoole again, who replied that he was Paddy's manager and that all the hard training had been done, and the few drinks were helping Paddy to relieve the tensions of the forthcoming Games. The lady appeared to accept the explanation offered by manager Drumgoole. She in turn asked about the date for the hammer throwing event and again Drumgoole rose to the challenge, whipping out a Games programme.

He duly found the information, the date and day of the competition. She promised she would have a particular interest in that event, now that she had met one of the athletes taking part. They were not to see the lady again. Nor indeed could Paddy Cullen's comments on the performance of one John Drumgoole be printed either.

The Cullen party moved off to their hotel for the duration of the Games, which they enjoyed immensely. The real Declan Hegarty, the Irish Hammer thrower, had a very disappointing start to the competition. Each athlete had three qualifying throws.

Declan's first throw failed to clear the cage, surrounding the thrower. His second throw was far more encouraging, over 233 ft, which was in fact, a record throw for an Irishman at an Olympic Games.

Declan's third throw was the important one, he knew if he was to qualify for the finals he would have to better his earlier effort. Declan, took great care with his wind up, and at the precise moment he unleashed the hammer. It not alone hit the side wire of the cage but to his, and everybody else's horror, it uprooted the entire structure, the first time in the known history of the Games that such a thing happened. The Cullen party had the height of sympathy for the Irish athlete, it just wasn't his day. Paddy Cullen's purchase of the pub was suitably celebrated in an Irish pub in L A before the party left for home. Paddy sold the pub some years later and is now the owner of a larger premises in Swords, County Dublin. He assured me that he would not be travelling to the next Olympics in Sydney in 2000, with John Drumgoole.

Retail Business Centre

70 Middle Abbey Street, Dublin 1. (Opposite Penneys)
Phone: 878 2080   Fax: 878 2660

THE 1 STOP SHOP FOR THE   SMALL OFFICE-HOME OFFICE

STATIONERY

- STAPLERS
- ENVELOPES
- PAPER CLIPS
- DIARYS
- FAX ROLLS
- NOTEBOOKS
- FOLDERS
- RING BINDERS
- COPIER PAPER
- PENS / PENCILS

CONSUMABLES

- PRINTER CARTDIGES
- PRINTER PAPER
- TYPEWRITER RIBBON
- FAX TONER
- MULTIMEDIA PRODUCTS
- PC ACCESSORIES
- SCREEN FILTERS
- PC CABLES

MACHINES

OKI	PRINTERS
CANNON	SCANNERS
HP	FAXES
SHARP	WORD PROCESSORS
PANASONIC	TYPEWRITERS
BROTHER	CALCULATORS

PHONES

- P2P MOBILE PHONES
- CORDLESS PHONES
- ANSWERING MACHINES
- TELEPHONES
- EXTENSION CABLES

BUREAU SERVICES

- COLOUR COPYING
- B/W COPYING
- FAXING
- LAMINATING
- BINDING

FURNITURE

- CHAIRS
- DESKS
- PC WORK STATIONS
- FILING CABINETS
- PEDESTALS

OPEN SATURDAYS 9:00 TO 5:30   # GIVING YOU MORE SINCE '64

Kevin Beahan of Louth

Not alone was Kevin Beahan, a brilliant footballer, but he was also one of the best free takers in the game and played a major part in helping his native Louth to All-Ireland football glory against Cork in 1957. He also figured on successful Leinster teams in the interprovincial series. Kevin, has another talent, he is an excellent raconteur and is able to recall great characters associated with Louth football and his native Ardee, and his St Mary's team. During his growing up days in Ardee everybody looked up to Owen Markey, who played on the Louth All-Ireland winning team in 1912. He was the only All-Ireland medal holder at the time in the county. But everybody looked to "Ian" (pronounced Oyne) and his views were always sought when a major game cropped up and "Oyne" was always willing to give of his vast knowledge. He was thrilled when Louth won the 1957 All- Ireland football title. with 5 Ardee men on the team, captained by Ardee's Dermot O'Brien. The 1912 medal winner claimed that the advice he had given, helped in no small way towards fashioning that famous victory. "Oyne" was not alone a legend in the town of Ardee but he was also the town wit. No matter where he appeared he was the centre of attention and was constantly asked about football in the "old days". "How big was the ball? "What was the football like?"How many aside?" etc, were only some of the questions asked, only to be posed a few weeks later again. As Kevin Beahan pointed out some of the answers strained credulity but the sincerity of the man was never questioned.

He was a legend, and that was it. Kevin asked him about his approach to a high dropping ball and how would he go about it: "Very simple" replied "Oyne" "I would bring the ball under me oxter to last Mass and slip in before the first gospel, but I would kick the ball up in the air before I would go in, and slip out before the last gospel and catch it."

"Oyne" would be asked, What would you do about speed and fitness. ? All eyes were drilled on "Oyne" as they awaited his answer: "Well, I would go out to the back garden with the ball, kick it over the roof of the house, run through the half door, through the kitchen and out the front door, over the road and catch it in my neighbour's orchard on the far side."

A favourite question posed to the legend concerned the size of the ball in his playing days compared to the present: "Ah, for Jasus sake, there is no comparison, it would take two of us to carry the ball up to the pitch." What about the size of the ball? "Size, do you know, I saw two of us carry the ball to Broad Lough (an old pitch near Ardee) and we looked at the size of the ball and the width of the gate, and we had to throw it over the ditch." "Oyne," we believe you had a great catch of the ball.? The legend took a big swig from his pint of stout. "We were playing a match over in 'Bellingham and I went up for this ball, I knew I went up high, but I didn't think I went that high."

The questioner looked a bit puzzled: "What do you mean, "Oyne?" The legend gave him a hard stare: " It is very simple, when I came down from my jump, what was I clutching?.... two crows"! " I was told you had a brave kick?" asked another of his audience: "Oyne" revelled in that question as he tried to explain about his huge kicks.

"They had to put me at fullback because of the length of my kicks. I had to wave at Petey playing at centre-field to move towards the other goal. He did move back out not enough. I waved to him again to move further and he did, to the small square, and then I kicked the ball over the bar. I waved to Petey to stay there." "Oyne" played with a local team called Volunteers in his young days. On one particular Sunday they were three points in arrears with time just up in a very tough championship match. Volunteers were awarded a 14 yards free and "Oyne" was called up to take it. He described the scene thus: "They called me up to take the free because they knew that I had the strongest kick. I lifted the ball from where the referee had placed it and had a good look at it. There was a rip in it, a bloody rip in it. I put the ball down again on the line where the referee had placed it. I moved back a few paces and hit it as hard as I could. The cover went into the net, the bladder went over the bar, and we won by a point!"

Kevin Beahan cites Patsy Coleman as being one of Louth's most feared defenders in the county's halcyon days, and heaven helped any brave forward willing to take him on. Playing in his role as a defender, Patsy invariably ruled strongly and firmly in a very physical way and believed in the old maxim of 'not taking prisoners.'

Facing Patsy in a local championship game was a young player who believed in another aspect of the game, it was, being spruce and tidy in dress. He was always beautifully turned out, nice clean togs, stockings, and clean football boots to match. He was a very neat performer. If he was given the opportunity of a goal, he'd opt for a point, ensuring that he had no physical contact with a defender.

The game wasn't long on when Coleman charged in and crashed him to the ground, ball and all. The young player, well aware of his opponent's track record, rose angrily, and shouted: "Look here, Coleman, I came here to play football." The doughty Coleman was turning away when the player's comment halted him in his stride and he retorted: " Then you have no f...k....g business here." !

Louth travelled to Navan to play a National Football League tie against Meath which Meath won handy enough. Patsy Coleman was, as usual, the rock on which many a Meath attack perished, but he was also warned by the referee for a few dangerous tackles on opposing forwards. Coleman kept his man scoreless from play.

When the game was over, a newly ordained priest, well known to some of the Louth players visited the dressing room, to give the players his blessing, and good wishes for the season ahead. Admittedly, it was not a regular practice, though Kevin Beahan did admit the team carried a few players who needed more than a few priestly prayers. Patsy Coleman was returning from having a shower, to be greeted by the priest who was just in the act of imparting his blessing. When the priest left the dressing room, Coleman turned to Kevin Beahan, seated next to him: "Jasus, Kevin, was I that bad that he had to come in to bless me." Louth have a second division grade in football, which is peculiar to the county. It's neither, junior, senior or even minor, and those playing in the grade can be "hasbeens, would-bes, what ever you like. Such a game took place in Glack, outside of Ardee, out in the bog. The playing surface was not too level, but matches played at the venue were invariably very tough. A strange referee officiated in a game involving the St Mary's, and during the course of the match the referee indicated that he was sending off one of the best of the St Mary's players for a misdemeanour. Naturally, being a new referee, he did not know the player he was issuing marching orders to or that he was a very good senior player. Half of the St Mary players surrounded the referee arguing against his decision, while the remainder surrounded the dismissed player, who was promptly being stripped of his jersey, and being handed a jersey taken off a substitute, who had come into the action a few minutes earlier. The substitute, now wearing the No 8 jersey, was marched across to the referee, who duly took his name and promptly sent him to the line. All was then well!

Kevin Beahan (second from left, in front row) and the St. Marys football team.

Wintergreen or embrocation, was a magic potion used by team trainers to cure all the ills which befell a player during the course of a match. It was used long before the advent of physiotherapists, sports injuries doctors, hamstrings and cruciate ligament problems.

The same wintergreen, a horrible concoction, was also a passion killer, a turn off for young players during the early stages of courtship. Girlfriends hated the smell which emanated from the boy friend, who, perhaps, earlier that day, had got a rub of the potion for an injury received in a match.Sitting in the dark confines of the local cinema that night, the pungent odour of the wintergreen, mingled strongly with the cigarette and the pipe smoke, but the magical rub potion easily overcame the weed, which brings me back again to Kevin Beahan and his experience with the same wintergreen.

The St Mary's, Ardee, club had a famous character called the "Bark" O'Brien, who was trainer and masseur. The "Bark" was a great believer in wintergreen, the only solution at the time for all known injuries. Kevin was only one of many players treated by the "Bark". Dermot O'Brien told me that it was better to get a rub of the wintergreen before going out to play from the "Bark" or suffer a double dose, should you needed treatment for a bruise after the game. One of the St Mary's players was nursing a groin strain and a team mentor asked the "Bark" to deal with the problem.

Unfortunately for the player, who was having his first experience of the same wintergreen, some of the solution strayed in the rubbing and got on to his 'you know what'.

A few nights later at training, the treated player stormed into the dressing room and demanded: "Where's the "Bark?" where's the bastard?", I'll kill him." A quiet voice piped up from the corner where he was giving a rub to another player: "What's wrong with you?" asked the "Bark: "What's wrong with me?, you rotten hoor, you. I had to keep a bucket of cold water at me bedside all night to cool my 'willie', it was so hot."

But the wintergreen trick had its good uses as well. The "Bark" was a famous character in his own right, apart from his official job as the Ardee team masseur. He also had an IRA pension, a British Army pension, and an old age pension. How he managed to have all three nobody knew. Louis Malone decided he wanted a rub from the "Bark" and visited him in a tin shed in the back garden of his house. The "Bark's" wife threatened to leave him if he did any 'rubbing' in the house. After a half hour of massaging, and the sweat on his brow, the "Bark" asked Louis at what venue was he playing that afternoon. Louis replied: "I'm not playing actually, I'm a sub, but I'll be in great form for the dance in Tallanstown tonight."

Kevin was invited to a Tyrone County Board dinner to honour the Tyrone senior football team beaten by Louth in the 1957 All-Ireland football semi-final. A number of the Louth winning team were invited. A great friendly rivalry exists between the two counties and invitations to various functions are reciprocated. The '57 function was a huge success and old friendships were renewed. There was the usual get-together among players and stories became the order of the night. Kevin recalled one story told about a certain player, playing with an army team. Also playing with the Army team was "Rosie" Devlin of Tyrone. The other player who shall be nameless was named as a subsitute on his Army team to play a Representative match against the Rest of Ireland. At half-time this player asked "Rosie" to go down injured in order to allow him play, so that he could always say he had played with the Army in that particular fixture. "Rosie" duly obliged, and ten minutes before the end the Tyrone player retired 'injured' and our friend was called into the action. Now anxious to show his capabilities, he went for a 50-50 ball and ended up getting an unmerciful kick in the private parts. He was in so much pain that he was whipped off to hospital, where the injured part was treated and bandaged. The sad part of the story was, that this man had a date to be married the following day, so, though still in considerable pain, he secured his release from hospital. His wife to be wasn't that interested in football, but she had appealed to him not to play in the Army v The Rest match. The wedding went ahead as planned even though he was still feeling the effects of his injury. The wedding was a big success and thoroughly enjoyable. Later that night the newly married couple prepared for bed. His new bride said to him that she knew he was a bit of a Romeo and that he had gone out with a lot of other girls. But she maintained that she always loved him: "I never went out with any other man, I always loved you and nobody else, and I am still a virgin." said the newly married bride. The groom meanwhile, lying in bed was still not feeling the best and he started to chastise his young bride: "Look, I'm fed up listening to you telling me that I am a Romeo, and me going out with other girls, and about your virginity and all that. Look " he said, whipping the bedclothes back revealing his bandages, "look, it's still in wraps."

Michael Henry of Tooreen Co. Mayo.

T he Henrys, are a famous hurling family from Tooreen, near Ballyhaunis, who have made a huge contribution to the spread of hurling in their native county. Michael, Tony, Vincent and Joe have between them amassed more county hurling championship medals than any other set of brothers in the country. Joe, the youngest, was selected and played with Connacht and was a reserve All Star selection. The Henry's, are best known for their dedication to the game of hurling and their great love for it. The club celebrated its 40th anniversary earlier this year. Like all good clubs it possesses a mini bus to transport players to and from venues where the team is playing. The driver is a well known character popularly known as "Knickers". How he came to have such an unusual appellation I was afraid to ask Michael Henry when I contacted him in London. where he is working as a Civil Engineer. There is a shop in Tooreen where players invariably meet to be taken to matches. A notice appeared in the shop window a few days before the match stating: "All players to assemble here for S.H.C. match versus Castlebar on Sunday. Knickers will be down at 2.30 p.m."

When Radio Eireann decided to broadcast commentaries of the All-Ireland football and hurling finals to Brazzaville in North Africa, it proved a boon to all those Irish missionaries working in remote parts of that vast continent in the early 1950s. Michael Henry often wondered how that was arranged, considering that Radio Eireann couldn't be heard at any time in England until technology advanced to allow him to get his home news.

Michael met a Galway man whose uncle was a missionary in Africa at an Irish function in London. The missionary was mad keen on hurling and when posted to his new assignment took with him a caman and sliotar. He loved the game and spent a lot of his spare time belting the sliotar around a clearing much to the amusement of the local natives. But gradually some of the young boys were given a chance of using the missionary's hurley and ball, and they became very proficient at it. Some miles away a young Cork missionary, operating in another village, got to hear of the Galwayman's success with the spread of hurling and visited his Irish neighbour. He also had a hurley and ball and was soon involved in teaching the young men in his own village how to use them. It generated great interest, and some of the older men began to take a hand in this new sport. The two missionaries met one Sunday afternoon after listening to a commentary by Michael O'Hehir on the All-Ireland hurling final and the local men of both villages were enthralled with the whole atmosphere and the excitement created by Michael's commentary.

During the course of the chat between the two Irish missionaries the Galwayman announced that he was writing to the Galway County Board for a set of jerseys and 30 hurleys and a few sliotars. The Cork priest thought it a brilliant idea, and when he got back to his own village later, he immediately wrote to the Cork County Board and explained the need for a set of jerseys, 30 hurleys and a few balls. Before taking leave of each other the Corkman suggested that since the natives had become proficient in the use of the hurleys why not stage a match between the two villages, which were in fact about twenty miles apart. The problem was they had no field or area suitable in which to stage a match. The problem was solved when one of the elders in the Galway man's village informed them that there was an actual clearing which would suit their purpose. It lay half way between the two villages, all that was needed was a mowing of the grass and both tribes would willingly assist in that important chore. Things were looking up in a big way for the two priests. The Provincial - General of the Order was visiting the areas where his missionaries had helped to bring Christianity to the natives and he would be arriving in about a month, giving both priest ample time to make the playing area ready for the big game. The Galway priest had written to the Bishop in whose Diocese they were carrying out their priestly duties and he was delighted to accept an invitation to be present to coincide with the visit of the Provincial General. The Bishop went a little further and insisted on providing a Cup and set of medals to the winners of the match, the Cup to be called "The Congo Perpetual Trophy". Naturally, both priests were over the moon at the latest turn in events. Not alone were they going to have a visit from the Provincial, the Bishop's presence would be a big morale boost for the two hard working clerics. May I digress for a moment in the story, to point out a very important side issue that even the two young missionaries knew very little about. They had replaced two older priests, who had worked in the country for many years, and were now retired. Another fact relating to this story must be put in perspective. Many years previously the natives of both villages became sworn enemies when women from one village were abducted by men from the rival village and that led to a war which lasted for a long time. It was only with the arrival of the missionaries that peace was eventually restored. Moving on in the story, the big day arrived for the big match which had attracted a lot of attention with the visit of the two church dignitaries. The "Congo Perpetual Trophy" and medals were also a source of great interest and the small platform which had been built for the visiting clergy gave a grandstand view of the whole playing area.

The two teams from the respective villages paraded on to the field, led by a motley band of musicians, amidst horn blowing, hoots and drum beats as the rival natives gave support to their kith and kin. The two teams were resplendent in their new jerseys while the traditional loin cloths were worn under the jerseys, all the players, naturally played in bare feet. The referee was a young priest who was accompanying the Provincial -General, he had experience of refereeing, having performed in matches in his seminary days. No, Faith of our Fathers" was not sung before this match because the teams were showing signs of the pressures of the occasion, and the referee decided not to waste time. The match started and the excitement mounted and the clash of the ash was barely heard over the din coming from the rival factions. Half-time was reached and neither side had succeeded in scoring. The two team managers immediately commenced their respective team talks emphasising the valuable trophies that were there to be won and how a little more effort could secure the valuable silver ware. Both teams were obviously hell bent on improving on their opening half displays and two very serious sides lined up for the second half.

Everything was going fine for ten minutes or so until a player on the Galwayman's team whacked a player from the other side across the legs; he happened to be, the son of the tribe elder. All hell broke loose, as the players turned on one another. This was the opportunity for old scores to be settled and the players got great encouragement from their respective supporters. The honour of the respective villages was now at stake. The poor referee hadn't a chance, and the constant blowing of his whistle was drowned, as both factions lay into one another. The referee had no option but to abandon the game. The free-for-all continued for a long spell afterwards until such time as sore limbs forced the retreat of both factions, who returned home to their respective villages. Both team managers were utterly devastated with the sudden turn in events. They were summoned to a meeting with the Provincial- General, who had to make his apologies to the Bishop, who, nevertheless, had never enjoyed an occasion like it, and wanted to know when the replay would take place. He was assured that it wouldn't be for some time. The meeting between the Provincial and the two priests was of more immediate importance, what was going to happen to the "Congo" Cup and medals. The Galway missionary accepted full blame for his team starting the row and suggested when tempers had cooled off enough they could arrange to have a replay. The Cork priest appealed to the Provincial, on the grounds of fair play, that his side were the victims, they had gone out to play the game in sporting fashion, but were made suffer the consequences of a vicious attack by the opposing team on one of his players.

When the shrewd Cork missionary produced his coup de grace. (Corkmen are noted for their knowledge of GAA rules) he stood up and declared: "Rev. Provincial, I am claiming the match and the trophies on behalf of my team, on the grounds that Father Tim did not comply with the rule that states: "that all team names be submitted to the referee on Irish water marked paper and the names of the players must be written in Irish." The referee can vouch for the fact that I did give him a list of my players written on the appropriate paper and in the Irish language, or as near as possible to same. Therefore, Rev. Provincial, having supplied irrefutable evidence relating to the disposal of the trophies and the awarding of the match, I hereby claim same." With that, the Cork priest sat down. His Galway counterpart was struck dumb and while the Provincial-General was genuinely sympathetic towards him, the power of the Corkman's case was far too convincing. Consequently the "Congo Perpetual Challenge Trophy" and medals were handed over. The Cork man didn't hear the words uttered under the Galwayman's breath: "wait until bloody next year."

Jack Lynch of Cork

He first played senior inter-county hurling with Cork in 1935, he was on the famous Cork hurling side which won 4 successive All-Ireland senior hurling championship titles in the early 40s, 1941, 1942 (when he captained the side in their win over Dublin), 1943 and 1944. In 1945 he played with the victorious Cork side which won their third All-Ireland Senior Football Championship title. Then, by helping Cork to win yet another senior hurling title again in 1946, he became the only player to play in 6 successive winning senior All-Ireland sides. He played on 2 losing Cork S H C finals, as captain in 1939, and again in 1947, thus becoming the only player to play in 7 consecutive senior All -Ireland finals. He also featured in the great Munster finals against Tipperary in the years of 1949 and 1950, before retiring in 1951. He won 3 National Hurling League medals, and 3 Railway Cup hurling medals with Munster, in 1942, 1943, (as Cork's fourth player to captain a winning side). He was elected into the Texaco "Hall of Fame" in 1983, the 2nd hurler to be so elevated. He also set up another record which may never be equalled. On February 20th 1944 Jack lined out with his club Civil Service against Eoghan Ruadh in a Dublin senior hurling league game. Because of his involvement with Munster later that afternoon at Croke Park, Jack started the league game in goal. He moved out to midfield where he and I had a few great duels and he took over free-taking for "Service" and scored a couple of good points. Eoghan Ruadh won the game at the finish. Jack headed for his digs on the South side of the city immediately after the match for a bit of lunch before heading for Croke Park. He waited for a 'bus to take him to the city but they were all full. He eventually got a 'bus and arrived into the Munster dressing room to find all the players ready to take the field. Jack was greeted by a more than anxious team trainer Jim Barry, who greeted him with a sarcastic: "Ah, there you are, Jack, it was very good of you to come." Jack played very well in the defeat of Ulster hurlers, notching several good scores in a one-sided semi-final match. He then turned out against the Ulster footballers and while he again figured on the scoring sheet, the Munster men had to yield to a better organised Ulster squad in their semi-final clash. But Jack Lynch achieved a unique distinction on that February 20th occasion. He played in three matches on the one day, and scored in all three, and that is a record that may never be equalled.

I remember travelling to Mallow in the mid '40s with Dublin for a National Hurling League game against Cork, then trained by the legendary Jim Barry. I was to meet him many times after that trip and we became very good friends.

Jim was a fount of knowledge about his native Cork and the teams that had passed through his hands. He told me about the 1942 Cork team that beat Dublin in the All Ireland final that year. "During training for that '42 final, Jack Lynch happened to go down among the forwards. Mick Brennan raced for the ball with Jack and happened to beat him for the ball, which he drove for the goals and scored. Turning to Jack, the bould "Mica" said: " This is a great game, when you learn how to play it." Jim recalled a particular Munster hurling final between Cork and Tipperary at Thurles where the referee's handling of the match didn't go down very well with Cork supporters or indeed with some of the players. As the referee was leaving the field, with Tipperary victors, one of the Cork players walked up to him and said: "Hi ref, where's your dog.? "My dog?" asked the referee: "Yes, your dog." "I have no dog," replied the referee: "what do I want a dog for?" "Well," replied the player: "You're the first blind man I ever saw going around without one."

Jack Lynch was an established senior player when he saw Christy Ring in action for the first time. "I remember we were playing a Munster championship match against Waterford. After togging out I went to look at the minor game in which Cork were involved Ring was on that team. He struck me as a perfect hurler even as a minor." Years later Jack was to sit and watch a much older and mature Ring in action in a senior game: "I had given up playing at the time and I was sitting on the grass behind the goal at a Munster final in Thurles. I had a perfect view of Christy Ring doing the most wonderful thing I've ever seen in hurling. The ball was hit from midfield. After Ring had seen it in the air, he raced in towards the goalmouth without watching it, he looked back at it in flight just when it was about 15 feet from him. Then as the ball bounced he caught it in his hand without even glancing down. He had his eye on three opponents coming at him. He shouldered the first, tapped the ball past the second, and beat the third for the greatest goal I have ever seen." Jack Lynch's last match in hurling or football was an unusual one. He was already nearing the end of his playing career when he decided to enter politics joining the Fianna Fail party, and he was elected in 1948 for Cork City North West: "After playing my last game in Ireland the 1950 county hurling final, I was named as a member of an Irish delegation to New York".

Continuing Jack said "out there they insisted that I should play one game and, although slightly unfit, I agreed to play for ten minutes, that ten minutes was to become an hour an hour during which I broke a rib and was in bed for most of the trip by liner back to Cobh. What a way to finish a career!"

Jack Lynch was one of the finest hurlers produced by Cork and he was also one of the most sporting. He could never be accused of pulling a bad stroke on an opponent although he himself, was subjected to more than his share of wild pulling. Cork played Tipperary in a Munster final at Thurles and during the course of the game he followed a high dropping ball into the square. The Tipperary goalkeeper Tony Reddan, was watching the ball as Jack Lynch came tearing in, and as Reddan caught the ball he was shouldered over the goal line and a Cork goal was flagged. As Jack was moving away, Reddan shouted after him: " If you try that again, Jack, there will be another by election in Cork City North West."

The Blackpool people gave Jack Lynch, their hero, a special homecoming after his election as Taoiseach, or, as the papers proclaimed at the time," another All Ireland for Cork." Thousands gathered near Dublin Hill to await his arrival in Blackpool. Tar barrel blazed in front of the Glen Rovers club house, and well wishers, young and old, pressed forward to shake the hand of the man who had brought the club so much honour and glory. Two groups of schoolboys and girls, in the colours of the "Glen" and St Nicholas clubs, lined up in front of the club house and welcomed the new Taoiseach by singing Irish ballads. Then with the crowd surging around him, Jack Lynch began to deliver his address: "What's he saying?" asked an old timer at the back of the crowd: " Yerra what's he saying" answered his pal " only that he's glad to be home and he'd play for the " Glen " in the morning if he could."

I met the former Taoiseach at a book launch at Croke Park some time ago where we chatted about old times on the playing fields. Jack was one of those skilful hurlers who was a joy to play against. He was elegant, fast onto the ball and deadly accurate when a scoring chance cropped up. He was a perfectionist in many ways and not given to the gamesmanship indulged in by some of our present day "stars" He also had a great sense of humour and loved stories of other players and other times. During our chat I happened to remark that he was looking in very good shape, to which he replied: " There are three stages of age ... Youth, middle age and be Jasus, you are looking well."

Sean O Siochain, who was in the company, wasn't long topping Jack's observation on getting old gracefully with his contribution. He started: "Well now, I can tell you this. There are four stages of age. Stage One.. when you forget names... Stage Two... when you forget faces...... Stage Three.... when you forget to button your fly ... Stage Four.... when you forget to open it." There was no answer to that.

Jack Lynch.

Jimmy Smyth of Clare

Over the years some of our best hurlers have failed to win a coveted All- Ireland medal even though provincial and other honours may have come their way. That observation equally applies to some great players who missed out on years when their respective counties succeeded in capturing prime honours, maybe because of injury suffered in a previous match or of not being selected for the grand prize. Numerous players fall into that category and the list is lengthy.

Jimmy Smyth, of Clare, would have been an automatic selection on present day Clare teams because of his outstanding qualities as a scoring forward and his imposing physical presence. Jimmy, a Munster Colleges' star with St Flannan's College, Ennis, came into the Clare team at a very early stage and for ten years 1954-1964 commanded a regular place on Munster hurling teams. It was the time of great Interprovincial competitions, a time of great hurling and hurlers. And Jimmy Smyth played alongside some of the greatest forwards in the game Christy Ring (Cork) Seamus Bannon (Tipperary) Dermot Kelly (Limerick) Willie John Daly (Cork) Seamus Power (Waterford), Paddy Barry (Cork) to mention some. Jimmy Smyth came from Ruan, a traditional hurling area in the county and he fondly recalls his growing up days in the parish.

He told me: "In our younger days we practised hurling every evening outside the churchyard wall at Ruan. Mickey, a neighbour, always wanted to be present but he still wanted to practice his violin mainly in order to keep his mother happy. So Mickey brought his violin to the session each evening and scraped and floundered painfully through a musical ritual before the real stuff of the evening commenced.

"Christy, another neighbour of mine, also attended, and took part in our hurling sessions. He was a great believer in the close bond that existed between the dead hurlers and the present, and he was ever conscious of the hurlers who had passed away, and who were buried in the nearby graveyard, which was close to the hurling pitch."

Christy also believed that those heroes of the past, who were buried nearby, were enjoying the clash of the ash, of hurley striking sliotar and the echo and re-cho reverberating around the area. Some years later Jimmy Smyth met his old comrade Christy at a match at Croke Park and inevitably the conversation hearkened back to their growing up days in Ruan. " Do you remember, Jimmy," he said, " when Mickie played the violin.

We knocked mortar off the graveyard wall." And then in a truly solemn tone ," There was no corpse lonely in those days."

The same Christy was a goalkeeper himself and was very proud of the fact that few goalkeepers could get the same length into a puck-out as he. Indeed he never failed to get his goal deliveries down to the opposing 21 yard line and more often than not, Jimmy Smyth and his Ruan forwards were able to collect the ball and score. His puckouts were certainly an invaluable asset. In those days the ball was far heavier than it is nowadays. The "Lawlor" ball was the most popular at the time. It was made from leather, had very thick verges and was quite heavy. On wet days the ball became heavier still. But times change and sliotars and hurleys change too. The "O'Neill" ball which came later was lighter and replaced the heavier edition. Ruan is about six miles from Ennis, and Doora is about two miles beyond Ennis. Jimmy Smyth recalls " Doora could well have been in

Africa because we never ventured beyond Ennis, so it was a long distance away and all we had were bicycles, ass and horse cars, and the odd sidecar."

Just a few years before Christy died, Jimmy asked him a very pointed question. What was the longest puck out he had ever struck.? He looked at Jimmy through and through without saying a word, thinking and evaluating the scale of the question. He didn't answer for a long time and continued to repeat the question posed to him, again and again.

"The longest puck out, ha h... the longest puck out hah ...? Eventually he glared at Jimmy with his steely blue eyes that had frightened many a forward who had dared venture into his territory. He looked at Jimmy and said with a certain amount of venom " If I had the "All Stars" ball that they have today I'd drive it down to effin Doora."

Naturally, there was no curb on the abuse or advice readily offered by the knowalls cramming the sidelines. Some of the advice was constructive enough and offered in good faith. The other kind was not meant to be helpful , but then it takes all kinds to make a world. I can relate to another story given to me by Jimmy Smyth but I'm sure there are other players country wide who have also had experience of similar advice.

Jimmy was playing in a local important championship match with Ruan. One of his best friends, Tom, who was also a great fan of his, kept shouting words of encouragement, while also urging on Jimmy's team mates. Things weren't going too well for Ruan, nor indeed was Jimmy's contribution up to his normal standard. There are days like that when everything goes well and you score without looking at the posts.

There are other days when it seems as if fate is conspiring against you and nothing can change the situation. Eventually the ball broke kindly towards Jimmy. He always had the strength to take defences on once he had the ball in his grasp, and that, invariably got the Ruan fans excited. There was only a point or two between the teams and the final moments were ticking away, when Jimmy grabbed possession and went tearing away on a solo run.

The amosphere was electric at the prospect of a major score. The advice was coming fast and furious from the Ruan followers, " Stick it over the bar, Jimmy," "Go for a goal, Jimmy," "Pass it to Henchy, Jimmy," "Burst the net, Jimmy, "Pass the ball to Power, Jimmy," Jimmy's prime fan Tom, had remained very quiet up to that stage, but now with an opportunity arising of a possible winning score, with Smyth in full flight, he could contain himself no longer. Standing up on his sideline seat and totally ignoring all and sundry, Tom cried out over the din: " Take no notice of them , Jimmy, make your own arrangements."

Jimmy Smyth.

Mick Wright of Offaly

A noted wing back on the Offaly senior football team, winning All-Ireland medals with the panel in 1971 and 1972. His haul of medals included 8 Leinster's, five senior, two u-21 and one junior. He is a native of Daingean and will always be remembered for his tenacious tackling, long dead ball kicking and tearaway style, which endeared him to the Offaly followers. Later in his career, he trained Senechalstown to win their first ever Meath senior football championship title. He performed a similar feat with Celbridge in Kildare. Mick also joined a growing band who were invited to play in the New York football championship. His host club was Donegal, who included a number of other prominent county players brought out for the championship. On a particular Sunday Mick lined out with his Donegal team and was chosen at centre back. The game was ready to commence, the backs were back, forwards in their places but the referee was in no hurry to start proceedings. He stood there and one of the players from the opposing side said to the referee "What's keeping you, ref, why can't we begin.?" The referee told him to take his time. After about another thirty seconds the same player again inquired about the delay as the players were champing at the bit to get the action started. "What are we waiting for,?" he said. The referee turned to him and said:" I haven't got a blooming ball, that's why" To which the opposing player said to ref; "Shure, what's that got to do with it, can't you blow the whistle and start it anyway.?

Mick played with Celbridge in his latter years and they were competing in the Keogh Cup competition in Kildare. They had just made up the fifteen and included on the side was Mick's son, Kenneth, at wing back, with Mick holding down the centre half berth. Young Kenny was actually making his debut at senior level. On that particular day, Jack Charlton's heroes were playing a World Cup qualifier and most of the players would have wished to be watching it on television rather than competing in this particular fixture. The referee was about to start the match when Mick clearly heard a voice in the opposing half- back line roar across to his brother on the opposite wing: " Right Joe, this is it, drop the blade, it's time to mow." Mick played with his home club Daingean in the Offaly football championship in Tullamore on a fine Sunday afternoon. The ball went into touch off a Daingean boot on the side of the field where there were concrete seats on the sideline. The referee was Jody Gunning, a former intercounty star, who was only after taking up the refereeing chore but was later to handle many important intercounty matches. A defender placed the ball to take a sideline kick, as he stepped back to take the kick, he was subjected to terrible abuse from a spectator sitting on the concrete benches.

The same spectator had been vilifying the player earlier in the game but human nature being what it is, the player about to kick the ball , stopped suddenly and walked off the pitch.

He mounted the steps, made straight for his agitator, hauled off and laid him out on his seat with a box to the jaw and then returned to the field of play. Referee Jody Gunning was waiting for him, with his book and pencil, demanding his name. The player said " What are you doing, Jody, the guy is a friend of mind, we work on the bog together I was only playing with him. He's always giving me stick at matches and this time I wasn't taking it." Jody wasn't impressed and gave him his marching orders.

Not so long ago Celbridge were involved in a Kildare senior football league match, but they were short one of their best players, who failed to get to the venue in time for the start of the game. The team had to take the field without him. He duly arrived ten minutes after the start, the manager told him to get ready that he was going to put

Mick Wright

him into the action. The manager said: "Ok, Tom, get warmed up before you go on." The player replied: " I'm warm enough, I have a good heater in the car."

Dublin played Offaly in the 1978 Leinster senior football semi- final in Portlaoise and Mick Wright was positioned at centre half- back. It was the day that Kevin Moran was pressed into action ten minutes into the second half by the Dublin selectors, a move which led ultimately to Dublin winning the game by a three point margin. Moran, back in his familar centre half-back role, though a signed Manchester United player, was asked to take a long range free. Jimmy Keaveney had moved out from goal and was closely watched by Mick Wright who moved in behind the Dublin sharpshooter. Jimmy kept backing into Mick Wright before Moran's effort came sailing in, and Wright said to Keaveney: "Come off it, Keaveney, you bloody fish and chips merchant," Jimmy started to laugh and replied " Now Mickey, you're earning your bleedin' living up there too." a comment which had both of them laughing.

Both teams went to the Killeshin Hotel after the game. Along with other members of the Offaly team Mick Wright headed for the bar where Jimmy Keaveney and Bobby Doyle were drinking pints of stout. Keaveney shouted to Wright: " What are you having to drink Mick," and all three started to talk about the match which Dublin had just won - such was the comraderie.

Celbridge were paired against Sarsfields in the Kildare senior football championship, a daunting task for Mick Wright's men. Sarsfields had the services of Dermot Earley, one of the finest players ever to decorate the football scene, not alone for his native Roscommon, but also in his adopted county, Kildare, where he served as a Commandant, in the Defence Forces. In many years watching Dermot play I have never seen him step out of line. He epitomised all that is good in the game and had an impeccable record for sportsmanship. The Celbridge team mentors knew that Earley was the man to watch. Instructions had been given before the game to mark him tightly, which they proceeded to do. Dermot gained possession and immediately was challenged. He turned left and right, played the ball on his toe, and tried to break through the shackles imposed by the close attention of his markers. Eventually Dermot wiggled free and passed the ball to a colleague, but the referee blew his whistle and awarded a free to Celbridge. Dermot asked the referee why had he blown him for a foul. Dermot was a bit incensed. The referee informed him that he had turned twice. Dermot fired back and told the ref that he was entitled to turn twice as long as he had played the ball, and that's what he had just done, and he was clear about the rule. The referee's reply was: " Well, you won't do it here." End of message.

There was a great old timer who frequented a bar in Rhode, County Offaly. A favourite practice of his was to put fifteen porter bottles on the counter and use them to pick his best Rhode football team of all time. This usually took all day in the bar but he had plenty of time to spare. As soon as he had nominated his players he would then proceed to put them in their positions. This involved moving the bottles around for hours on end, until eventually the barman said to him: " Dinny, I've been watching you all day. You have been moving every one of the bottles around, except one, Johnny Mooney, Paddy McCormack, Eugene Mulligan, Martin Heavey, everyone in fact, but the corner forward, why is that." ? The old timer looked at him and gave a grimace: " That's young Dinny my son, and God Almighty wouldn't move him."

Jack O'Shea of Kerry

When I set about choosing my best midfielder in my "Best Football Team" in a previous book I ran into a major headache. There were so many talented players vying for any one of two posiitions that it took me quite a while to decide on the players I felt fully measured up to the qualifications necessary for the positions. I finally settled on two players, Brian Mullins of Dublin and Jack O'Shea of Kerry. The two players went on to play major roles in the pursuit of major honours for their respective counties. Brian Mullins was well established as the country's top midfielder before Jacko made his All- Ireland debut with Kerry in the 1978 final. I made Jacko my choice instead of his Kerry colleague Mick O'Connell. I suppose you could describe O'Connell as the artist extraodinare, O'Shea as the artist cum artisan. Some players tend to lose the head when greatness is thrust upon them; it can never be said of O'Shea who still remains the unassuming player he was when he first hit the senior scene in the mid 1970's. Indeed Jacko's first meeting against Brian Mullins came just a few weeks after Dublin had beaten Kerry in the 1976 All-Ireland final, a victory which helped to exorcize the memory of the '75 defeat at the hands of the Kingdom. Dublin's first National Football League game was set for Tralee just two weeks after their great win in the All-Ireland final. Jacko remembered it well because he was pitted against Mullins, and had the satisfaction of scoring a point right from the throw-in at the start of each half. Later in the game Mullins soared up for a ball in the centre of the field and as he was moving away with the ball Jacko caught Mullins jersey and glove. A furious Mullins threw the glove at Jacko with the comment: "O'Shea you should be still in school."

But the bould Jacko suffered a telling- off of a very different kind during a local championship game between Jacko's team, St Mary's of Cahirciveen and Kilcummin, near Killarney. Present Munster Council Chairman, Sean Kelly figured at midfield for Kilcummin, and while small of stature for the midfield position, he was noted for his never - say - die- spirit when contesting possession. Sean's uncle, also Sean, played full- forward on the 1953 All Ireland winning Kerry team which defeated Armagh Present on the occasion of the St Mary's- Kilcummin match was another uncle, a local parish priest, who, incidentaly, was later to baptise Jack O'Shea's young sons, Kieran and Aidan. There was nothing between the two teams coming up to half - time when Jacko went to field a high dropping ball. He invariably timed his run in order to arrive at the vital moment as the ball began to drop. Jacko never spared himself in that kind of situation.

He went flying in, scattering players in all directions including Sean Kelly, who was unfortunate to bear the brunt of Jacko's charge. Kelly had to receive attention but recovered quickly. At half- time as the teams made for the dressing rooms Jacko was accosted by a furious Fr Kelly, Sean's uncle, who thundered: "O'Shea, you should be locked in a cage."

Jacko in action for Kerry.

Dave Guiney - A man of many talents.

I grovelled in my efforts to coerce David Guiney into telling me the source of the following story but he refused point blank to reveal the characters named in the story. The only concession I finally extracted was a hint that it happened in one of Dublin's most famous GAA clubs. I keep telling Dave that he shouldn't attempt a Dublin accent with his lilting Duhallow cadence. I told him I have never heard Jimmy Keaveney, for instance, telling a Cork joke, with a Cork accent. However, that's by the by. Dave swore to me that this story is true. This club had a Treasurer, who had served with outstanding distinction for over 40 years. He decided to retire and he duly tendered his resignation. Without advising the Treasurer, the other officers of the club met to consider the letter. After a long discussion the Chairman, a man of good old Dublin stock, made the suggestion that in recognition of his 40 years of great service, the Treasurer should be given an honorarium. This was greeted with almost unanimous acceptance but the Chairman noticed that one member present appeared to have some reservations about the suggestion and he put the direct question to him: "Are you against the honorarium?" "Not exactly" said our man-" but I have known our Treasurer for most of the 40 years, and I have never known him to be interested in any form of music. Before we give him the honorarium, I think we should find out first whether or not he can play one." It goes without saying that Dave Guiney is a well known sporting figure, former Olympic athlete and author and spends quite a lot of time giving talks to various organisations and corporate bodies. They are occasions not to be missed, because of their humorous content. He was invited to a GAA function to his native Cork, where he immediately renewed old friendships. He espied Willie John Daly, one of Cork's legendary stars, who had just walked into the function, rushed over to him crying: " Willie John" and with arms outstretched, enveloped his old friend in a bear like hug. They exchanged the usual greetings, asked about one another's health, had a brief chin wag and Dave moved on to greet another friend Frank O'Brien who brought him down to earth when he and said to him: "Listen Dave, are you losing your marbles, that's not Willie John Daly, that was John "Kid" Cronin you were talking to." Dave was flabbergasted when the error was pointed out to him. He immediately rushed across to where "Kid" Cronin was talking to some friends of his, pulled him aside, and began to apologise profusely for his terrible mistake in mixing him up with Willie John. Admittedly, Dave hadn't met "Kid" Cronin for some time but genuinely thought it was Willie John who had walked in to the reception. The "Kid" Cronin put his hand on Dave's shoulder and said: " I wouldn't worry about it, Dave, to be mistaken for Willie John Daly is a great honour."

Dave attended a major function in Cork. Former GAA President Con Murphy, holder of 4 All Ireland medals, 2 Railway Cup medals, All-Ireland referee, and later to become Cork County Secretary and Chairman of the County Board, was being made a "Freeman of the City". The very large attendance included former great stars from other counties who had played against the great Cork defender, and of course, all shades of Cork sporting life were present. Dave mingled with old friends during the reception and met Willie John Daly, whom he had known for many years. They started talking about old times when they were joined by none other than Tipperary's Mick "Rattler" Byrne. The Tipperary man hadn't met Willie John for some time and they were delighted to renew old acquaintances. " Rattler" Byrne started the ball rolling when he invited Willie John to look at his forehead: " Do you see that scar, Willie John, I had to get five stitches, you did that in the Munster final in Thurles." Willie John, not to be outdone pulled up the leg of his trouser displaying a vivid mark of an old wound: " Will you look at that "Rattler". You gave me that in Limerick in a Munster semi final." Dave sat there listening to the pair of them. "Rattler" opened his shirt and pointed to his shoulder: "Have a look at that, you nearly smashed my collar bone when you gave me a shoulder, illegally, when I went for a ball "

"What are you talking about " said Willie John, "look at my hand, you broke a finger when I put my hand up to catch a dropping ball. " Served you right" said the "Rattler" you should have had more sense " on and on they argued, until Dave thought it time for him to leave their company. Just as he did, the "Rattler" Byrne put his arms around Willie John and said "Willie, isn't wonderful, the dust on the square has settled at last."

Dave refused to tell me the name of the character involved in another story. Sufficient to say, it happened to one of the "country" players on the Cork team. In Cork, there are city players and "country players" or players who live outside of the city. This "country" player was walking down main street in his local village when he suddenly realised that the local parish priest was heading in his direction. There was no way that he could avoid him. The priest, not too gently, began to chide the player about the fact that he had been somewhat remiss in his essential religious duties in recent months. Fortunately for the player, and before the parish priest got properly into his stride, the Angelus Bell rang out and halted proceedings. The player whipped up his hand, made a rapid "Sign of the Cross"- and within a matter of seconds, he promptly crossed himself again... and waited patiently. The parish priest in the meantime, had made the "Sign of the Cross", solemnly, ceremoniously and slowly. And he was slower still as he said his silent Angelus. Several minutes passed and then the parish priest again with solemnity and ceremony and time, crossed himself again.

With the sternest of faces and clear disapproval, he looked at the player and said; "That was a very quick Angelus, you know." And without even a flicker of a smile the unabashed player replied:. "Practice, Father...... Practice" ..... and with that he was gone, moving smartly towards his destination and safety. In 1972 Kilkenny gave Cork a hammering in the All- Ireland senior final, an event which Corkmen generally prefer to forget. As Dave was struggling to get out of the ground he found himself in the middle of his own, a very subdued Cork crowd. A plaintive accent, that echoed Blackpool, Spangle Hill, Guranebraher, or their environs, raised itself in pain behind him. "You know something" — it whined — "If we didn't have Ray Cummins, we'd have been murdered." Perhaps two or three seconds later, a second Cork accent, as richly endowed as the first, piped up in equal anguish, " Come here" — it said — " we WERE murdered."

My late "Evening Press" sports editor, Longford- born Paddy Flynn and Dave Guiney had two regular seats in the Hogan Stand. They had just turned into Jones Road when Paddy nudged Dave and said: " Would you look at the two culchies"? forgetting for a moment, that both of them qualified as "culchies". The two men that he pointed to were striding along the road, their white shirts gleamed whiter than white and there was a glow on their faces that could only have come from the fields and the wind and the sun. " You don't see men like that nowadays, "said Paddy, "they're up for the day and they'll make the most of it." They followed Paddy and Dave into the queue for "Press Tickets only". Dave was about to tell them that no money would be accepted at the particular stile when he noticed that they had tickets. Obviously they were men of substance in either Kildare, Meath, Offaly or Wexford. But they were football men, as Paddy and Dave did a bit of eavesdropping. "I'd say Meath have a good chance of winning this one." "I wouldn't be too sure about that, they're not as good now as they were last year." "But what do you make of Kildare? They're up one minute and down the next. You never know where you are with them." "Still they might be good today and that wouldn't be a bad thing at all." I'm glad it's the first game. We'll be out of here by 4o'clock and on our way home." "Aren't you in a fierce hurry? The hurling game will be good." " I have no interest, good, bad or indifferent in it. Wexford will crucify them. It won't be a game at all." Still,I think we should stay on and have a look at it." "All right,but only for a few minutes of it anyway. At the most, a quarter of an hour." " Ah now, we could stay for half of it. It might be a great game. A half is a long time." "Indeed it's not. We'll stay for one half and then we'll head for a pint and home." "Great. That's grand. And which half will we stay for? The first or second?"

I pop into Dave Guiney's house in Sutton for a chat occasionally which is only a brisk walk from my abode in Raheny (I have to admit, I take the car) and while his long suffering wife Phyl is making the coffee, we exchange our usual pleasantries. I remember meeting David for the first time when he visited our house in Fairview along with another Corkonian, Danny Lucey, who was anxious to meet my father, Sean Senior. Since then Dave and I have remained the best of friends and we soldiered together when he worked with the "Irish Press Group".

Dave being the excellent raconteur that he is, loves telling stories, and with a little persuasion I got him to tell me the one about a Miss Jane Reid. Someone in the "Mirror" Newspaper in London suggested that Dave was the ideal person to contact when she arrived over from London to write articles on famous Irish sporting personalities. The said Miss Reid had much to recommend her, tall delightfully endowed, and fetchingly beautiful and would, unquestionably, be made effusively welcome by the average Irish sportsman, particularly the single one. The ever galant Dave, immediately set the wheels in motion and contacted all the major sporting figures of his acquaintance whom, he felt, would do the nation proud. The response from all those well known sportsmen was magnificent just as Dave had expected. In time, the charming Miss Reid did all her interviews and even managed to get hold of the elusive Mick O'Connell on Valentia Island and in the fullness of time she packed her bags again and disappeared back to London her assignment completed. But Dave's problems were really only beginning.

With her lack of knowledge of Ireland, Irish sportsmen, and Irish sport, particularly hurling and Gaelic football, the lovely Miss Reid dropped a few resounding and indeed, at times, hilarious "clangers" in some of her stories. One, in fact, succeeded in creating a distinct coolness between one person and his girl friend, another came close to setting off a miniature tribal warfare in a certain part of Ireland. The upshot was that Dave Guiney was drawn unwillingly back to the scene. Before any further stories were published Dave had a succession of telephone calls from Miss Reid's office in London to check on facts and on statements that the lovely Miss Reid had made and which, while on the surface might have appeared innocent, could possibly be misconstrued here in Ireland.

Then one afternoon another call from the "Mirror" in London seeking a David Quinney, a version of his name Dave Guiney was not prepared to accept. He wasn't long putting the caller right on that score. The arrogant voice on the phone, had all the undertones of Eton, Harrow, Cambridge, Oxford, the British Royal family, horses and hounds and tally-hoes to boot. Dave conjured up visions of a plum-coloured face, a bristling moustache, the cutaway Norfolk jacket, the drainpipe whipcord trousers, even the silver box of snuff: " I believe you have been of some service to one of our ladies?" the voice asked.

Dave Guiney, far right, seen here at the presentation of the National Irish Bank / G.A.A. Personality of the Month Award to John Leahy (centre), also present Jim Lacey, of National Irish Bank.

"You do know Jane Reid, old boy?" One thing Dave hates is being called "old boy" so he quickly asked his caller the reason for the phone call: " It's like this, old boy. Miss Reid has written an excellent story for us about one of your famous sportsmen, Eddie Key-Hur is the name, old boy.- recognise it? A rather splendid story, damn well written. Seems to be quite a man this Eddie Key-Hur, old boy. You probably know the chap? Dave managed to scrape in a little "Yes". But the caller was in full torrent, and there was no halting him. " It seems he plays hurling. A bit like shinty I imagine. It sounds a damn good game, old boy, and he is quite a star. But there are a few things I would like to check with you. Miss Reid says here that he comes from inisty-oogee in County Kilkenny and that his father was stationed there with the Irish Guards." Efforts by Dave, for the benefit of the population of Inistioge, to get in the correct pronunciation of that delightful place, went unheeded as the Londoner pounded away. " Damn it all, I think there must be a mistake here, I was in the Guards for years, you know, and I can't recall they were ever stationed in Kilkenny. Fine regiment and all that, old boy, jolly fine record, splendid chaps." Dave's London caller, was in full flow: "You know, old boy, that several of your lads won the V C, not only in the last show but also in the first one.... you know, the one that was to end all wars, and all that sort of things." He went on and on and Dave had to suffer hearing about the Irish Guards history, chapter and verse. " It's possible Miss Reid made a slight error. She should have written Gardai instead of Irish Guards " suggested a by now weary Dave Guiney. That halted him most effectively and allowed Dave time to explain the word Gardai. " Of course, of course, old boy. By Gad, that's it. Knew damn well it couldn't have been our crowd. Never stationed in Kilkenny, you know. Fine chaps, great regiment." It must have been 10 minutes later before Dave got the chance to get his caller off the line, claiming his services were needed elsewhere: " But of course, dear boy, how jolly of you to talk with me for so long. splendid, splendid, absolutely marvellous. Knew I couldn't be wrong about the Guards. Wonderful regiment. Knew they were never stationed ... Dave hung up. My good friend Dave, to this day has never asked Eddie Keher if he read the story, which Dave hadn't. He dreaded to think of the outrage that might have been perpetrated on our beloved Eddie Key-Hur of Inisty-oogee.

I was drinking a cup of tea in the GAA hospitality suite in the Hogan Stand, prior to the start of the All -Ireland senior hurling semi final between Waterford and Kilkenny. In my company was that doyen of rugby writers Edmund Van Esbeck formerly of the " Irish Times." Edmund has two sporting passions, apart from his love for rugby- hurling and Arsenal soccer team. For years I have been chastising him gently about his allegiance to the "Gunners" pleading with him to change over to Manchester United who at least were picking up trophies as if there was no tomorrow. Last season Arsenal won the Premier League and Cup, and Edmund grew a foot taller as the Man Utd cupboard remained bare. Opposite to us in the hospitality suite were colleagues Dave Guiney and Paddy Downey, both of whom were engaged in a very animated discussion. Edmund turned to me and said quietly: "will you look at the pair of them, I never let them forget about the hammering my native Waterford dished out to Cork in the first round of the Munster championship in 1967. Did Dave mention it at all to you for your book?" I admitted that he hadn't but I made a mental note to broach the subject to the same Dave, which I did many days later.

Dave remembered the occasion well (I didn't tell him how the subject arose or the involvement of one Edmund Van Esbeck.) Dave then proceeded to tell the story. On the morning of that particular match in 1967 Dave, Paddy Downey of the "Irish Times", John D Hickey of the "Irish Independent" and Donal Carroll of the "Evening Herald" set off for Waterford to see Cork, then the reigning All Ireland hurling champions, take on Waterford at Walsh Park in the first round of the Munster Championship. Donal Carroll, the teetotaller in the party, was on that occasion a back-seat passenger(normally he would have been coerced into driving his colleagues to the match) Dave was a regular drinker at the time, a habit shared by Paddy and John D.

All three were more than reasonably fortified by the time they arrived at Walsh Park for a match which turned out to be an absolute and total disaster not just alone for Cork but also for Paddy Downey and Dave- and of course for every Corkman who had made the journey to Waterford that day. Cork were riding high at the time following their All Ireland win over Kilkenny the previous September, Waterford were going through bad days- and the general feeling was that Cork, even in second or third gear, would romp away to the easiest of wins. The first half supported that feeling with some assurance. Cork, without any undue pressure, looked the part of All-Ireland champions and there was not even a faint hint of trouble on the horizon.

Sadly for the two Cork scribes, the second half was to become a raging nightmare. Cork's full-back, the utterly reliable Tom O'Donoghue was sent off... John Kirwan blasted in a goal for Waterford... Tom Cheasty belted over a point ... and in those few explosive minutes a potentially beautiful picture for Cork became an ugly and mutilated canvas. Waterford went delightfully mad, ran poor Cork ragged in every area of the field and by the time a merciful final whistle put an end to the rout, they were ahead by eight points. It was a sobering and chastening experience for Dave Guiney who was close to despair when he filed his report on the game. Once that was completed he promptly retired to the bar to drown his sorrows. There, sometime later, he was joined by John D Hickey and together they disposed of a few more Irish whiskies, while they waited for Donal, who had gone for a walk, and for Paddy, who was still composing his epic report for the "Irish Times" In time Paddy arrived at the bar, more whiskey was consumed and when Donal turned up to remind his colleagues gently that they had still to face the journey to Dublin, the others were, to put it mildly, more than well fortified.

The four of them got into Paddy's car, took off in the general direction of Dublin- and into further trouble. They arrived into Kilkenny to find out that it was the final night and the extravagant climax to the Kilkenny Beer Festival. It was clearly a welcome and handy excuse for further drinking- and against the vote of the affable Donal Carroll - they decided the Festival's closing night would not be complete without all three.

Donal Carroll in his excellent wisdom, decided to remain in the car. With the luck of John D, Paddy and Dave- they saw it as good luck, Donal would have dismissed it as bad luck- they ran into the cast of the 'Riordans' a popular RTE TV soap at the time, in the hotel. They were the guests of honour at a reception, and they gladly joined them. The hours slipped by gently, the drinks came and disappeared until, eventually, close to midnight, a halt was called. In the very best of form, Cork's humiliating defeat at Walsh Park was now in the past, the three scribes made their way slowly to the car - and to Donal. And from Donal, there was not a word of criticism, not even a suggestion of angry frustration. So they made their way towards Athy and on towards Dublin. Peace was supreme in the car. And it remained like that until Donal, in the back seat, pointed out, with all the politeness within the man, that the car was slightly on the wrong side of the cat's eyes in the middle of the road. Paddy corrected the flow of the car but within a few minutes there was that little fade away again to the right. Donal reminded him that they were back on the wrong side of the cat's eyes. At that stage, unfortunately, Dave added the comment that it was normal in Ireland to drive on the left side of the road- and that, sadly was the moment when the straw within Paddy finally cracked. He jammed on the brakes, brought the car to a savage halt, exploded into a raging condemnation of his three passengers- and ordered them out of the car. Those of us who are in the trade are well acquainted with the fury of P K Downey going back to the Bank of Ireland All-Stars Selection days when he would bring his walking stick crashing down on the table we sat around, to vent his anger on those who went against his player selection. But Dave said on that night, on a bleak hill overlooking the town of Athy he was at his best- or perhaps his worst. The fires of Goleen flared in Paddy, he gave his three unfortunate passengers his multicoloured opinions of all three in language that was far removed from parliamentary and in a towering inferno of rage, he was adamant that all three remove themselves from his car. And so they did- and Paddy, in immense dudgeon drove off. I can well picture the scene. There they were, the three scribes, standing in the dead and darkness of night, far from Dublin, marooned on a lonely hill and suddenly terrified. What could they possibly do.? But Paddy, fair play to him relented. Within a few minutes they saw the car reversing towards them and when it came to a halt they entered timidly and quietly. And the silence reigned until they were about a mile from Athy. Then Paddy exploded again- happily not this time at them. He had forgotten to get petrol in Waterford, had forgotten again in Kilkenny and now his petrol gauge was showing empty. The problem now was whether or not they could make it all the way to Athy. But they did make it. The first petrol station was in darkness, so was the second.

There was no life showing in the third garage they tried so matters were beginning to look pretty serious. In desperation Paddy came to a halt just outside the local Garda station and all three went to the door. They had to knock a few times, loudly, before it was eventually opened by a slightly surprised man, who at that particular moment, looked as though he had just got up from a comfortable bed. Indeed on that point Paddy claimed that he could see the tips of his pyjamas peeping out from the end of the Guard's trousers. But the Guard emphasised what they had feared and were fearing. There was not a petrol station open in Athy at that hour. Their only hope, he explained, would be to get to the Naas Road to Dublin - and that was, as they knew, possibly 20 miles or more away. On what was left in Paddy's tank at that moment killed that hope stone dead.

Their gloom was close to zero- until the Guard provided just a tiny light. He remembered that he had a can of petrol in the station. It might be enough to get them to the Naas Road. But when the can was produced, another problem arose. The can had no spout, they had no funnel to transfer petrol to the tank- they were still in trouble.

Then Dave had a brain wave. He had bought a "Sunday Press" starting out and it was somewhere in the back of the car. A quick search and it was found. By rolling it up, could it not be used as a funnel? The operation after that was executed smoothly and was well carried out. Some petrol was lost in its transference to the tank but, thankfully, most of the petrol went into the tank. Dave still remembers very vividly John D 's remark as the last precious drains of petrol went safely into the tank. " That's the first time in its history that bloody newspaper was ever of any use to anyone." From then on it was plain sailing to Dublin. They made the Naas Road petrol station with comfort, filled up and duly reached the city in the late hours of Monday morning. And there they parted to go their separate ways. During all that time there was never a word of criticism nor remonstrance from Donal Carroll. Naturally the three scribes were left with the distinctly embarrassing measure of guilt, made more acute by returning sobriety, that the three of them had thoroughly spoiled his day and night. But who was it said, there is repetition everywhere and that nothing is found only once in this world of ours? So help us, with their guilt well behind them, they did it all a second time to the patient Donal. Some years later the four of them, again with Paddy in the driving seat, took off for a Leinster

Championship game in Paddy Flanagan's home town, Mullingar- a matter of just fifty miles from Dublin. The day was uneventful, they did their reports smartly and without delay and left Mullingar for the run of an hour and a quarter or so to Dublin. John D, however, suggested a break of a few minutes at Enfield for a quick drink and with the voting power of three-to-one, the decision was made.

Donal declined to go into the pub, being the non-drinker of the party. He would go for a walk, have a look around and wait for the other three. And with all due respect to the charming town of Enfield, one walk up and down the main road would be more than sufficient to absorb and enjoy everything that Enfield has to offer. The quick drink became a succession of quick drinks. Then to add strength to the proceedings Johnny Butler and a few of his friends in music, dropped into the pub and in no time at all, with Paddy Downey as always contributing his well known party piece "Skibbereen" the evening became quite an entertaining affair.

At one stage Paddy indicated a little worry about Donal and to ease his mind, Dave went out to have a look. There was no sign of Donal, and he assumed that he had taken a lift from someone- and that assumption got total agreement from John D and Paddy. As far as they were concerned Donal was now safely back home in Dublin.

The evening finally ended and they stumbled out to the car and there was Donal-still patient and still waiting. Again there was no criticism, no recriminations- but the rest of the journey home to Dublin was made in silence- deep, deep silence. Their guilt had returned.

(Dave no longer drinks. He has joined Donal and me in the teetotallers stakes. More power to his elbow.)

Of course, being a teetotaller has its advantages and disadvantages. On social occasions you become very popular when the need arises for a sober driver It is very helpful on other occasions when intoxicating drinks are being pressed on you and your "I don't drink" reply can save a lot of hassle. But I do respect a person's right to have which ever drink they prefer, in moderation of course. I was the only member of my family growing up who abstained from intoxicating beverages which prompts me to tell a story in which the 'teetotal' factor plays an unwitting part. I have also been persuaded by good friend and RTE colleague Fred Cogley to include this true story in this collection He has told it many many times to his friends. My wife Ann and me were invited out to lunch by friends of ours we hadn't met for some time. While the order was being taken for the meal, the question of having wine with the meal cropped up. A choice of wine was agreed so I pointed out that I was a teetotallar and I suggested my own tipple, a non alcoholic beverage called "Madison" which is popular with a lot of non drinkers. The contents of the small bottle fills a wine glass.

We had a very enjoyable meal and we were delighted to renew an old friendship with Patrick and Veronica. Many months later a very close friend of Veronica's, a Mother Superior of a confraternity of nuns in New York came to visit her in Dublin. During the course of her stay she was invited out by her hosts to an evening meal. While awaiting their table the visiting nun was asked to have a beverage but she declined pointing out that she was a teetotaller and intoxicating liquor had never passed her lips. Her friend Veronica casually mentioned a possible way out. She told the nun that her friends the O Ceallachains had been out with her, having a meal, and that Sean Og had a non-intoxicating drink on that occasion. She wasn't too sure of the brand, but she did remember that the name of the beverage related to a place in New York starting with the letter "M". "Manhattan, would it have been Manhattan" asked the nun.? "That's it, " said friend Veronica " I knew it was named after somewhere in New York." The waiter took the order, sherries for the home couple and a "Manhattan" for the visiting nun. When the drinks arrived the "Manhattan" stuck out like a sore thumb. The glass had a rim covered in fine sugar, a twist of orange, lemon and a cherry were speared by a cocktail stick and chunks of ice tinkled in the glass. The hosts, Patrick and Veronica, agreed that the "Manhattan" beverage was far more impressively presented than when they last saw it in the company of Sean Og and his wife Ann. Mother Superior Helen was also impressed and asked in a timid questioning voice: " and this is a non-alcoholic drink."? She was readily assured that Sean Og was a teetotaller and he drank it when in company and enjoyed it.

Mother Helen picked up her glass, raised it to her lips and took a swig and swallowed it. She closed her eyes momentarily and put the glass back on the table. Her friend, Veronica asked her was the drink alight. Mother Helen assured her that it was and posed the question :" and you tell me that it is non-alcoholic?" She was assured that is was non intoxicating and their friend Sean Og, a member of the Pioneer Total Abstinence Association always drank it. That it seemed, was good enough for Mother Helen, who proceeded to finish her drink, mentioning in passing, that a very nice warm glow accompanied the end of the liquid. She suggested she would have another before the meal. " I must say I really enjoyed that drink, I wonder do they sell it in New York? It's very palatable." A second "Manhattan" arrived for Mother Helen and she was well into it when the waiter arrived to say their meal was ready. Mother Helen, knocked back her drink and proceeded to rise from her chair, only to flop back again in her seat. She succeeded at the second attempt, dismissing the incident in a light hearted manner, and blaming it on the jet lag. Patrick, Veronica's husband, was more concerned and as the two ladies proceeded him, he slipped over to the bar man and asked him about the drink which Mother Helen had consumed:. " That "Manhattan" which our friend had, it is non alcoholic, isn't it.?" The bar man looked at Patrick and laughed "are you joking me, too many of those would have you up here dancing on the counter." Patrick was a bit distraught: " But what is the name of that non alcoholic drink, the name starts with the letter M.? " he asked. The reply explained his worst fears. " The only soft drink that I know of starting with the letter M is "Madison", a very nice drink with an apple taste."

Patrick shook his head slowly: "Tell me, what goes into a "Manhattan"? "That's a very nice cocktail " said the bar man" made up of two parts Vermouth and one part Bourbon with ice." On the way back to join the ladies, Patrick was wrestling furiously with his problem. Should he tell the visiting nun about the ghastly error that they had been part of or should he leave sleeping dogs lie and leave the innocent nun in her ignorance. He decided on the latter course of action.

(Footnote: Some months later, Veronica and Patrick got a phone call from New York from Mother Helen, thanking them profusely for her very enjoyable stay in Dublin. At the end of the call, Mother Helen asked Patrick for the name of Sean Og's non alcoholic drink which she had enjoyed so much but had forgotten the name of it. She would like to buy it in a store in the "Big Apple." Patrick, in a very weak voice, said he would try and find the name of the drink and would be in touch- some time.)

Paddy "Bawn" Brosnan

The 1947 All Ireland football final between Cavan and Kerry was an historic occasion due to the fact that the final was played in the Polo Grounds in New York, the one and only time that a final was played outside of this country. The championship matches that year were fiercely contested with the added prize of a trip to America for the would be finalists. Cavan beat Roscommon in their semi final while Kerry easily accounted for Meath. Kerry had a very strong full- back line in Dinny Lyne, Joe Keohane and Paddy "Bawn" Brosnan. The "Bawn" and Keohane were a formidable pair and many an attacking forward line perished at the hands of both, who were known not to have stood on ceremony. During the closing stages of the semi- final against Meath, with Kerry well in control, an attack started on the left wing as a Meath forward came sweeping in on a solo run. The "Bawn" sidled over to Keohane and whispered quietly: " Joe, do you see something coming in here". To which Joe replied: "I do". and The Bawn added, "I don't know where he is going but we are going to New York."

During the course of the New York All- Ireland between Cavan and Kerry Joe Stafford said to Peter Donohoe: "I'll take the The "Bawn" and you go for the ball." As events transpired a high ball came floating in to the Kerry full backs. Joe Stafford jumped in and floored The "Bawn" with two knees to the chest. and Peter Donohoe got the breaking ball and kicked it over the bar for a point. The "Bawn" gave Stafford a dirty look which the Cavan forward clearly recognised. There was no where he could hide and he waited for the inevitable tit- for- tat exchanges. The next ball came via a handpass but as Stafford moved to collect it he slipped and The "Bawn" hit him a full blow on the top of the head. Joe got to his feet and as he was turning away, said to the "Bawn:" " Paddy, too light, too light." and to prove it, he dashed across to the other wing and helped to set up another scoring opportunity for Peter Donohoe.

The "Bawn" was playing for Kerry in a National Football League game against Cork at Tralee. Naturally, both counties had a great respect for one another. It was the time of the great Kerry teams that were winning All- Irelands handy enough. When the teams lined out for the Tralee encounter, Cork had a number of newcomers on duty. A young Cork newcomer made his way down to corner forward where his immediate opponent was going to be the "Bawn" Brosnan. The two players shook hands and the "Bawn" said to the young Cork forward: " Do you see that line ?" pointing towards the 21 yards line 'dont' come inside that line, that's my territory, come in at your peril." Shortly after the game had started the young Cork forward got a pass and was heading for goal when he was stopped in his tracks by a Paddy "Bawn" charge and flattened. While he was being attended to the "Bawn" looked down at him and said: "Sonny, did you not hear me the first time?"

I do not know when the hamstring was "invented" or when it became one of the most talked about ailments that a sports figure incurred during his or her playing career. It was unknown during my playing days and indeed a number of my contemporaries agree with my sentiments, when I suggested, that it would have proved a boon if one needed an excuse to miss out on a fixture that had clashed with another important personal engagement. I may also add that pulled ligaments, crusciate knee ligaments were all unheard of during my playing days. I am glad to report that I am not the only former player to emphasise his ignorance of the phenomena which feature daily in newsprint and on radio and television announcing the absence of a prominent player from a team selection. Former Kerry County Board Chairman Gerald McKenna, former Dublin football star, Tony Hanahoe and Paddy"Bawn" Brosnan, met in a Dublin hotel prior to an All-Ireland final and in the course of conversation the issue of the "hamstring" entered the discussion. Tony mentioned that the team opposing Kerry that weekend would badly miss the services of one of their best players... out of action because of a pulled hamstring. Paddy "Bawn" turned to Tony and Gerald and said: " The two of ye gentlemen are intelligent men, can ye tell me something, when did they invent the hamstring.? 'Tis an awful pity it wasn't there in my time, it would have been a bloody great excuse for missing matches in order to drink porter." Mick "Rattler" Byrne, the doyen of Tipperary defenders, belonged to my era and he too never heard of "hamstrings" during his playing days. " Do you know something, the only time I ever heard of "hamstrings" was one hanging outside a butcher's shop." he told me. Gerald McKenna recalled a story about Paddy "Bawn" Brosnan, who played in a local championship match in Castlegregory during the war, and in the course of the match he ran into a tackle and suffered a split nose. At the time there were no such things as plasters or other means of dressing wounds of that nature, especially since the nose was spouting blood. However a team official tore a strip off the local newspaper," The Kerryman" and stuffed it up the "Bawn's " nose and that did the trick. It stopped the blood flowing. He continued playing on and finished the match. He went off drinking his favourite brew after the game and the following day , the injured nose began to give him considerable pain. So he decided to visit a Dr. Scully in Dingle,who was well used to attending the "Bawn's" ailments after matches. Dr. Scully quickly diagnosed that the nose was indeed broken. Paddy Bawn asked the pertinent question: "Was the injury serious?" To which the good doctor replied: "Well, Bawn, the most difficult part facing me now is, to get the "Kerryman" out of it" .

The Kerry All-Ireland team of 1938. Paddy "Bawn" Brosnan (third from right, back row) and Joe Keohane (sixth from left, back row).

Tall Tales & Banter

The Game of Hurling

While many will argue about best teams and best players I still cling to the view that the most exciting period when hurling was really at its best was in the 40s and 50s. The 1947 All Ireland hurling final between Kilkenny and Cork for instance, had everything, high drama, alternating scores and a heart palpitating finish. It is still recalled and judged to have been one of the most exciting ever played between the two great rivals. I remember reading an account of a hurling match between Cork and Kilkenny in Tim Horgan's " Cork's Hurling Story". and it typified the nature and the character of the game around that time. Fr O'Brien of the Doneraile club found himself sitting beside a total stranger in the Cork Athletic Grounds."It was a beautiful day of brilliant sunshine, a white ball and an unusual amount of delightful hurling, a truly splendid specimen of the game, in fact. The stranger had never seen the game played before and I was explaining the points to him. He had seen numerous other codes- rugby, soccer, ice hockey, baseball and cricket. He was watching very intently. There was one particularly brilliant burst of hurling. Three times the ball travelled the length of the field, from one goal to the other, in beautiful overhead play. A man never handled the ball and eventually there was a wonderful point for Cork. The stranger sat back with a big cigar in the corner of his mouth. "My goodness" he said, "It's a game for the gods."

In 1912 Kilkenny beat Cork in the All- Ireland senior hurling final, and the game marked the retirement of Billy Mackessy. A native of Duhallow, he had the rare distinction of winning All- Ireland senior medals in hurling and football with his native Cork. Standing around the 5' 8" mark, he was sturdily built and had tremendous reserves of speed and strength. After his retirement he countinued his association with the GAA and his restaurant in Oliver Plunket street became the setting of many Cork victory celebrations right up to the time of Christy Ring. It also served as the background to one of his favourite GAA stories.

Two penniless Cork city 'characters', a father and son, went into Mackessy's to try and get a free pint each. The father spotted Billy Mackessy talking to a customer at the far end of the long counter and approached him while the son waited at the other end of the bar: " Excuse me, Mr Mackessy," he said," but the son and myself were arguing about hurling and football and he won't believe me when I tell him that you won two All- Ireland medals with Cork. He thinks you only won wan. "Wasn't it two, Mr Mackessy?" "That's right" said Billy, "it was two, one hurling and one football." The man thanked him and walked back to his son and then called the assistant barman: "Mr. Mackessy said to give us two pints" he announced. " Who are you trying to cod?" asked the barman, who knew the pair well.

"He did, I'm telling ya," said the father and beckoning Billy Mackessy at the other end,. he shouted : "Mr Mackessy, wasn't it two you said?" " That's right," Billy replied, "two." " There you are now," said the father to the barman, "Two pints," And with that, they got their two pints.

A clan of Cork supporters were travelling up to Thurles for a Munster final between Cork and Tipperary. Seated amongst them was an old man who was enjoying the good natured banter. There was an argument between two of the fans over the number of medals won by various stars and the names of Christy Ring, Noel Skehan of Kilkenny and John Doyle of Tipperary cropped up. The old man said to one of the two fans engaged in the medal controversy " Can any of ye tell me what Corkman holds an All Ireland hurling medal and an FA Cup soccer medal?" " That's a good one, sure enough," one of the fans replied, as they all racked their brains for an answer.

Was it Noel Cantwell?" someone ventured. " No" said the venerable gentleman. "Tommy Kiernan?.... Christy Ring?.....Charlie Hurley?.....Jack Lynch?.... Miah Dennehy?...."Not at all" the old timer said until finally the fans had to give up. "Okay," they all cried" tell us the name of the Corkman who holds an FA Cup soccer medal and an All Ireland medal"The pawnbroker at the foot of Shandon Street," was the reply.

Another Munster final story concerned Michael "Gah" Ahearne, rated by many as one of the greatest forwards of all time, reputed to have scored more goals than any other Cork forward of his vintage. On one occasion when Cork was playing Tipperary in a Munster hurling final the full team went to early Mass and Holy Communion and afterwards the players received a special blessing from the priest. At breakfast, "Gah" Ahearne was silent and not eating well, still thinking of the solemn blessing:."What's wrong with you, "Gah?" asked one of the players. "I don't know what to say to it" he replied, "But if we can't bate this Tipperary team, we shouldn't be there at all." Beating Tipperary on the field was something that took Cork three games to accomplish in 1926. "Gah" Ahearne played a prominent part in every one of those matches and, no doubt,he relished the Cork victories as much as anyone else, even though spiritual aid had been invoked to get the better of Tipperary.

Jim Hurley was another of the top performers to make an All- Ireland debut in 1926. Jim remembered a game he played in around that time in which he broke a finger.

He ran back to the captain, the legendary Sean Og Murphy, for sympathy and advice: "Look at this Sean," he said "I think the finger is broken" "Get back to your place and stay there," was the curt response from Sean Og, and without another word, the young peerless defender did what he was told and played on to the end of the game.

Eamonn Cregan of Limerick

Eamonn scored 2-7, playing at left corner forward in the 1980 All-Ireland Senior Hurling Final against Galway but he finished up on the losing side. He was placed at centre half-back and helped Limerick to a storming victory against Kilkenny in the 1973 All-Ireland Final. Eamonn won 3 Bank of Ireland All-Star awards; 3 Railway Cup medals and 1 National Hurling League medal. His father Ned, won a Senior All-Ireland medal in 1934. Eamonn's brother Mick, trained the 1973 All-Ireland winning team. He also captained Claughaun to county title success with brothers Eamon and Conor in the team. All players are subject to the whims of nature at one time or another, colds, flu and of course, injuries, picked up from match to match. A dreaded ailment which can strike at any time is gastro-enteritis, a very debilitating dose which has its after effects. Three weeks before Eamonn Cregan lined out with Limerick against Clare in the 1974 Munster Senior hurling final he was smitten by a bout of gastro-enteritis. Foolishly, he admits, he thought the matter would clear up in the matter of days, so he didn't bother getting treatment for it. Coming up to the final against Clare, Eamonn still had his problem, in fact his weight had dropped from a tidy 12stone 4lbs to 11 stone 10lbs. His health had also suffered and he lacked stamina and showed signs of fatigue. He was spared the tough training grinds as the team mentors knew of his complaint. Eamonn was a very key figure on the team and his services were very much needed. On his way to the Munster final, which was played in Thurles, Eamonn had to break the journey on no less than three occasions. The Claughaun man was a non drinker so alcohol was out of the question but he was still in a very weakened state. An hour before the Munster final, Eamonn was prevailed upon to drink a glass of brandy, purely for medicinal purposes, which he did. He felt fine going out onto the field. He took his place at centre half-back and his immediate opponent was Noel Casey " I must confess, I felt great after the brandy" Eamonn told me," but I wasn't given to any heroics. I ran, when I had to, but rather gently. Had Noel Casey been aware of my problem, I'm sure I would have got the run-around. Happily I managed and played until the final whistle We won by three points. But as soon as the final whistle sounded my complaint returned and I had to make a quick dash for the dressing room. I went to the doctor immediately I returned from the game, something I should have done weeks before the match. I was very silly to ignore the signs. The treatment I got cleared up my complaint in a matter of days. Where ignorance is bliss 'tis folly to be wise."

One of Eamonn's most embarrassing moments was not on the field of play but off it. Mick Mackey and Eamonn were very close friends. Mick was a county selector and also a Munster selector and he was always free with his advice during Eamonn's playing days. Mick Mackey's death came as a major blow to all followers of sport in the county and beyond. On the morning of Mick Mackey's death, a member of the family phoned Eamonn to tell him the sad news. Mick's widow, Kitty told Eamonn that the family were burying Mick in his Munster blazer but they needed a GAA tie which they would like to put on Mick's shirt in the coffin. Eamonn told her that he had a number of the ties that she requested and he would give her one. Later that evening Eamonn went to the Mackey house to offer his condolences, bringing the tie with him. There were quite a number of mourners in the house. Kitty took the tie from Eamonn and she proceeded to place it around Mick's neck in the coffin. The prayers were being said as Eamonn turned away to join the mourners. For some unknown reason that Eamonn to this day couldn't fathom, he whispered to Kitty that there was no need to give him back the tie. She stared at Eamonn for a second, and then blurted out, with the mourners listening: "What do you mean?" said Kitty "the tie is going down with him to the grave."

Eamonn Cregan on the sidelines, during his spell as Offaly manager.

Pat Fanning of Waterford

Pat was President of the GAA 1970-'73 during a period when relationships between the Central Council of the Association and New York GAA were at a very low ebb. Efforts to heal the rift were tried by Pat's predecessor Seamus O Riain and they were successful. An uneasy truce still prevailed when Deiseach Fanning took over the helm. A motion from the Civil Service football club in Dublin calling for the removal of the ban on "foreign games" was listed among other motions at GAA Congresses for years. Pat Fanning was a staunch ban defender and articulated the views held by many leading GAA officials at the time. Pat always offered strong support for the pro-ban lobby and the motion calling for its retention was well supported at county conventions. Tom Woulfe, the Civil Service spokesman, waged virtually a lone battle to have Rule 27, the ban rule, removed from the GAA statute books. He consistently succeeded in getting the motion passed at Dublin Conventions but when it appeared on the Congress clar, it inevitably failed to get the necessary support from other counties. In 1971 Tom Woulfe attended the GAA Congress in Belfast, presided over by Pat Fanning, who was in the second year of his three year term. 30 counties had tabled motions calling for the removal of the ban and it was in the light of that pressure that the mood of Congress had changed as regard to Rule 27. Pat Fanning addressed the assembled delegates and his speech was described by "Irish Press" journalist, Padraig Puirseal, "as Pat Fanning's finest hour." At the end of his address he called for a proposal to remove Rule 27. Con Shortt of Armagh proposed the abolition of the ban and it was seconded by Tom Woulfe of Dublin. Congress erupted with applause, ironically, initiated by Pat's erstwhile opposition of the ban issue, Tom Woulfe, who stood up and clapped the President, a gesture which brought all the other delegates to their feet. It was, without doubt, an historic occasion in GAA history. Pat Fanning had, over the years, met John Kerry O'Donnell when he was New York GAA President and invariably, despite the friction which had arisen between the New York and the Central Council, got on fairly well with him. But John Kerry's mood had many swings when he operated on his own turf in Gaelic Park. A request by New York GAA to stage a game, with the proceeds going to relieve hardship on the dependants of the internees in the North, was sanctioned. President Pat Fanning agreed to send out a team for the occasion and sent the then Financial Controller, Pat Canton, to oversee the gate receipts, as there were strong suspicions that Noraid were trying to get involved, and the GAA at home were having none of that. The atmosphere in Gaelic Park with the arrival of Pat Canton, was to say the least, icy and John Kerry was affronted that the GAA had sent an official for that particular event.

The charity match had attracted a lot of attention both in Ireland and in the States and it was that factor which prompted the GAA to have Pat Fanning in attendance, and he was accompanied by Tommy Mellon of Derry, a well known GAA figure in the North of Ireland. They arrived in Gaelic Park, not to a fanfare of trumpets, but to a very cool reception. Pat Fanning addressed a meeting of the New York Board and when he was finished he got a standing ovation, which pleased Pat Fanning greatly and it lifted a lot of the pressure he was under from his arrival in the Big Apple. The following day Pat got a phone call to say that his speech the previous evening had been taped and was he aware of it? Naturally, Pat was not aware of any such thing. He was told that John O'Shaughnessy, John Kerry's right hand man in Gaelic Park, who looked after the maintenance of the place, the pitch and other functions, had wired the microphone to a tape recorder for Fanning's speech, which was a thoroughly uplifting one, as only the Waterford man can give.

A lunch meeting was arranged the following day with John Kerry at which Pat had hoped to sort out some of the difficulties which had arisen between the two Bodies. Both were collected by former President Terry Connaughton and brought to the lunch venue. John Kerry was waiting, they shook hands and when they were seated Pat put the question to his New York opposite " By the way, John, was there anything on the tape that I shouldn't have said.'"? John Kerry was stopped in his tracks, the hard face which had greeted the two visitors, suddenly changed and was replaced by a broad smile " No Pat " he said " nothing that you couldn't have said in church." The ice was broken. Pat Fanning enjoyed the lunch and most of the business in hand was successfully completed.

The two major figures were to meet again at the Bank of Ireland All Stars banquet in the Burlington Hotel later in that year. During the reception John Kerry appeared in his Knight of St Gregory uniform, an honour accorded to him by the Pope, for his great contribution to charity functions in New York. Pat Fanning walked over and greeted him. While the two had crossed swords many times, as the saying goes, they still had great respect for one another's viewpoints. "You are looking very resplendent in that uniform" said Pat to John Kerry " but I didn't think a Knight of St Gregory would come improperly dressed" John Kerry gave him a quizzical look: " What do you mean?" he asked:. "Well " said Pat, with a grin, "you haven't got your sword on." John Kerry regained his composure and fired back at Pat: "If I had it, I'd use it on the likes of you." But normal relations resumed between the two later at the dinner.

Tony Wall, one of Tipperary's great half-backs contributed an article to the "Gaelic Weekly", a paper devoted to Gaelic Games, in which he slated New York for the poor condition of the playing surface at Gaelic Park, in the Bronx. He said that the pitch was in a dreadful state, without any grass, and it was dangerous, and somebody would suffer a serious injury if something wasn't done about it. Admittedly, during the very hot summers in New York, the Gaelic Park pitch suffers a lot. The grass had long gone and was replaced by a green weed-like growth which withstood the hot conditions. Still, the pitch was pockmarked from overuse. Soccer and rugby games were played there during the week at the request of visiting teams, who naturally had to pay for the privilege of playing there. John Kerry O'Donnell took grave exception to criticism of Gaelic Park, especially the playing surface. I remember paying him a visit at the ground early one morning to find him holding a water hose and douching the playing pitch. He took none too kindly to Tony Wall's criticism, a copy of the "Gaelic Weekly" had been sent to him containing the article, and he did not like what he read. It can be said of John Kerry, he never forgot things, and years after the event he would dredge it up and remind a poor unsuspecting individual of something he had said or written many years previously. Tipperary, were playing New York in the final of the National Hurling League, over two legs, in Gaelic Park. Tipperary centre back that day was Tony Wall who was now back again playing on the pitch he had criticised in the "Gaelic Weekly" article a few years previously.

Watching the arrival of the Tipperary team onto the pitch from the stand was John Kerry O'Donnell. For some unknown reason, Tony Wall was at the end of the line of players running on to the pitch and as he appeared, John O'Shaughnessy, the ground maintenance man, ran ahead of Tony Wall, carrying a watering can, sprinkling water in his path all the way on to the pitch until the can was emptied. As O'Shaughnessy trooped off, he looked up at the stand to get a wave from John Kerry.

Pat Fanning and the then Director- General, Sean O Siochain were invited to the Corkmen's Association dinner in London. They took an afternoon flight and were late getting to their hotel because of very heavy traffic. Sean immediately contacted an official from the Corkmen's Association to let them know that their two guests at the function had arrived safe and well. It was only then that Sean was told that the dinner was a formal affair and neither he nor Pat had brought the required formal wear with them, assuming that the occasion, like many they had attended in the past, would be informal. Sean had a very dark suit and bought a bow tie to match in the hotel shop. It was too late for Pat Fanning to secure a dress suit.

His lounge suit was perfectly suitable for an informal occasion but not this one. Pat decided that he couldn't attend the dinner under the circumstances So the decision was taken, Pat would have to stay in the Hotel, much to his disappointment, and Sean would attend the dinner. Pat retired early but slept fitfully. He was not a good sleeper but he was aroused by the telephone ringing in the bedroom. A Cockney voice, asked him did he know a Mr Sheescan or Sheescaun or a name like it. Pat, still not fully awake, demanded to know who was asking the question and what time it was. " It's 12. 30 a m and I'm the night porter" said the voice "and I have a gentleman here who says you can vouch for him". Pat, now fully awake, told the porter to send Mr Sheescaun to his room, realising immediately that the late intruder was no other than the Director General. The Cockney porter arrived at the door of the bedroom with Sean, and Pat explained, that in their anxiety to prepare for the function, Sean had neglected to sign himself in. All was well, but the porter did tell Pat that he was on the point of ringing the police, thinking that his late visitor was a gatecrasher. Sean, who had enjoyed himself immensely among his own, and liberally supplied with uisce beatha, was also enjoying the exchanges between the porter and Pat Fanning. When the porter had left, Pat said to Sean: " My God, what was up with you atall, I thought we had signed the register together?" Sean, was all apologies, and explained that he forgot to clock in. He immediately undressed and climbed into bed. In the space of minutes he was asleep and snoring. That was the start of Pat Fanning's ordeal. If he hadn't slept very well before Sean's arrival, there was no way he was going to succeed then. Sean's snoring filled the room and perhaps the adjoining bedrooms as well. Pat made a vow there and then, that if ever he had to travel anywhere with Sean O Siochain he would make doubly sure, that Sean's bedroom was at least a mile away from his. Pat Fanning's successor as President was Dr. Donal Keenan of Roscommon, who though a gifted footballer and winner of two All- Ireland senior titles with his native county, was a great lover of hurling. During a very acrimonious meeting of the GAA Executive (now known as the Management Committee) matters were nearly getting out of hand. Pat intervened and said, "Gentlemen: for goodness sake, be a bit more sensible, after all it's only football we are discussing." It was the worst possible thing he could have said. A very angry Dr. Donal rounded on him: "So it's only football is it, if it was bloody hurling,

Pat Fanning

you wouldn't be talking like that."

Declan Goode, former great All- Ireland hurler, retired as Secretary of the Waterford County Board at the County Convention in 1971, after serving 33 years in the office. He was succeeded by Seamus Grant. Declan, when announcing his decision to step down, explained to the large gathering at Convention,why he had served 33 years, 32 for the number of counties in Ireland and the 33rd for the number of years Christ had spent on earth. Declan's retiral came during Pat Fanning's term as GAA President and he and Declan were invited by the Waterfordmen's Association to a function in New York. Declan had taken up the game of golf and one of his great wishes was to play one of the American courses. He got his wish when one of the local Deise men invited him to play on his home course in Auburn, upstate, New York. Declan joined his friend and two other members, and a very enjoyable match ensued. Declan happened to mention that he was anxious to buy a present to bring home to his wife, Honey. He was immediately directed to a local store which catered for everything and everyone. When Declan later arrived at the store,he headed for the ladies dress department because his wife, Honey, had said if he saw a nice dress that might suit her to buy it. He was approached by a stunning Afro-American lady assistant,tall, svelt,with a figure to match. Declan became a little flustered when she asked: "Can I help you, suh.?" Declan, quickly regained his composure, and explained that he wanted to purchase a dress for his wife to bring back home to Ireland: "Certainly, suh, would you know her size?" Now Declan may have been a smashing hurler in his day, and a highly respected County Secretary for 33 years, but when it came to remembering his wife's clothes size, he could only stare blankly at the vision in front of him: " I'm afraid I don't " said Declan. The lady assistant remarked very sympathically: "I'm sure your wife will be dreadfully disappointed, suh." But Declan was not to be outdone. He got an inspiration. He looked at the lady assistant and then measured her slowly up and down, (not a practice to be recommended in a ladies dress store) much to the lady's own amusement, and blurted out: " God, if it will fit you it will fit her." And the dress he bought Honey did fit her too.

The Home Team.

GER CANNING

MICHEÁL Ó MUIRCHEARTAIGH

MICHAEL LYSTER

CON MURPHY

MARTY MORRISSEY

BRIAN CARTHY

You may miss being at the game, but you won't miss a single piece of the action with RTÉ's home team. (And if you do there's always action replay!)

RTÉ provides comprehensive GAA coverage a our team of expert commentators offers in-dep analysis on both Television and Radio.
It's an all round performance that's unbeatabl

RTÉ
RADIO TELEFIS EIREANN

Kevin Heffernan of Dublin

A legendary Dublin figure. In 1974 he became the first non-player ever to be voted as "Texaco Footballer of the Year". He helped Dublin to win 3 National Football League titles in 1953, '55 and '58. He captained Dublin to win the 1958 All Ireland Senior football crown. He won 7 Railway Cup medals with Leinster (a record for a Dublin player in either code). He managed the great Dublin teams of the '70's, when they won the All Ireland title in 1974, '76 and '77. A free scoring roving full forward, he scored 52 goals and 172 points in 119 games for the Dubs in the 7 year period from 1955 to 1962. He was a selector when Dublin won the All Ireland Senior title in 1963. It was Jimmy Grey, the then chairman of the Dublin County Board, who persuaded Kevin Heffernan in 1973, to take over as manager of the Senior football squad at a period when Dublin fortunes had slumped to an all time low. It is now part of football history how Heffernan became the 'Messiah' who led Dublin out of the wilderness to All Ireland glory. Kevin quickly spotted the potential of the O'Connell Boys goalkeeper named Paddy Cullen and he was installed between the post, where he became one of the best goalkeepers in the game. Cullen's talents were also recognised by the Bank of Ireland All Stars selectors, who, late in 1973, selected him as an All Star substitute on the All Star team which travelled to San Francisco. He was the first Dublin footballer to be chosen on the All Stars Selection.

Cullen revelled in that role and constantly reminded his luckless Dublin companions of the honour that had been bestowed upon him. When training started for the historic football championship of 1974 at Parnell Park early in that year, Kevin recalled during a training session, an Aer Lingus 'plane flew over the ground, and Paddy Cullen, the joker of the squad, pointed up at it "There it is, lads, there's the All Stars 'plane that I was on." And then he had to run for it, as footballs were kicked at him from all directions. Six Dublin players, including Paddy Cullen were to win All Star Awards that year, in their own right, for that '74 All Ireland victory. Kevin Heffernan, teamed up very effectively for many years during his playing days with St Vincent's and Dublin, with the renowned Ollie Freeney, who figures in other chapters of this book. Both players were playing for Leinster against Munster in a Railway Cup match. The great Paddy "Bawn" Brosnan of Kerry filled a corner back role and was getting a bit of a roasting from Ollie. Kevin remembers the "Bawn" collecting a ball in defence, shaking off three heavy tackles, and with the ball under his arm, he made a ferocious lunge at the waiting Ollie Freeney. The Dublin man stepped back a pace, stuck out a foot and sent the "Bawn" crashing to the ground, and a free out was awarded. Ollie sidled over to Kevin Heffernan, while getting bulls looks from the "Bawn", and said " I think, Heff, I will be concentrating more on the right wing in the second half."

Liz Howard of Tipperary

I presented the "Sunday Game" for two years on RTE television, an experience I enjoyed very much. My hurling analyst on the programme was the vivacious and articulate Liz Howard, a very knowledgeable young lady, and an All-Ireland camogie player of note with her native Tipperary. Her father was the legendary Garret Howard, winner of 5 All-Ireland medals, 3 with his native Limerick, 1921, '34 and '36, and two in between for Dublin (1924 and 1927). He thus won more All Ireland medals than any other Limerick born player. He also won 5 National Hurling League titles and two Railway Cup medals, one with Leinster in the inaugural year in 1927, and one with Munster 4 years later. In 1982 he joined Mick Mackey as the first two Limerick men to be selected as the Bank of Ireland All-Time All-Star award winners. Liz was a very competent hurling analyst, and with her love for the game, her measured comments were always very well received. She found herself in a very unusual situation in 1979 when we were showing highlights of the Leinster senior football championship final between Dublin and Offaly. Just before half-time Dublin full-forward Jimmy Keaveney was sent off for an elbow offence on Offaly defender Ollie Minnock, and referee Paddy Collins (Westmeath) had no option but to dismiss him. Former Galway All-Ireland football star Enda Colleran, a brilliant games analyst, was in two minds about Keaveney's dismissal. Liz Howard left viewers in no doubt that the sending off was very harsh, and felt that there were other incidents in the game which were allowed to go unpunished. Liz's comments were picked up by the "Irish Press" at the time. They had a banner headline "TV personality supports Jimmy Keaveney" over a front page story. Jimmy Keaveney was invited to attend a meeting of the Leinster Council Disciplinary Committee, to explain his actions resulting in his sending off. The Dublin County Board asked Liz Howard to attend the meeting and give evidence in support of Jimmy Keaveney. Liz readily agreed and so, too, did Ollie Minnock of Offaly, who attended the meeting in a supportive role, seeking a lenient outcome on behalf of his Dublin adversary. The combined efforts of all three failed to sway the disciplinary body and Keaveney was suspended for a month. Liz Howard was genuinely disappointed with the verdict reached in Keaveney's case. She had been cross examined by the disciplinary committee and she had given, what she thought, was a clear and honest assessment of the situation as she had viewed it. She was a bit taken aback by questions relating to other incidents, not related to the Keaveney case. Ollie Minnock, the victim in the case, also made light of the incident and he, too, pleaded for leniency for the Dublin player. It was all in vain, Jimmy Keaveney incurred a month's suspension, which put him out of the All Ireland semi-final against Roscommon a few weeks later.

It must be said, that much of Dublin's successes on the football championship from stemmed from the accuracy of Jimmy Keaveney's free taking and his scores from play. Any team aspiring to All-Ireland greatness must possess an accurate free taker, and Keaveney filled the bill to perfection in Dublin's case. On the day of the All Ireland semi final between Dublin and Roscommon the usual huge Dublin following made its way down Jones Road, in route to the 'Hill. There were queues for the Hogan Stand and quite a number of Dublin fans, dressed in all kinds of regalia, sporting the Dublin colours carried on good natured banter with rival Roscommon fans. Liz Howard was standing

Liz Howard

in an adjacent queue, which was reserved for members of the Press, and working media, and she was enjoying the exchanges between the rival fans until she was recognised by a Dublin fan. He wore a Dublin jersey never intended for his build. Rolls of fat protruded over his trousers, and obviously, he had spent some time slaking his thirst before heading for the Hogan Stand entrance. The Dublin man gave a roar and pointed to where a horrified Liz Howard was standing, waiting her turn to be admitted in the queue. All eyes turned in her directions, especially when the Dublin fan shouted: " Jasus, will you look at her?, there's the wan that shafted Jimmy Keaveney" If ever someone wanted the ground to open up in front of her, it was Liz Howard. It wasn't the time to run over and explain to the same gentleman, that she was the 'her', who had tried to save him, so she had to grin and bear her embarrassment. It was, in the words of Liz: " one of the most embarrassing moments of my life." Dublin, without Jimmy Keaveney's free taking expertise, beat Roscommon in that All Ireland semi final by a one point margin.

Matt Spain of Birr

"The Hurlers" is a well known Golfing Society, formed many years ago and naturally had its origin in the famous home of hurling, Thurles, and a number of former great Tipperary hurling stars were among those who helped to launch it on its successful way. It grew in strength and most of the counties who were, and are, to this very day proficient in the game send teams to play in the competition on the eve of the All Ireland hurling final at the Thurles Golf course. I must put it on the record, and say that the Society is unique and is open to golfers who have played with their respective counties. The most enjoyable aspect is the close friendship that binds the members who may have been once great rivals on the field of play but who now meet in deadly rivalry out on the golf course. My abiding memories are of those players whom I played against many years ago, and whom I hadn't met for years. It was a great thrill renewing old friendships and listening to great old stories, which now form the basis of this book. The "Hurlers" Golfing society plays a major role in bringing all those great players of the past and the present together and the social evening that follows is something not to be missed. That's why I am lucky to be still a member. I met Matt Spain of Offaly there, a former great hurler in his own right, played with Faughs, in Dublin and like all those rogues that make up the Society, possesses a fund of stories, some of which appear in other sections of this book. Matt enjoys telling this one about Canon Hamilton of Clare, a major figure in GAA history, the man who succeeded in getting Congress in 1947 to stage the All Ireland senior football final in the Polo Grounds, New York. In 1957 the Tipperary Hurling team travellled by ship, the S S Ryndham, to New York to play New York in a St Brendan Cup match. It was Mick Dunne's and John D Hickey's first visit to the States to cover a game for their respective newspapers. Canon Hamilton, a member of the Central Council at the time, accompanied the team. Paddy Leahy, the well known Tipp selector and wit, was as usual a member of the travelling party. Shortly after the ship had left port for its destination, an American lady approached a Tipperary contingent on deck. She announced that she had just had a most enjoyable holiday in Ireland, but she had one major regret, she failed to make the journey to kiss the Blarney Stone, that she had heard so much about.

As usual the ever helpful Paddy Leahy took command of the situation.: " Well now, mam," he said, " you cannot possibly go back to the United States and tell your friends that you were in Ireland and you never kissed the famous Blarney Stone" The lady, who earlier had a resigned look now became a little bit more interested, following comments of Leahy. The Tipperary official, sensing her earlier disappointment, held up his hand and said to the lady: " But all is not lost, mam. What if I told you that there is still a way out of your dilemma?." The American lady's face brightened quickly. She became all ears and looked hopefully at the Tipperary man, with the hat tilted enjoying the focus of everyone's attention: "The fact that you missed kissing the Blarney Stone doesn't really matter," said Paddy, " as long as you kiss somebody who has kissed the Blarney Stone, do you follow me?" The lady looked very relieved and confessed that she hadn't heard that suggestion in her travels: "But where can I find a man who has kissed the Blarney Stone?" she asked innocently," have any of you men ever kissed it?" "I'm afraid we haven't" said Paddy, "but you are a lucky woman" said the bould Paddy, "do you see that priest standing further down the deck" pointing in Canon Hamilton's direction: " he has kissed the Blarney Stone. Go down and tell him your problem." The very " helpful " Tipperary official watched as the flamboyantly dressed American lady approached the good Canon and told him her tale of woe. The Canon, realising that his leg was being pulled, after noticing the grins on the Tipperary men's faces, apologised profusely to the lady and said " I'm very sorry, mam. I have never actually kissed the Blarney Stone, but I have sat on it."

The famous Faughs hurling teams of former years always trained in an open space in the Phoenix Park, beside the Army Ground, which faces the Wellington Monument. The Faughs club has now well laid out grounds, and a spacious Social Centre over on the South side of the River Liffey in Willington Lane. Matt Spain played with the Faughs junior hurlers and the team included many famous senior players who were well into the autumn of their hurling careers, but who nevertheless, loved the old game of hurling. Faughs were playing a junior league match in the Phoenix Park, which is adjacent to the Army ground, and the condition of the Hurling Ground was to say the least, unsuitable for hurling. The playing surface was littered with potholes filled with surface water, and parallelogram was a no go area - it was a quagmire. Tommy Moore, an All- Ireland hurler with Dublin, and owner of a famous hostelry in Cathedral St, in Dublin at that time, was in charge of the Faughs team. Faughs weren't doing too well in the game so Tommy sent in one of his selectors to tell a player, who wasn't figuring too prominently in the match "to lie down". (To the uninitiated, to get in a replacement.) The message was duly delivered and after about ten minutes Tommy sent in the messenger again, ordering the player in question to "lie down" because he was being outplayed: " Tell him to take his bloody time, until I find a dry place to lie in" said the player sharply, whose pride was wounded. Matt travelled from Dublin to Birr in the train for the 1947 All- Ireland hurling semi-final between Kilkenny and Galway. The whole carriage was filled by Faughs players who had arranged to travel together for the match, which Kilkenny duly won. Prior to that game, the Faughs had played the previous Sunday in a junior match, and they had to bring in all the oldies, Tommy Leahy, Jack Walsh, Mick Gill, Bobby Donoghue, to mention just a few, and the match was the subject of great amusement amongst the players on the way down on the train Bobby Donoghue, also with the party in the carriage, spoke up and said: "How in the name of God, could we have won that match,I looked one time, and there was Tommy Leahy and Jack Walsh kneeling near the line, and I think they were discussing how they sowed spuds down in Mooncoin." Quick as a flash Jack Walsh put in his spoke, and said to Donoghue: "Aye, and yourself and Mick Gill were showing us how ye dug them out in Connemara."

Clareen, the home of the famous Dooley brothers and the Coughlans, who have made and still continue to make a major contribution to the All- Ireland successes of the county since the start of the 80s, were late taking the field for a local championship match The referee was getting impatient, constantly blowing on the whistle, to get the Clareen men out on the pitch. One of the officials, big PJ Grogan, who won an All- Ireland junior medal with the county in 1929 came into the dressing room and remarked: "Come on, lads, get out, or you will lose the match,what's keeping ye?" Clareen had a hurler playing with them then called Paddy McDonnell, known as the "Maggot" and he acquired the nickname because of his size. He was a little over five foot, and slim as a bean pole and weighed about seven stone. P J was told the problem, they had no jersey for the "Maggot" P J quickly solved the problem: "What jersey do ye want, can't you put a stocking down over him."

Mike McInerney, who hurled for Galway in the full- back line, some years ago, trained to be a teacher. He came home for holidays and a local club official asked him to play in a minor hurling championship match that weekend: " But, I am over age "said Mike,"I was nineteen last year" "Don't let it worry you" said the club official, " you'll be alright, you're the youngest we have anyway." Famous Tipperary hurler "Sweeper" Ryan took up refereeing after he had retired from the game and was very much in demand as a knight of the whistle. "Sweeper" who liked to lay it on the line for the competing teams before the start of the game and invariably got a quick round of applause, ended his remarks by saying: " Now lads, there are four ways of refereeing this match, there's the right way, the wrong way, there's your way and there's my way, so, we'll do it my way now, so, backs back." Kilkenny, played Tipperary in a League game at Thurles and Noel Skehan, perhaps the best goalkeeper in the game of hurling, was beaten by a ball shot home from an acute angle, much to Noel's disgust. "Pa" Dillon, playing in front of him said: "You should have stopped that one, Noel." To which Noel replied: "Well, didn't it pass fourteen of ye before it came to me." Limerick were invited to play Cork in a hurling tournament in Cork but they had to travel without their best goalkeeper. So an emergency plan had to be put into operation. The team bag man, who hadn't played for years was pressed into service. Before taking the field, the instructions to the Limerick defenders were, " take the man and let the ball in to the goalkeeper" But the bagman had his own ideas, he said to full back Mick Hayes " You take the ball, Mick and let the forwards in to me."

Dermot O'Brien of Louth

Dermot, from the famous Ardee St Mary's club, carved a niche for himself when he captained Louth to their first All Ireland senior football title success for 45 years in 1957. A very skilful centre-forward he thrived on the good supply from Kevin Beahan at midfield, a combination which grew successfully from their club days with St Mary's. Dermot won two Leinster championship medals in 1953 and 1957: captained Leinster in 1958; captain of the Ireland team versus Combined Universities in 1958. A famed accordionist and dance band leader, he has played all over the United States and lives in New York. Dermot has a fund of stories relating to his own playing days and recalls great characters. Ardee, of course, had great players who were synonymous with Louth teams. Dermot had a great admiration for Sean Boyle, who was on the Louth team beaten by Mayo in the 1950 All-Ireland final. He told me about the excitement that Sean would create whenever he got a new pair of football boots: " There would be upwards of fifty or sixty people in the field watching Sean. He would get three or four footballs and bring them out fifty or sixty yards, and when he would put one over the bar, those watching would say, "boys, he's getting the feel of them now, he has it." The "boys" would be old-timers, nodding their heads and smoking their pipes, watching one of the longest kickers of a dead ball going through his paces. Dermot, also awed by the kicking of Boyle, would rush back to the town with the news, "Sean Boyle has a new pair of boots and he's hitting the ball a mile." When Dermot won his first county senior football championship title with St Mary's in 1951, he was just nineteen years of age. He was to win two more in 1956 and 1960. Dermot knew some great characters who became part and parcel of the game's history in Ardee. Take for instance, Jamie Farren, who had a bad right knee but wore a knee band on the left knee so that the opposition would concentrate on the good knee. Dermot clearly remembers opening the windows of his house in Ardee so that people could listen to Miceal O' Hehir's commentary on a match involving Louth: " My heroes were Jack Bell, Paddy Markey, Sean Boyle, Johnny Malone, Nicky Roe and the "Gua" Mooney. O 'Hehir would say," on the square for Louth today is Ray "Gua" Mooney, they were all household names" said Dermot. "Gua" Mooney left an indelible imprint whenever he played. It was claimed that he moved so fast after a ball that his knees never bent."

Dermot got a great kick out of stories in which "Gua" was the central figure. Dermot is in no doubt that "Gua" Mooney was indeed a great forward who believed very strongly in the old maxim," that it takes two to create a score"- which really meant in "Gua's " eyes, that if he passed the ball, he expected to get the return pass for him to go on and score. He also felt that in the interest of fair play, should he pass the ball, it was imperative that the receiver should immediately pass the ball back- a mathematical problem nobody could fathom.

Dermot O'Brien

Tall Tales & Banter

Tom Ryall of Kilkenny

om has been supplying Kilkenny GAA results for my Sunday Radio "GAA Sports Results" programme for many years. Tom is also the author of the Kilkenny GAA History - 1884 to 1984, a very detailed book, containing reports of matches from the foundation of the Association, and accounts of All Irelands, Leagues and tournament games involving the famed Black and Amber Brigade. Tom is a great man to tell a story about his native county and county men. Dave McGrath, better known as "Daw" was a great Cork hurler in the 1900's. Cork were playing Tipperary in the Munster championship. There was a priest associated with the Cork management team and he asked all the players to go to confession on Saturday night and Holy Communion on Sunday. The priest said Mass for the team on Sunday morning and asked the Lord to look after them that afternoon. Some time later the priest noticed that "Daw" seemed down in himself. He asked "Daw" was there anything wrong with him. " Not really" replied "Daw" " but you asked the help of the Lord this morning at Mass, but to tell you the truth, Father, I would rather bate Tipperary fair and square on the pitch." Two fellows from Kilkenny who had no interest whatsoever in hurling went to Cork and as luck would have it, they went into Billy Mackessy's pub. Billy was one of the great Cork All Ireland stars who had played against Kilkenny many many times. The two visitors to the pub ordered their drinks and while Billy was getting them ready, he asked them from where had they come. "We are from Kilkenny" said one of the men. " In that case" said Billy, " the drinks are on me. Tell me, how is Jack Rochford keeping"(a great Kilkenny hurler). The two boys looked at one another, never having heard of Jack Rochford. Billy realised they had never heard of Rochford as well. " Give me back those drinks" said Billy " ye are not from Kilkenny, ye are frauds." Johnny Leahy (Tipperary) and Sim Walton (Kilkenny) were opposing captains in the 1916 All Ireland hurling final and were marking each other. At the end of the game Sim, in congratulating Johnny on their victory said "Leahy we were the better hurlers." "That's right " said Johnny " but we were the better men."

Kilkenny beat Waterford in the 1963 All Ireland hurling final in one of the highest scoring deciders in years which was indeed a thriller all the way. Ironically it followed on similar lines to the traumatic 1957 final in which Kilkenny pipped their neighbouring rivals by the narrow margin of one point. In 1963 Kilkenny lined out against Dublin for their opening round National League game at Nowlan Park and a huge crowd turned out to give the newly crowned champions the welcome they deserved. The teams paraded before the match, led by a local band, and they were greeted enthusiastically. The teams were joined at the end of the parade, as they marched around the pitch by about 300 young children, and efforts to remove them failed. Once the teams had reached the centre of the field, the young admirers scattered. Kilkenny, needless to say, scored a decisive victory to make the occasion worthwhile. At a subsequent Central Council meeting the matter of pitch encroachment arose and it was stated that the referee's report of the Kilkenny- Dublin League match made reference to hundreds of children invading the pitch and following the teams in the parade. The Chairman asked for a comment from the Dublin delegate who simply said that having hundreds of young children running around behind the teams was not conducive to good arrangements for such an important game and a trifling upsetting for the players. Paddy Grace of Kilkenny, when asked for his comment,agreed that a lot of children had indeed encroached on the pitch and apologised to Dublin if they had in any way upset them. He then added " But wasn't it a pity that it wasn't 500 kids just to show what winning an All Ireland means to a county."

Phil "Gunner" Brady of Cavan

The "Gunner" Brady was easily one of the toughest full backs in football, and to put it mildly, was one of a number of hard hitting defenders in the game at the time, "not given to taking prisoners". I remember the Ulster senior football championship final of 1951 between Cavan and Antrim in Clones and the duels between the "Gunner" and Antrim's Harry O'Neill helped to pack the Clones venue for that decider. The Antrim full forward was as tough as nails and was noted for his no nonsense approach towards score taking. It was said of him that he would go through a wall in quest of a score. The "Gunner" and O'Neill had been very keen rivals around that time and it was a case of the immovable meeting the irresistible. Both counties were great rivals and were not to meet again in a provincial decider. Antrim secured their last Ulster success that year. But a year later I was able to have first hand experience of the same "Gunner" when I refereed The Ulster final between Cavan and Monaghan. In fairness to the "Gunner" he played an exemplary role in helping the "Breffni" men to victory and I never had to issue one word of caution to the burly Cavan giant during the game. In fact on two occasions I had to admonish one particular Monaghan forward for needlessly charging at the "Gunner" as he was about to deliver a clearance. It was to my surprise, many years later, that I saw the "Gunner" refereeing a tournament match between Louth and Dublin at Drogheda. He hadn't long taken up refereeing but was later to become very proficient in the job. Dublin- Louth matches were never kid gloves affairs and this one played in Drogheda, was an exception. There wasn't a single incident of discord and the game was very exciting and sporting until a few minutes before the end. Kevin Heffernan, charged in towards the Louth goal to meet a high dropping ball only to receive a Tom Conlon uppercut, which floored Heffernan and he had to get medical attention. Louth full back Conlon didn't wait for the referee to decide his punishment,he simply walked off the pitch. The match continued and Dublin edged the verdict. Some years later I met the "Gunner" at a game and I asked him about the Tom Conlon walk off. Said the "Gunner" " I didn't know what to do? Conlon went before I could speak to him. The gas part of that was, I was only going to give him a caution" said the bould "Gunner" with an impish grin.

"Muckle" McKeon

M"uckle" was an outstanding player with his native Louth, who will always be regarded with fondness by the county supporters, for his services to the county over a long period. Michael "Muckle" McKeon was a very polished forward who produced on the big occasion. He broke the heart of many a defence and could always be relied upon for a spectacular score. He was never given to gamesmanship, he played for the sheer love of beating an opponent, without recourse to the tactics employed by some of today's forwards. He turned to team coaching after retiring from the game, and became a highly respected manager. He was one individual who believed in putting something back into the game, after his playing days were over. His advice to teams going out on the field was simple enough, "G'up for the ball and don't come down without it."

Watching his team on one occasion he noticed a fellow standing beside him on the sideline who was supposed to be on the injured list. "Muckle" inquired after his wellbeing, to which the player responded: "I'm suffering from a hamstring." " You have a what?'" Muckle asked. " A hamstring," replied the unfortunate player . " Muckle" looked him up and down and said: " Listen, sonny, when we were playing, and if we had one of those yokes, we'd ate it." "Muckle" had another piece of advice for his players before taking the field: "Keep your high balls low into the wind. "Muckle" noticed one of his players wasn't togging out, so he inquired the reason, to be told: " I'm injured." "Muckle" quickly commented: "Well, I don't see any bandages."

Babs Keating of Tipperary

Michael 'Babs' Keating of Tipperary fame can never be accused of not putting something back into a game he adorned with such pride and distinction, not alone as a brilliant hurler, but also as a footballer of note with his native county. "Babs" has used his flair and talents in the capacity of team manager and has been associated with successes, not alone in his native Tipp but also with a number of other counties. During a spell with Tipperary as team manager, he was trying out a number of newcomers in a League game against Kilkenny at Semple Stadium, Thurles. One of the newcomers on trial at full back was getting a roasting from burly Kilkenny full forward Christy Heffernan. Manager Keating decided enough was enough and called the young player ashore. The player was taking his place on the subs bench when he turned to "Babs" and said " You should have left me on, Babs, I was doing well on him, anyway, he was afraid of me." Babs never batted an eye lid and said " He was afraid of you, well, you must have been telling him ghost stories."

"Babs" travelled with a Tipperary team which played Kilkenny in an important hurling League match at Nowlan Park in the mid 60's. It was a very strong Tipp team which had won the All Ireland title in 1964 against Kilkenny, so naturally there were a few old scores to be settled. "Babs" was part of a very imposing forward set up which included

Jimmy Doyle, Larry Kiely, Donie Nealon, Mackey McKenna and Sean McLoughlin. They were up against an equally imposing Kilkenny defence, very well marshalled by "Pa" Dillon at full back. "Pa" was as hard as nails and made score getting very difficult. He was a player who was never afraid to call a spade a spade, nor was he afraid to use what ever means available to him to keep forwards at bay. The game developed into a contest of championship vigour with very little between the two teams but pride alone, and the scoreboard reflected that situation as well. Time was drifting on and the visitors needed a score badly but the Kilkenny defence, and particularly "Pa" Dillon was unyielding. "Babs" slipped across to Mackey McKenna, and suggested to him to move in to the full forward berth for a spell but Mackey was having none of it. Said he to "Babs" " I will in my arse, Dillon is in there sharpening the edge for me."

Michael Keating

Tom Woulfe of Dublin

By tradition the GAA was wedded to a Spartan culture. Up to the 1960's club grounds with running water and sanitation were the exception. But it has to be said that these facilities were the exception in many parts of rural Ireland too, in those days. By the same token, recreational buildings up to the 1950s, were subject to a statutory maximum outlay of £750, due to the shortage of building materials in the wake of World War 2. Today, recreation throughout society at home and abroad, has become a major industry. Players in traditionally professional games are traded in millions, where previously a 'few thousand pounds' was the going rate. Quite recently Rugby Union, by tradition, a bastion of the amateur culture has gone professional. Down the years in the Rugby Union ethos, a player who turned to professional Rugby could never again be admitted to the amateur ranks as a player, nor was he eligible for membership of an amateur club, once his playing days were over. The GAA, apart from its notorious ban on 'foreign games' had its social norms too. Tom told me until after World War 2 the ladies were, in practice, excluded from the festive table. But it has to be said that they always enjoyed the parity of esteem at the turnstiles. Up to World War 2 "Smoking Concerts" were a feature of male recreation in the GAA. A group would book a large room in a hotel for a social gathering laced with drink and songs. I'm told, that at one of these functions a young Corkman was asked by the M.C. to contribute a song. He hesitated initially with a promise to respond later. In the interval he consulted a friend about his problem; a problem rooted in the rigidily exclusive nationalism of the day. His favourite song was "Bonny Mary of Argyle" and since ' 'Mary' was a 'foreigner', he feared that she might not go down well in the company. In the event, no audible objection was raised "Smoking Concerts" disappeared early in World War 2; wartime cigarettes, rationing etc. saw to that. By the way, medical knowledge in regard to the terminal health hazards of smoking was in the womb of time at that point. May I now refer to a social function organised by the Dublin County Board that ran amok cost wise. The year was 1942, a particularly good year for Dublin. In keeping with the culture of the day, it was an exclusively male presence - apart from the waitresses.

The senior footballers and hurlers qualified for their respective All- Ireland senior finals. The hurlers lost to Cork but the footballers made amends when they beat Galway in the decider, a victory, which was very much hailed in the capital. Nineteen years had elapsed since the previous win in 1923. It was decided at a meeting of the Dublin County Board in November to honour both teams at a function in Clery's. The function which was confined to the teams and officials was, a very enjoyable affair despite the war time restrictions. Treasurer of the County Board at the time was Tom Woulfe, and his Civil Service colleague Sean O Braonain was County Chairman. The County Board supplied the drink at the dinner but because of rationing, no whiskey was served Guinness stout was the order of the day. At around 11. 30 p m Woulfe was approached by Paddy "Beefy" Kennedy, a Dublin player, who had played in both finals in 1942, a unique record. The drink had run out and the company felt that a few more bottles wouldn't break the County Board. Woulfe set off in search of County Chairman O Braonain to explain the crux which had arisen. O Braonain took out his notebook and tore a leaf from it. He surveyed the crowd and wrote an order for the store man to supply a further 12 dozen of stout to the tables. At that stage there were about 70 people still in the function room. "Beefy" offered to take the written order for more stout to Clery's store man whose job it was to look after such details at functions. The chairman was leaving the festivities around 12, 30 a.m, and although a strict teetotaller, O Braonain couldn't fail to observe the behavioural transformation throughout the hall that the - as he thought- meagre transfusion had effected. A sedate gathering had become a rollicking party in no time. He mused aloud that perhaps he was witnessing a repeat of the "Miracle of Cana". A month later the bill for the function arrived from Clery's. The drink item was staggering. Woulfe knew that "Beefy" had changed the 12 dozen into 72 dozen of stout. The party was still going strong at 4 am in the morning. The Chairman was furious when he saw the cost of the drink and asked Woulfe about it. Tom responded that he only transmitted the order as instructed. Woulfe claimed later that he applied the old Chinese proverb to delicate situations: " Those who know don't talk, and those who talk don't know". It was a night to remember.

Tom Woulfe

Paddy McFlynn of Magherafelt, County Derry

Derry born Paddy, represented Down as Central Council representative for many years. He got involved with the GAA from a very early stage of his career and achieved the pinnacle of that involvement when he became President of the Association in 1979 to '82. Paddy was born in Magherafelt and became Secretary of the Derry County Board while he was still playing football with his club. He went on to become a teacher and took a teaching post in Guildford in County Down and was to become very much part of the GAA in his adopted county. Paddy was no mean footballer, and excelled in filling various roles on the field whenever the need arose. He was known as a very committed footballer as many found to their cost, be it as a defender, midfielder or forward. In 1942, Paddy played with his club O'Donovan Rossa of Magherafelt against Glenullen in the Derry Senior Football Championship final in Dungiven. There was very keen rivalry between the two clubs. Rossa, were favourites having won the title previously in 1939. The referee appointed was none other than the County Chairman, Paddy Larkin, and to make the occasion more interesting, Paddy McFlynn was the County Secretary at that time, but was still very active on the playing field. The Rossa forwards were a bit on the small side and they were finding score- taking a little bit difficult against strong fielding Glenullen defenders. Paddy McFlynn, was told by his team captain to move to the attack in order to bring a little order to chaos. Matters improved immensely with the presence of McFlynn and gradually the Rossa forwards began to click and their tally mounted. As the game entered the final stages the Glenullen full -back rose to field a high ball, only to be met by a full- blooded shoulder charge from one Paddy McFlynn, who not alone put the opposing full- back over the end line but into the the railing surrounding the pitch. Referee Paddy Larkin immediately took McFlynn's name and sent him off. The rash challenge earned Paddy McFlynn a month's suspension. Rossa went on to win the game and the county title. Referee Paddy Larkin, who was brought to the match in the O'Donovan Rossa coach, wasn't the most popular passenger on the way back. Naturally O'Donovan Rossa celebrated their great victory in due course. A meeting of the Derry County Committee took place a few weeks after the county final and it presented a few problems. Paddy McFlynn was the County Secretary but because he had incurred automatic suspension for his dismissal in the county final, he couldn't attend the meeting in his capacity as County Secretary. He had brought all the relevant books and reports, meticulously prepared,and handed them to the County Chairman , but Paddy was instructed that he would have to sit outside the room during the meeting.

Little did the County Committee know of what was to follow. The normal one hour County Committee meeting was about to become a marathon four hours. It was the longest ever held in the history of the county. As every item on the order paper cropped up, a member of the committee had to go outside the room to consult with Paddy.He then had to advise the committee member on the next step in the order of business There were so many queries that committee members had to make frequent trips out to the waiting County Secretary. At the end of the marathon affair the suggestion was agreed, that there should be some rule in the Official Guide which permitted a County Secretary to attend a meeting even though under suspension because of a playing rule misdemeanour.

Paddy must have created some other kind of record, after being sent off in a match refereed by his own Board chairman. The appearance of the All- Ireland champions of past years, who are introduced to the massive atttendance at Croke Park on All-Ireland final day, have been, for the past 20 years, a major attraction The man responsible for that innovation was the late Mitchel Cogley, the then Sports Editor of the "Irish Independent". Mitchel met Paddy McFlynn at a GAA function one evening and floated the idea of inviting All Ireland winners on the occasion of the silver jubilee of their victory to Croke Park on All Ireland day. Paddy thought there was great merit in the suggestion and promised he would bring the matter up at the next meeting of his Committee. In the meantime, Mitchel, on his own initiative, approached Michael Fingleton of "Irish Nationwide Building Society" an ardent GAA follower, who readily agreed to sponsor the former All-Ireland Champions appearance at the big game. He would also host a dinner for them on the eve of the big event. Mitchel , communicated the good news to the GAA President. Paddy McFlynn was delighted and a date was set for the launch of

Paddy McFlynn

Mitch Cogley's brain wave. The launch took place at a Dublin hotel which was attended by the media and representatives of the former champions who were getting the invitation that first year. President McFlynn thanked all those who had attended the get together and singled out the sponsor, Michael Fingleton, for his sponsorship of the inaugural event in the GAA calendar. He left the originator of the idea, Mitchel Cogley, last on his list, because he wanted to pay a special tribute to him, for coming up with the suggestion. Unfortunately, as the old saying goes, "there are many slips between cup and lips." Paddy started to pay a special tribute to Mitchel, off the cuff, which can be fatal at times Paddy called him Mitchel Geoghegan, who was a great character known to Paddy back in Guilford in County Down.

Oblivious of the mix up in names, Paddy continued to lavish praise on a now very embarrassed Mitchel Cogley, who, it must be said, took it all in very good heart. When Paddy stepped away from the lectern to join the party, he was met by GAA PRO at the time, Pat Quigley: " Who in hell" said Pat "is the Mitchel Geoghegan, you have been praising for the past ten minutes?" Paddy McFlynn was taken aback and only then realised his error, and the mix up in names. He immediately went over to Mitchel Cogley who was in the company of Michael Fingleton, and apologised profusely for his terrible mistake, explaining about the other "Mitch" in his home town. Mitchel Cogley, always the gentleman, took it all in good spirits, and demanded two extra tickets for that year's All-Ireland final, which he got. GAA Presidents suffer the same demands as other major officials of the Association when the question of All-Ireland final tickets arises in the course of conversation. Paddy McFlynn found that out at a very early stage of his stewardship. He was travelling to Cork to honour a commitment, the presentation of medals at a club function. Paddy's chauffeur was Billy Byrne, who drove him to all his engagements during his three year term. There was a bit of an urgency attached to the trip to Cork because fuel was running a bit low, and Paddy was hoping that he could get a ' top up' before going to the function. Former Cork star Paddy O'Driscoll, was Chairman of the County Board and he persuaded Paddy to allow him to drive the visitors to the club function. Paddy also told the President that he would get plenty of petrol at an all night filling station in Fermoy. The club function was very enjoyable, helped by the social evening which followed, with tenor Sean O Se, the guest artist. It was late when President McFlynn took off for his date with the filling station in Fermoy. But horror of horrors, when they reached O'Callaghans Filling Station in Fermoy, the place was closed and locked up for the night. Paddy's driver Billy Byrne took charge, and drove to the Garda Station which was open, and told the night duty sergeant about the petrol predicament and the important passenger he was driving. The Garda could not have been more helpful, and indeed explained, that he always kept a stock of petrol in case any of his visiting relatives were in need of a top up late at night. Billy Byrne accompanied the Garda to his house, where he duly produced the petrol and Paddy was delighted to pay for services rendered. The Garda was a Roscommon man and the inevitable question was shyly posed, would there be any tickets going for the All-Ireland football final? True to his word, Paddy sent the Fermoy Garda on two tickets for the All Ireland final, and as luck had it, Roscommon played Kerry in that final, so it turned out to be a very satisfactory situation all-round. Paddy McFlynn got his petrol for his return journey and the Sergeant was the recipient of two All Ireland tickets and saw his native county play Kerry, the ultimate winners.

Dr. Con Murphy of Cork

Dr Con, tops the 6 ft mark, and is one of the more familiar figures attached to Cork hurling and football teams. He is also one of the nicest medics you could meet. Dr. Con is a noted medical practitioner and is very much in demand in his Cork city practice. He is also astute when it comes to discussing prospects of Cork teams for up coming championship matches, and after listening to his logical conclusions, you are none the wiser because of shrewd Cork villainy. Most counties boast of great characters who become legends irrespective of the sport that they become involved in and Cork is no exception. They had John "Kid" Cronin. He was an all rounder, boxer, hurler, footballer, team trainer, you name it, he was part of it. The "Kid" was a well known figure in GAA circles and became part and parcel of Cork activities, always attending games involving the county. Dr Con Murphy remembered an incident which happened in 1983. It was the year that Dublin agreed to travel to Pairc Ui Chaoimh to play Cork in the All- Ireland senior football championship semi-final replay. Joe McGrath was a well- known coaching figure and game analyst, and he was attached to the Cork team. Joe arranged a meeting of the players to discuss team tactics, and other means of clipping Dublin wings on the big day. Thirty players turned up for the team talk and Joe decided that each player would make a contribution lasting not more than two minutes. It turned out to be a lengthy session, with a lot of repetition. The defenders stressed that the onus lay on the forwards to put away scores, the forwards indicated the importance of the defenders keeping a tight rein on the Dublin forwards, and so on. Nearly two hours into the session, having looked at videos of Dublin matches and Cork games Dr Con felt that the limits had been reached and suggested to the coach that the session be wound up before the players got too bored. It was agreed. Present at the session was trainer "Kid" Cronin, as usual, but he had dozed off midway through it. Dr Con made the final contribution and Joe McGrath called on "Kid" Cronin for his comments only to be met with snores. The good doctor shook the "Kid" gently, he woke up with the startled comment: "what's up?" Dr Con explained that they wanted a comment from him on the big game that Sunday. The "Kid," fully awake at that stage, sat up in the chair and proclaimed: " I have only one thing to say" and a chorus of voices asked: "And what's that, "Kid" ?". There was a pregnant pause as the "Kid" looked round the room and declared: "Brian Mullins is over the top." Dublin won the game and Brian Mullins was the star at midfield, and the "Kid's" after match comments were never recorded.

There was a growing myth, not alone in Cork, but outside the Rebel County in the 70s, that the Leesiders never took the National Hurling League seriously but Cork men will always deny it. Cork travelled to Thurles to play Offaly in a relegation play- off, a very important fixture for both sides. John Horgan was a striking figure on the Cork team at the time, tall with fair hair, he was one of the best defenders of his era. John had another claim to fame, he never got injured, and he never visited Dr Con, a qualified Sports Injuries practitioner for attention or advice. Cork defeated Offaly in that relegation play off and after the game reliable masseur "Kid" Cronin spoke to Dr Con and asked him to have a quick look at John Horgan's leg, that something was wrong with it. Dr Con meticulously examined Big John, his knees, thighs, hamstring, groin, leg muscles' every

Billy Morgan ... former Cork footballers and manager.

movable part but could find nothing wrong with him. Dr Con told the "Kid" that Horgan appeared to be fine. "Look at his boots," asked the "Kid." Dr. Con looked at the Cork player's boots, which were sitting beside his other playing gear, they were two 'left' boots, which Big John had thrown into his bag that morning and he had played the full sixty minutes wearing those same 'left' boots. The "Kid" Cronin lost his wife many years ago and spent most of his afternoons visiting the local cinema, indeed it is fair to say that the "Kid" had seen every film that came to town and was an authority on them. On Saturday nights Dr Con and the "Kid" always met in a local hostelry for a few pints. Cork travelled to Dublin for an All Ireland senior hurling semi-final and the "Kid" as usual, shared a room with Dr Con, an experience the good doctor had become well used to, especially waking up in the morning. to find the bedroom covered in dense cigarette smoke. He believed the "Kid" smoked in his sleep. There was little happening in the afternoon but the "Kid" suggested to Dr Con that they look at a TV film. Dr Con thought it a very good idea. The film showing at the time was "An Officer and a Gentleman" and Dr Con admitted that he had never seen it. The "Kid" assured Dr Con that it was a great film. The film was running for about fifteen minutes when the bould "Kid" said to his bedroom mate: "Con, you won't believe this." "What is it, "Kid?" asked the good doctor: "Do you see yer man in the uniform with the moustache, he hangs himself later on in the film." End of film for Dr Con. The "Kid" always helped out by giving Cork players a good rub before taking the field. Shortly before the 1988 All Ireland senior football final against Meath the Cork team manager, Billy Morgan, stood among a circle of players in the dressing room and while addressing them, he kept throwing the ball to each player, who threw it back to manager Morgan.

Dr. Con Murphy, also stood among the circle of players, and he was drawn into the ball throwing exercise when Billy threw the ball to him, as he stressed to the players the importance of being alert and being focused at all time on the business on hand. Dr Con threw the ball back to Billy. There was only one other person who hadn't sampled Billy Morgan's ball throwing exercise and that was "Kid" Cronin, who was a little tired having given the players on duty a good rub. He was standing at the end of a broken circle of players when Billy threw the ball to him but the unfortunate "Kid" dropped the ball only to have abuse hurled at him by the annoyed Cork manager. Niall Cahalane turned to Dr Con and whispered "Jasus, is he thinking of using him". When John "Kid" Cronin died some years ago, the funeral was the biggest seen in the city for years. The attendance included all the hurlers and footballers who had passed through his hands. Cork haven't won an All-Ireland since the "Kid" died and the hurlers maintain to this day, that it was the footballers who broke his heart. "Kid" Cronin was a much loved character and took great pride in his membership of the famed Glen Rovers club where Christy Ring was one of his idols. He started his inter county career as trainer at the behest of Donie O'Donovan, when he was appointed manager of the Cork football team. One man who knew him well was Gerard Lenihan, father of Donal, Ireland's 6th most capped rugby player, with 52 caps, who was born in Cork. Ger played football with St Nicholas, he also won senior and junior Munster heavyweight titles in Boxing and represented Ireland in those grades in the 50's. He was the recipient of the Jury's "Hall of Fame Award" for boxing some years ago. "Kid" Cronin was a professional fighter, who fought in booths in England to make a living. Ger and the "Kid" became very close during the former's boxing career and the "Kid"s knowledge of the boxing game was invaluable, a fact very much acknowledged by Ger. The" Kid" was very gentle with children and Ger recalled an incident which typified the man. He was competing in the National Championships in Dublin and the "Kid" and himself on a walkabout in the city came upon a young child being heavily scolded by its father, and the child was crying. The "Kid" put his hand in his pocket and brought out a bar of chocolate and gave it to the young child. The "Kid" will always be remembered by those who knew him as a kind, warm hearted individual who would never do any one a bad turn.

Gerald McKenna of Kerry

Gerald is one of the finest GAA officials it has been my good fortune to meet and our friendship stretches back a long way. Having spent over 40 years writing on Gaelic Games in the "Evening Press " since its inception in 1954 until the company closed it down, with a loss of 600 jobs in 1995, I had the good fortune to meet leading GAA officials from all 32 counties, both at County Board and club levels. Gerald McKenna was one of those officials, but in one way, he was something special. First of all he is a gifted orator and his contributions at annual GAA Congresses are pure works of genius. If a very contentious motion would crop up for discussion the Kerry maestro would bide his time and allow matters to run their course before making his entry into the arena. Once called upon to give his view by the President the assembled delegates would lapse into silence.

Gerald would then proceed to air the Kerry thinking on the motion in question, praising the proposers of the motion for the businesslike manner in which they had put their case, and at the same time paying tribute to those who had opposed the motion, pointing out how the democratic process, which has always been the corner stone of the Association since its foundation in 1884, would see justice prevail.

Gerald's words appeased both sides, naturally, and then his closing argument, containing words of wisdom, would eventually strike an instant chord with the neutrals, who invariably agreed with the Kerryman. The motion would either go through or fall, depending on which side the Kerryman's logic laid the most emphasis.

During Gerald's tenure as Chairman of the Kerry County Board I had to phone him occasionally about Kerry matters, changes on teams, reasons for players being dropped, and other matters relating to a match taking place on that particular weekend. It was the policy of the "Evening Press" Sports Department that my copy would include comments from team coaches/ trainers, managers or influential county officials from both participating counties or clubs. Contacting Gerald McKenna presented no problems, being a National School teacher,it was a simple case of ringing him after school hours.

I followed that procedure for many years, getting the necessary "quotes" and comments that I had requested. I got to know Gerald's line of reasoning to the stage where I could have written the "quotes" myself. Gerald always praised the opposition and highlighted their strong points while playing down the strength of his own team. On one occasion, Gerald said to me: "Look, Sean, you know me well enough now, you can write your own "quotes", and I'll stand over anything you may write, if I'm not contactable at any time." I knew Gerald held me in high esteem but to give me licence to write something he hadn't personally said to me was very gratifying.

Some years later a crisis did arise when Gerald was not contactable because of a Telecom Eireann strike. The phone circuits were inoperable and it was impossible to get a call through to any of the regions outside of Dublin. Unfortunately, the strike coincided with a major Championship game involving Kerry and there was no way of contacting Gerald at his home in Ballyduff or indeed at his school for his comments on the upcoming match. Remembering Gerald's very generous offer of quoting him should he not be available, I wrote my piece about the match in question, and I included liberal comments from the Kerry Board chairman, just as I felt he would sum up the match and his county's prospects for that weekend. My article appeared on the Saturday in the "Evening Press" and the Sports editor at the time, Paddy Flynn, was delighted that I had broken through the telephone crisis in order to get the required "quotes" from the Kerry chairman, the only paper to carry such comments on the Dublin newspaper circuit. A colleague of mine, working for one of our competitors phoned me a few days later demanding to know how I was able to get "quotes" from Gerald McKenna on the match on that weekend, " when every bloody phone in the country was down" He told me that he had been hauled over the coals by his Sports Editor, and shown a copy of the "Evening Press" with Gerald McKenna "quotes" in my preview of the match. Trying to explain away his reasons for not having a quote from Gerald fell on deaf ears as far as his Editor was concerned, "If Sean Og could get to Gerald for his quotes, why couldn't' you," he was told. I hadn't the heart to tell my suffering colleague about the secret arrangement I had with the Kerry chairman, who, incidentally , when I met him after the game in Croke Park on that Sunday, was very satisfied with the "quotes" attributed to him, making the comment " I thought I summed up the game very well in your column last night." Needless to say Kerry had won the match. There was great jubilation in the Kingdom in 1978 when Kerry beat the reigning All Ireland champions Dublin in the All- Ireland final. It was a particularly gratifying win for the Munster men, who had suffered defeat at the hands of the "Jackeens" in the previous two years. A third defeat in a row would have been catastrophic from a Kerry viewpoint and certainly heads would have rolled, had it happened. Happily, all was well, and "Micko" and his men came out on top and so saved face for every Kerryman dreading the humiliation of a third setback at the hands of the mighty "Dubs".

The welcome given the Kerry team on its arrival home with the coveted "Sam Maguire" surpassed all previous homecomings by successful Kerry teams. Manager Mick O'Dwyer and each individual member of the team was accorded unprecedented applause by the huge throng of supporters who had turned out to greet them. The Chairman of the Kerry Board, the genial Gerald McKenna, couldn't help but think at that moment of those weeks before the All- Ireland final, when a local retreat was taking place in the parish of Ballyduff, his own parish. Naturally the occasion was a pious one, and everybody was feeling holy during retreat week. One evening walking to the church a friend joined him and said: "Do you know Ger, what's going on now reminds me of a prayer. 'Tis a case this week of "Glory be to the Father, to the Son and to the Holy Ghost, and next week it will be the very opposite, " as it was in the beginning, is now and forever shall be" That thought sprang to the mind of Gerald MCKenna, as the last player on the panel had been duly acclaimed and the Chairman of the County Board was called upon to deliver the final few words, before the coach and the players moved off to the next port of call. Gerald"s rousing speech to the multitude really caught the mood of the occasion, and if the supporters had been ecstatic before his appearance, Gerald's speech brought out the human emotions of the vast crowd, followed by rounds and rounds of sustained cheering and applause . Gerald, caught up in the excitement of the moment, suddenly grabbed hold of the Sam Maguire Cup, and holding it aloft for all and sundry to see, proclaimed: "And we will hold this Sam Maguire Cup, as it was in the beginning, is now and forever shall be here in the Kingdom of Kerry ". And so they did keep it for the next three years.!

Pat Stakelum / Mickey 'Rattler' Byrne / Paddy Kenny of Tipperary

I never pass through the town of Thurles without saying a quick hello to Pat, who will always be ranked as one of the finest centre half - backs in hurling. He captained Tipperary to win the 1949 All- Ireland title against Laois. He added two more, in 1950 (against Kilkenny) and 1951 against (Wexford). Pat had the unique distinction of never playing on a losing Tipperary All- Ireland final team. His talents were quickly recognised in the early 40s when he was brought to Dublin by the Young Irelands club, along with Seamus Bannon and the Kenny brothers Paddy and Sean. Their presence on the Young Irelands team brought crowds flocking to matches involving the Tipperary star hurlers. I remember playing against them when they made their debut in a senior hurling league game against Eoghan Ruadh at the Civil Service Ground at Islandbridge. I had a great battle against Seamus Bannon, who was operating at centre- field, while my brother Seamus had his hands full with Paddy Kenny. Pat Stakelum was as solid as a rock in the Young Irelands defence, and the packed ground witnessed some of the finest hurling seen in the capital from the Tipperary men. I happened to be in Thurles last year when I again renewed acquaintances with Pat Stakelum and Paddy Kenny, but a surprise addition to the party was Mick "Rattler" Byrne who became a legend in his own time as one of the great Tipperary defenders, winning four All- Ireland titles with the county. Mickey, was fearless and played on some of the best forwards in the game around that time. When you got a rattle, a good shoulder from the bould Mickey you knew you were in a match. When you sit down and begin reminiscing with former hurlers the stories begin to flow and it was no different on my meeting with the three Tipp stars that day in Thurles. The "Hurlers" Golf Society always comes into the equation and is used as a backdrop for most of the stories tossed around. Pat Stakelum remembered driving to Gort for Miko McInerney's Captain's prize. Travelling with him and a few other golfers was Society secretary Mutt Ryan. As they approached Gort, the question arose, how to get to the golf club. Pat said to Mutt, who was sitting in the front seat: " Let down the window and ask someone how do we get to the golf course." Mutt, whose mind was always on hurling matters, stopped a few men on the side of the road and asked: "Where is the hurling field, lads."? Incidentally, a visitor to the outing that evening was the renowned Josie Gallagher of Galway hurling fame, who turned up for the after golf meal and brought the house down. There was great excitement in the county in 1957 when Tipperary flew to New York after winning the National Hurling League. Included in the travelling party was a great Tipp follower, Maurice Whelan, from Carrick-on-Suir, who had never missed a match involving his native county.

He followed Tipperary everywhere and one of his greatest wishes was to visit New York, a place he only dreamt about visiting. His wish came true when the opportunity arose for a trip to the Big Apple with the Tipperary party. Maurice was a bit apprehensive about the trip but the players rallied around and he was readily assured that the 'plane journey, was a " piece of cake." The 'plane duly left Shannon and there was no more excited passenger than the same Maurice Whelan who sat back and luxuriated in the comfort of his surroundings, even disdaining the offer of a free drink as he contemplated visiting the city of his dreams. The 'plane was 650 miles out from Shannon when the pilot decided to return to his departure point because of an engine fire due to an oil -leak. The 'plane landed safely at Shannon and there were fire engines and emergency units standing by as it came to a halt. The story is told, that Maurice, a kind, decent man, got out and said, looking all around from the top of the passenger steps: "Well, thanks be to God, I've lived to see it, it's everything they said about it."

Tipperary played Dublin in a National League game in Croke Park and while the puck around was taking place, Mickey Byrne was eye-searching to see what his immediate opponent looked like. He spotted the number on the Dublin player's jersey, a big tall newcomer who topped the six foot mark and he was very impressed, while immediately planning how to deal with such a challenge. Shortly after the start of the match, the Dublin forward gained possession and came charging at Mickey who stopped him with a full shoulder to the chest area, and laid him out. When Mickey was asked about it after the match he said: "Well, when I went over to have a look at him, to see if he was alright lying his full length on the grass, I was only the size of Willie Carson, compared to him."

Tipperary played Cork in the annual Wembley, London Board sponsored Whit weekend game, and like all Tipp-Cork clashes, there were no punches pulled. The match was played at a lightning pace as both teams strove, might and main, to gain an advantage. Two English men who watched the game in awe couldn't get over the exchanges and yet no one was getting injured. Said one of the Englishmen: "Blimey, if that's sport in Ireland, what's their bloody wars like"? Meanwhile up in the broadcasting box, well known English rugby international Jack Hyams, who was invited to view the game, was asked by the commentator," How would you like to be in there with a hurley"? To which Jack answered "I wouldn't like to be in there without one."

In 1949, Tipperary met Cork in the first round of the Munster senior hurling championship the player Tipp feared most was the renowned Christy Ring. The task of marking Ring fell to Tommy Doyle, who had earlier indicated to the Tipperary selectors that he was retiring from the game, but he was prevailed upon by selector John Joe Callanan to postpone his decision until after the Cork match. This Tommy agreed to do in a once - off gesture. Little did Tommy know what he was getting into as the sports writers at the time were certain that Ring would crucify the Tipperary defence, and veteran Tommy Doyle, and lead Cork to another famous victory over their great rivals. But for once

Mickey 'Rattler' Byrne (fourth from left, front row), Paddy Leahy - selector (first from left, front row), Pat Stakellum (fifth from left, from row) and the rest of the 1949 Tipperary All-Ireland winning team.

the script writers were caught on the wrong foot. When the final whistle sounded, the sides were level, and 'veteran' Tommy Doyle had accomplished the noteworthy feat of holding the Cork maestro to a solitary point. The replay was another thriller with Doyle again charged with the task of marking the Cork wizard. The game ended in another draw and this time Christy Ring was held scoreless from play. Extra time had to be played at the end of which Tipperary emerged victors with Christy Ring the scorer of only one point. So after 150 minutes the name of Tommy Doyle entered the Hall of Fame books for his magnificent performance in containing the Cork maestro, and apart from one point, rendering him ineffective from a scoring viewpoint. Tommy Doyle's commitment and indomitable spirit had prevailed to help his side achieve a victory which eventually led to All- Ireland honours under captain Pat Stakelum that year, ably assisted by Mickey Byrne and the Kenny brothers, Sean and Paddy. But the victory over Cork was not to be forgotten and the team got a rousing reception with Tommy Doyle, the recipient of major praise. On the day after the Cork match Mickey Byrne and some of the players met as usual in Liberty Square in Thurles, where the match against the Leesiders was again the main topic of conversation. Tommy Doyle, who was known as the "Rubber man" joined up with his team colleagues and he was lavished with praise because of his performance against Christy Ring. But Tommy was rather dismissive of all the attention and back slapping, according to Mickey Byrne, and said to his colleagues: " You know, I'm getting more congratulations for holding Christy Ring for 150 minutes, yet I have been holding my wife, Nancy, for thirty years and there's not a bloody word about it."

There was always great rivalry between Moycarkey-Borris and Thurles Sarsfields at Tipperary senior hurling championship level. Former All- Ireland defender Johnny Ryan always had a big say in the selection of Moycarkey sides. He was a very influential figure and invariably swayed opinion on how best to line- out the team on the occasion of a major test even though he was not a selector. But the officials in charge felt obliged, out of respect for the former great player, to tell Johnny about the Moycarkey line- up before going out to play Thurles in a championship match. There was great excitement in the Moycarkey dressing room as the players got ready for the big game. Johnny Ryan made his appearance and was approached immediately by one of the team selectors John Hayes: "Johnny, it was a very tough job picking this team, it was very hard to know who to leave in or who to leave out. But after a few nights deliberations this is the team we finally picked," handing the slip of paper to Johnny Ryan. He looked at it and said: " Well, what ever team ye picked or what ever team ye didn't pick", putting his hand in his coat pocket and taking out a match box with his team written on it, " this is the team that will be playing today" and handed it to John Hayes. The games between the two teams were rarely kid gloved affairs and if an indulgent referee was in charge, he would turn a blind eye to several incidents which needed reprimand, claiming that continuity of play was more important. The local doctor was always busy after such events as he looked after a broken finger, cut foreheads, gashed legs etc. One Sunday evening as he entered his surgery he was surrounded by injured players which prompted him to remark " Tell me, do ye play the ball at all in these matches"? And that led to another story which I recalled when visiting Thurles many years ago while doing interviews for an All- Ireland Special for Radio Sport. I had made arrangements to meet several Tipperary players who were going to be involved in that particular All- Ireland inal. I mentioned to them that I was also interviewing Most Rev Dr Kinnane, Archbishop of Cashel and Emly, who was Patron of the GAA at the time. I was encouraged and dared to ask the Archbishop about his seminary days, and a story, told to me by one of the players about the Archbishop during his period in Maynooth. Some of the matches played here were more than competitive, they were tough and a number of prominent hurlers, who played in them were brilliant minors, who were later to go on to figure in All- Ireland finals during their priesthood days.

There was a lot of county rivalry apparent during the student days at Maynooth and it was reflected in the exchanges at some of the matches. Archbishop Kinnane was a fierce competitor during his student days at the famous College and he left his mark on some of those occasions. On this particular day tempers became a little frayed between a Munster selection versus the other provinces. The seminary infirmary was a busy place as the doctor in charge applied liniment and plasters for injured players. When the first of the injured appeared the doctor asked: " And what happened to you"? as he prepared to apply treatment. " Oh, Kinnane of course" A few minutes later another player arrived needing a stitch or two and again the doctor asked how was the injury incurred, to which came the reply: " That fellow Kinnane" A third player arrived later with a cut over his eye and the doctor said: " Don't tell me, Kinnane did this"? " No, No, " said the player " I'm Kinnane."

Denis Conroy of Cork, who was to become Chairman of the County Board in his latter years, was a constant guest on the "Marion Finucane Radio" programme. Denis was a great character and a noted wit and it was always extremely difficult to put one over on him. He always had an answer to the most awkward question and was never found wanting when asked for his opinion on the most contentious of issues which arose during his stewardship. On one of Marion's programme he was asked: " Denis, if one of your sons went off and played Rugby, what would you do"? "Marion, " said Denis "I would go home and ask his mother who the lad's father was." Denis was a great attraction when- ever he visited his local pub and was always ready to apply the put- down when such action was needed. A group of old timers were sitting around his favourite watering hole in Blackpool and they started comparing the standard of hurling away back in the old days with that of the present. Some of the oldtimers believed that the standard of hurling even in Denis's day was better than that of the present and the question was inevitably posed to Denis: "When did the change come about, in your view."? Denis looked around at his audience and declared profoundly: " When they took them off the tit and put them on Cow and Gate."

Mick Moylan of Dublin

You wouldn't meet a nicer guy than former Dublin star defender Mick Moylan A prodigious kicker of a ball, he remained a great favourite with Dublin team supporters apart from the sterling service he rendered to his club St Vincent's I remember on one very windy day at Croke Park he took a kickout from the Dublin goal from the Canal end. The high wind carried the ball well over midfield and opposing half- backs and forwards and untouched,ended up wide over the line at the Railway end near the Cusack Stand and Hill. I have never seen the feat repeated. Like a number of those Dublin players of the '50s, Mick enjoys a holiday in Kerry where he renew acquaintances with Kerry players of that period. Remarkably, there is even a greater affinity between the Dubs of the 70s and the Kerry players of that era and that exists to this very day. But I digress.Mick Moylan and his wife Peggy and children were returning from a very enjoyable holiday in Inch, Co. Kerry, a beautiful holiday resort on the wild Atlantic. My wife Ann and I often visited this coastal holiday spot and were taken by a sign displayed there near the beach, which simply says: "Dear Inch, must I leave you I have promises to keep;Perhaps miles to go to my last sleep." When Mick Moylan and his family were leaving Inch to make the long journey home to Dublin the rain was only bucketing down. Standing by the roadside in the rain,thumbing a lift was an elderly man and Mick stopped the car and offered him a lift. The man was only too delighted and told Mick that he was on his way to Tralee when he got caught in the heavy rain Mick assured him that he was on his way to Dublin and would drop him off in Tralee The conversation got around to football and Mick learned that his grateful passenger was actually catching a train to Cork for the Munster football final between Kerry and Cork. He hoped to stay in Cork and get to Pairc Ui Chaoimh in plenty time the following day for the annual contest between the great rivals. Mick's passenger had a very thorough knowledge of Kerry teams and was able to recall great games of the past and the famous individuals who had made impacts on those winning occasions. This inevitably brought up the famous 1955 All- Ireland final between Kerry and Dublin and Mick had given no hint that he had been a member of that particular Dublin team. His Kerry passenger made no bones about the fact that the '55 victory was probably one of Kerry's most famous wins ever against the Dubs: " There was so much talk about it and what Dublin' new style of slick football would do to Kerry's old style of fetch and kick " he said

He also emphasised the power of the Kerry forwards on that occasion, the accuracy of Tadghie Lyne from frees and play, the speed of Paudie Sheehy and the strength of Jim Brosnan. The he added for good measure:" And young Johnny Culloty gave the Dublin corner back a torrid time and that was also most important." Mick smiled and said nothing, remembering only too well the battle he had on that occasion against the same "Young Johnny Culloty". The conversation turned to the 70s and the epic matches between the Dubs and Kerry and the Kerry passenger was loud in his praise of the Dublin winning teams and manager Kevin Heffernan and conceded that the Dubs had got ample revenge in the wins over Kerry in the 1976 final and the '77 semi final. It was on that the journey ended for Mick's passenger whom he left at Tralee railway station. Mick extended his hand in parting which was grasped warmly by the Kerryman who said n a quiet voice: " Thank you Mick Moylan, for the lift, and safe journey home to Dublin."

Mick O'Dwyer of Kerry

My wife Ann and I stayed in the " Villa Maria Hotel" in Waterville, owned by Mick O'Dwyer's wife, Mary Carmel, along with Sean O Siochain and his wife Kathleen. Sean and I were naturally taken in hand by Micko and for the remainder of our stay we fought out many stiff battles against Micko and his golfing partners on the challenging Waterville Links. To put matters in proper perspective, Sean and I hadn't a chance winning the wager against Micko, who knows every blade of grass, every line to the hole and the vagaries of the wind on his home patch. Sean and I soon became reconciled to the fact that we were two "Dublin lambs" being led to the slaughter.

had to chastise my partner on a couple of occasions, gently of course, for needless coughing as Micko was about to take his putt. The unintentional dropping of clubs at precise moments didn't seem to faze our opponents either and in the end we had to give up and try and beat them at golf—again to no avail. Micko was, at the time, up to his tonsils training the Kerry footballers for the All-Ireland semi-final against Derry, and a probable meeting with Dublin in the final. Staying in the "Villa Maria" at the time was well known Cork soccer star, Donal Leahy, who played with "Evergreen" and Cork Celtic. He was a genuine sportsman, a lover of all games as Corkmen most surely are, and he was marvellous company. We looked forward to our chats in the "Villa Maria" kitchen late at night. Mary Carmel provided a marvellous treat, piping hot apple tart, which she had baked and tea, served in a friendly atmosphere. Donal and I compared notes one evening as we sampled the delicious late fare on how we both trained for important matches in our respective codes. We had to agree that the type of preparation indulged in by the footballers of Kerry and Dublin, was indeed far removed from what we had experienced in our playing days, especially the physical aspects of match preparation.

had attended many of the Dublin training sessions at the time, conducted by selectors, Kevin Heffernan, Lorcan Redmond and Donal Colfer. Quite honestly I never thought the human frame could take such punishment over a period of two hours. It must have been sheer hell and there was no let up either in the intensity of the workout. The session started at seven in the evening sharp. On one occasion, a key figures arrived ten minutes late. He trotted over to manager Heffernan to explain his late arrival. Kevin had a few words in his ear and sent him back to the dressing room, later he watched the session from the sideline. The player told me afterwards that "Heffo" had reminded him that training started at seven sharp and not at ten minutes past the hour. Needless to say, the player was never again late for training. I explained to my good Cork friend, Donal, about some of the extreme exercises which the Dublin players had to endure.

I said to Donal: " Jimmy Keaveney is perhaps the heaviest player on the Dublin team, over 14 stones, and he could run from one sideline across to the other side in Parnell Park in a little over eleven seconds, that's approximately 70 yards." I could see my good friend, Donal, was very impressed, and I emphasised that I was a spectator and saw him do it. Donal and I resumed our nightly dissertations on sport over hot apple tart and tea and one night he confided in me that he was very impressed with my comment on the Dublin training methods until he heard what the Kerry players had been subjecte to by Mick O'Dwyer: " Do you know, Sean, " he said in his soft Cork accent: " tha Micko makes the Kerry players run from one sideline to the other in Fitzgerald Stadiun Killarney, in 12 seconds, carrying concrete blocks.!" He paused and looked for m reaction. I told him I was indeed impressed and I said no more.A few days later I wa out with Sean OSiochain again on the Waterville links trying to extract a few shilling from the bould Micko and I chastised him over his nonsensical propaganda about "Kerr players carrying concrete blocks and running the distance in 12 seconds etc" When w reached the ninth tee I turned and said to Micko: "Listen, a Mhic,I will be prepared t add a few more seconds to Jimmy Keaveney's dashes in Parnell Park, if you are prepare to drop the concrete blocks bit." He agreed. Imagine using an innocent Corkman lik Donal Leahy to try and put one over an equally innocent Dub. You would be never u to those Kerry fellas.!

Mick O'Dwyer

Ned Wheeler of Wexford

Ned was a big man, huge frame, forceful as they came and was fearless in the tackle. I was glad that I had bowed out of the game when he began to make his mark on the inter- county scene. Ned was a native of Laois, but played all his hurling in Wexford where he assisted the Faythe Harriers club. He figured at centre forward, midfield and centre half- back and won 3 All- Ireland senior hurling championship medals with his adopted county and two National League medals, apart from provincial and Oireacthas trophies over a sixteen years span. In my period on Dublin teams, when selected at midfield, I invariably played on Ned's midfield partner Jim Morrisey, a very stylish and commanding player. Most players taking the field for a match, and I can include myself in this observation, quietly bless themselves. It is a regular act which becomes a habit. Ned Wheeler, at 17 years of age, was playing with Piercestown against a neighbouring parish of Killinick His immediate opponent was one of those old stagers who had been around for a long time, and at 37 was still performing. Ned, full of enthusiasm ran down to his position, and on his way, blessed himself, which he always did. The old stager gave Ned a hard look and said very quietly: "It's too late for prayers now, sonny!" Ned never regarded himself as a footballer, but he loved playing games, be it hurling or football. He was cajoled into playing a football match by an old selector (Ned claimed, that in his youth, all the selectors appeared to be old stagers.) Bobby Donoghue played with Ned Wheeler on club teams in the early '50s and he was also a selector. At half time Donoghue was giving the team a few words of encouragement, he turned to Brendan McGrath and said: "I'll be bringing you in for the second half, Brendan." "But I have already played in the first half" said a bewildered Brendan: "well, in that case, will be bringing you off in the second half." Bobby Donoghue was a very good forward. He was very fit and never stopped chasing balls. Faythe were playing Nick O'Donnell's team, St Aidan's in a League match in New Ross. Bobby secured possession and was hell bent on scoring a goal. He rounded one of the half- backs and made tracks for goal, and just outside the 'square' as he was about to shoot, when his jersey was pulled by big Nick, as he was in the act of striking the ball. The shot went harmlessly wide. Bobby shouted at the referee and appealed for a free, claiming his jersey was pulled. But he got no sympathy from the official in charge, who told him he had allowed him the advantage. Bobby's anger wasn't appeased when the referee, moving away said: " Anyway, Bobby, from where you were, my mother would have scored."

Wexford were playing Kilkenny in a National Hurling League game at Enniscorthy. Ned was going through for a score when he was fouled and the referee awarded a free to Wexford. Nicky Rackard was the free taker. Nicky, as usual took a few steps forward and blasted the ball to the right side of the Kilkenny net. The referee immediately blew the whistle and disallowed the score, claiming there had been an infringement by one of the defenders. He indicated to Nicky that he wanted the free taken again. The ball was placed on its spot again, Nicky took his usual few steps forward, and blasted the ball to the left corner of the net. As the referee was moving outfield Nicky said to him: " Would you like me to take it again?" The " Harriers" were invited to play a Dublin Civil Service selection in a challenge match at Parnell Park, Dublin. A great old character who travelled with the club, a retired Guard, Paddy Breen of Wexford offered to drive Ned Wheeler and a few of his team mates to the match. The car Paddy Breen was driving was an old Ford V8 and its top speed was 30 miles per hour. Before going to Parnell Park, Paddy had to call in to see his wife in a Dublin hospital. She had complained to him that she wasn't able to sleep and would he bring her a few sleeping pills. Paddy got the required pills for his wife from a local chemist. He also had a small vial of pills for another ailment. He was inclined to drop off asleep at the toss of a coin, so he got pills which kept him awake for long journeys - quite the opposite problem to the wife. The hospital visit over Paddy drove to Parnell Park and Ned Wheeler and his team mates played the challenge against Civil Service, which they won. After an enjoyable meal provided by the host club Paddy Breen and his passengers headed for the county of Wexford. Ned Wheeler noticed on the drive home, that chauffeur Paddy was constantly lowering his window and slapping his face. It was now 12.30 a.m. and the 30 miles per hour had dropped dramatically to 20mph at times. It was easily known, said Ned, that the car was originally used for funerals. Ned and the passengers were getting worried about the lateness of the hour and they were still a long way from Wexford. It was only then that Ned discovered that chauffeur Paddy had taken the wrong pills for the journey home. He had given his wife- not the sleeping pills- but his own pills for keeping him awake, while he had taken the sleeping pills meant for his wife. From that moment on, Ned and his team mates opened all the windows in the car, and Paddy got the odd slap in the face to ensure that he was wide awake. "We eventually got to Wexford at half past five in the morning, the longest journey it had ever taken me to go from Dublin to Wexford. Do you know something" said Ned: " I could have walked from Dublin to Wexford in half the time."

Dick Doocey of Tourin

Dick played around the time of the brothers Fives, McGraths and Powers in Waterford hurling when no quarter was given and the exchanges were uncompromising. The quality of inter county hurling was very high then, and players like, Jim and Charlie Ware John Keane, Christy Moylan and Andy Fleming were regular choices on Munster teams around that time. Tourin reached the Waterford County Final which created a lot of excitement at the time in the village. As Dick Doocey pointed out, they lived in a tightly knit community and the side was drawn from virtually three families. The final was set for Walsh Park, Waterford, and Dick, who played at centre half - back, was one of the non drinkers on the team. It carried a responsibility too. He was delegated, when the team arrived in Waterford for the match, to keep an eye on a couple of players who might have fancied a quick trip to the bar of the Hotel where they were having a pre - match meal. In fairness to the players, they had trained diligently and social drinking was kept to a minimum during the course of the campaign. Players are always edgy before a big game, so Dick decided to bring the players he had under his wing, for a short walk to help break the monotony of the waiting period. They passed a church and Dick suggested a brief visit and a short prayer as a little help from the Good Man above might not be out of place. The church was empty, and as they walked around they heard a familiar voice coming from a side altar. They stopped and knelt behind the figure known to them as "Shiner", a character named Jack Connors, who was also known to visit pubs more often than a church. "Shiner" was lining up the Toorin team with candles, by placing them in their positions on the floor at the small altar, naming them as he went along "in goal, Johnny McGrath, left corner back, Danny Murray, full- back, Davy Walsh, right corner, Conal McGrath, centre back Dick Doocey and may Christ help the man inside who passes you." There were brothers who lived in Tourin and they bought a new radio to listen to Miceal O'Hehir's commentary on the 1948 All-Ireland senior hurling final between Waterford and Dublin, which I had the pleasure of playing in. Waterford, were doing very well in the opening quarter and when they were awarded a free, one of the brothers would scream at the radio: "Let John Keane take it," and he felt justly vindicated when John duly obliged. Waterford were building up a good lead at the time when one of the brothers decided to answer a call of nature: " Listen, Johnny, switch off that radio until I get back, I don't want to miss any of the Waterford scores.

There was an old character living in Tourin called" Winger" Barry. He fought in the Boer War. He was always brought to matches when the local side was involved, and rarely missed one. He was unable to attend one particular game, but he heard in Cappoquinn that Tourin had won. He was very pleased and said it was good enough. Later on that day he met two old acquaintances who also informed him about the Tourin success and stressed that they had played very well and were extremely good. The old character replied profoundly: " They were always good, but they must have been greater this time."

Seamus O'Brien, the then Secretary of the Western Board in Waterford, was present at a local hurling championship game between Tourin and Dunhill and he had brought with him a few American visitors who were keen to see a hurling match. Seamus, pointed to the players and explained that sets of brothers were not uncommon on both sides. He wanted to prepare them for a physical confrontation but he also explained about the rules and how the game was about to be played. He pointed to the Dunhill players and mentioned that there were a number of Powers playing on the side, brothers, cousins and brothers-in-law. He brought the visitors over towards the Tourin players and again stressed the inclusion of the McGrath brothers, Jack, George, Johnny the goalie and Bob but Seamus could see no trace of Bob, who was behind a bunch of players, tying his bootlaces.

The Americans visitors were intrigued with all the preparations that were taking place on the field as Seamus spotted Bob, and hurried over to where he was completing his lace- up job explaining to the visitors that he would like them to meet Bob: "Well, Bob," said Seamus, "what kind of form are you in"? No reply. " What kind of form are the lads in?" No reply. "Are ye good enough to win it?" That sparked a reaction from Bob, who jumped to his feet, his hands holding the hurley, citeog style, and he took a few steps backward and then proceeded to make swipes at the top of the grass. He turned to Seamus and said: " I'll tell you something for nothing, Seamus, there will be more blood shed here today than was shed at the siege of the GPO in 1916" They were brave words but the game did not end in the blood- bath predicted by the bould Bob, who was playing at corner forward. Tourin, were under pressure entering the closing stages as they held on to a one point lead when Dunhill forced a 70. Dick Doocey, who was operating in his usual berth at centre back began to marshal his forces. Some of the Tourin forwards dropped back to lend a hand including Bob McGrath. Dick called out to his defenders: " I'll go for the ball let ye watch the break." Back came the rejoinder from Bob McGrath: " Dick, there will be no breaks but the forwards neck."

Jim Barry, the legendary Cork trainer, was appointed circulation manager of a well know Sunday newspaper for the Munster area. It was late in Jim's life when he learned to drive a car, but luckily, he was offered the post soon after taking up driving. The car came in handy when Cork had to travel to play matches, and Jim invariably carried some of the players. Coming home from a match one Sunday evening, the players he was driving became a little nervous about Jim's antics. He was taking corners at high speed and appeared to be in an awful rush: " Steady on Jim, " one of the players said, " we want to get home all in one piece." Jim was all apologies."I'm sorry, lads, I didn't want to say it to ye, but I'm very low in petrol, and I want to get home before the engine cuts out." Shortly after the last war, a Waterford hurling team was invited to Belfast by the then Antrim Board Chairman, Padraig McNamee. It was a very enjoyable experience for most of the Waterford players, visiting Belfast for the first time. The team travelled by coach, and on the return journey, Declan Goode, the Waterford County Secretary, insisted on stopping at the Border to take a few photographs. He was immediately prevented from doing so by an RUC officer. Declan began to remonstrate with the RUC man but was ordered back into the coach, by the chairman Fr. Tom Cummins: "I will, Father, I will, but we'll take the bloody photos on the other side" and he pointed at the RUC man and roared: " and he can take a running jump at himself" as the coach roared across the dividing line. Tallow in County Waterford, was renowned for the number of citeogs, or for the uninitiated, left-handed hurlers. The Sheehans were a typical example, who featured on the club sides. Pat Sheehan was playing against local rivals Lismore in a championship match on a Sunday afternoon. When the two teams are drawn against one another they would toss for choice of venue, either Tallow or Lismore. On this particular occasion, Lismore had won venue advantage and staged the match. Prominent for Lismore at the time was Joe Duggan and he provided plenty of headaches for the opposing Sheehans. Well known Waterford tenor, Frank Ryan, who was chairman of the West Board, was present at the match. He had recorded "The Rose of Tralee", which turned out to be a best seller in the music market. The game developed into a ding dong battle between the two great rivals, neither of whom were taking any prisoners, and naturally tempers became frayed at times. Frank Ryan, who was sitting on the sideline, was very unhappy about the way Joe Duggan from Lismore was behaving against Pa Sheehan from Tallow. When play moved to Frank Ryan's vantage point he roared at the Lismore man: "Duggan, we didn't come here from Tallow for you to blackguard us "But unperturbed by the comment from the West Board Chairman, Duggan, turned and belted the ball towards the Tallow goal and then turned and roared back at Frank Ryan: " and you stick to your " Rose of Tralee."

Holycross is still a mighty force in Tipperary hurling and in Pat Stakelum's era they were a match for the best in the county. They were pitted against Boherlahan in a championship game and Holycross were streets ahead on the scoreboard at half-time. The big stumbling block was Stakelum, who hurled rings around everybody in sight, and no matter who was switched on to him Stakelum performed regally and the Boherlahan score sheet remained very meagre indeed. It was crisis time in the Boherlahan dressing room at half-time, and the whole discussion centred on Stakelum. How were they going to face the second half and the rampant Stakelum.? Something drastic had to be done, but what.? Sitting in the corner on a seat was team character Jimmy Mac, pulling away on a cigarette and listening to all that was being said. Up he jumped with a shout: "Listen I'll mark Stakelum if ye mark the other fourteen."

The Kerry county football final was being played in Tralee between Dr Crokes and Austin Stacks and sitting in the stand was a Dublin man on holidays witnessing his first Kerry county final. Both teams spent much of the time hand passing the ball around and there was very little of the famed 'catch and kick' for which Kerry teams in the past were famous. The Dubliner turned to a spectator sitting beside him and inquired: " Where are all the footballers gone"? He got his answer: "The grave yards are full of them." Newly elected Kerry T D Jackie Healy Rae was asked during the course of the elections who was he representing and he replied: " the ordinary people of Kerry" But the questioner came back at him looking for something more definitive and asked: "who are the ordinary people of Kerry?" Healy Rae never batted an eyelid and remarked: "They are the people who have their dinner in the middle of the day." There is a well-known hostelry in London frequented in the main by Irishmen working on the building sites. They are drawn from most counties and bitter arguments break out regularly about the outcome of matches involving their respective counties at home. It is not unknown for fights to break out either when somebody oversteps the mark, and treads on the toes of another acquaintance. In one such incident a row developed between two men who had been drinking at the bar, both had a lot on board. They had been slagging off each other's county, until one of them rounded on the other and said: "Kerry is it,? nothing good ever came out of Kerry but whores and f....k...g footballers." With that a burly figure, topping six foot and as broad as he was long, stood up from a table and grabbed him by the scruff of the collar and said in a loud voice "My mother comes from Kerry" "And what position did she play in?" asked his half strangled victim.

Ollie Freaney of Dublin

Ollie was, in my book, one of the best centre half-forwards in football and was also one of the most popular players ever to don the Dublin football strip. He was also the least liked among opposing sides, especially defenders, some of whom got a roasting from the burly St Vincent's player. He was an untidy dresser, socks around his ankles, and jersey, half in and out of his togs. But he was deadly taking a ball and making tracks for the opponent's goal. He relished taking on defences, rarely was dispossessed but when fouled, he would pop the resultant free over the bar. He had a peculiar gait, a side to side roll, and looked slow yet few defenders could catch up with him when he went on a solo run. I played with him on Dublin football teams in the late 40s and early 50s and I can certainly say it was a pleasure to watch him in action. Ollie had another side to his football character. For some unknown reason he would try and intimidate his immediate opponent, by either a comment about that player's occupation or stature. Some of the stories relating to the Dublinman were figments of some fertile imagination and some got better in the telling. There were some stories that were true. St. Vincent's played an Army team in the Army Grounds in the Phoenix Park, the first time that an Army team had entered for the championship. Ollie was in his element on that occasion, teaming up with Kevin Heffernan and Johnny Joyce, and before half time the game was well beyond the Army team's reach. Ollie, had scored three great goals so the Army sideline mentors took off their centre half-back, who was well over the six foot mark, and sent in instead a smaller substitute, who immediately after taking up his position, started to elbow and shoulder Ollie. The St Vincent's man looked down on this new addition to the action and roared across at Kevin Heffernan: "Heh, Heffo, they must have run out of men in the Army." He was master of the put down. The Army figured in another Ollie Freaney story which my good friend, Eamon Young verified. It was a Dublin versus Cork National Football League game and Army man John Cronin at centre half-back was pitted against Ollie Freaney. When Ollie ran down to take up his position he said to big John:" Well, soldier boy, I see you are not soldering today" a comment that immediately raised the hackles of the placid big John. The game wasn't long in progress when the inevitable happened. Ollie came soloing in towards the Cork goal and he was met by a shoulder from Cronin that flattened the Dublin man. Big John, he stood about 6' 4", looked down on the prostrate Ollie, and said: "Now Ollie, the next time you come soloing down here, and when I say jump, you jump". Many years later, Ollie Freaney was sitting in on a Board meeting in his very successful Accountancy firm on North Strand when one of the young receptionist rang him to say that a Mr Cronin was looking for him.

Ollie went out to the reception room to find Big John Cronin waiting for him. They greeted each other and John said: "How are you Ollie, would you have any job for me? "What do you do" asked Ollie. Big John was a bit non committal so Ollie said," speak to that girl there and she will fix you up" John was duly fixed up with a job and was rarely seen around the offices, but appeared on a Friday to pick up his wages. Twelve months later Cyril, Ollie's brother, went out to lunch together and Ollie told him that Big John had left, hadn't turned in for a week and nobody knew his whereabouts. And that was the last that Ollie saw of his former Cork footballing foe.

Nicky Purcell of Kilkenny

Nicky takes great pride in the fact that he is an out and out Tullaroan man. He was chairman of the Kilkenny County Board for ten years from 1959 to '68. It was a very good period for Kilkenny hurling. I didn't have to remind him of the great rivalry which existed between Tullaroan and Mooncoin and how it effected the selection of Kilkenny teams for All Ireland duties. It was the time when clubs represented counties at All Ireland level and the club strip of the county champions was worn. The two clubs dominated Kilkenny hurling and there was no love lost between them. When Tullaroan were county champions they would exclude some Mooncoin players from their All Ireland final team, and Mooncoin operated the same system when they had the selection. But there was a compromise in 1907 when Kilkenny played in the Tullaroan jerseys. The county final had ended in a draw. Tullaroan claimed at a subsequent County Board meeting that they had scored a point which hadn't been recorded and the Board sided with Tullaroan and they were awarded the match. A compromise was reached when the captaincy of the county team was given to Mooncoin's Dick "Drugs" Walsh and Kilkenny won the All Ireland that year. Relationships between the two clubs deteriorated and there was constant bickering and disputes between them for long periods as Mooncoin players refused to play in the Tullaroan strip, which was a white jersey with a green sash, and Mooncoin had a green jersey with a white sash. So when did Kilkenny change over to the black and amber striped jersey which is worn to this day? Kilkenny P.R.O and historian Tom Ryle supplied the answer. A well known Carlow farmer, John Drennan, owned race horses and he won a major National Hunt championship race in 1911 and a substantial sum of money. His riding colours were striped black and amber, colours worn by his jockey. John Drennan had a set of black and amber jerseys made up and he presented them to the Kilkenny County Board, and they were gratefully accepted. Kilkenny had reached the All Ireland final that year but they got a walk over from Limerick. The new Kilkenny jerseys were worn the following year in 1912, when Kilkenny beat Cork in the final. They were to become the famous "Black and Amber" brigade that dominated the hurling scene and continue to do so to this very day. Kilkenny and Cork were always great rivals and respected each other whenever they met at All Ireland level. One of Cork's great players Jim Hurley, whom I mention in another story, and winner of four All Ireland medals, was a prominent figure in the famous 1931 All Ireland final win over Kilkenny, which went to three cracking matches.

Jim Hurley died some years ago and his funeral drew huge crowds. There were stars from all the leading hurling counties represented at the funeral Paddy Grace, Nicky Purcell, Lory Meagher, Paddy Larkin and Jimmy Langton travelled to Cork to pay their respect on behalf of Kilkenny. Nick Purcell, Paddy Larkin, Lory Meagher and Jimmy Langton went to the Bon Secours Hospital where Jim Hurley was laid out. Sitting beside the bed was Jim Hurley's widow and Christy Ring, a very good friend of Jim Hurley, stood behind her chair. He greeted the Kilkenny men as they came into the room. They knelt for a moment at the bedside and said a silent prayer for a man they respected highly. Nicky introduced his companions to Jim Hurley's widow. When Lory Meagher's name was mentioned, she stood up and leaned across the bed, grasped Lory's hands in her's and said, " My heavens, Lory Meagher, you are the the most often repeated name in our house."

Kilkenny travelled to New York to play New York in the National Hurling League final and they were quartered in the Manhattan Hotel on 42nd Street, where most GAA teams visiting the "Big Apple" stayed. It was the time when each of the travelling party got a daily allowance and he used it as he preferred. The players had their meals in the" Van Dyke" restaurant, Dutch owned, but it had good food and reasonably priced. When Nicky Purcell asked about a place to eat he was assured by Ollie Walsh that "Van Dyke" was indeed the place, having discovered it four years previous, and it was near the Manhattan Hotel. Ollie insisted on bringing Nicky to the eating house. When they arrived into the eatery they sat at the counter and were soon approached by a coloured waitress, who wore her hair in a bun. She had a pencil stuck in the bun as she moved towards Nicky and Ollie. Ollie shouted " Howya Honey" The waitress was stopped in her tracks. She took one look at Ollie and said, with a big grin " Don't say you're back in town" Kilkenny had been invited out for a bit of sight seeing and most of the party had assembled in the lobby of the hotel early one morning. Missing was Fr. Tommy Murphy who had been invited to a function the previous night, and was late getting in. He had no knowledge of the sight seeing trip and so Ted Carroll decided to rouse him from his slumber. Carroll got the name of a sports columnist from the "New York Times" and phoned Fr. Tommy's room. Half asleep, half awake Fr. Tommy answered the phone to hear a nasal voiced New Yorker, giving him his name, and he was in the lobby of the hotel, and hoping to get an interview with the priest playing in the big ball game. Fr. Tommy told him he would see him in the lobby in a few minutes. Ted Carroll put the phone down and alerted the other lads to what was happening. Sure enough, out of the lift hurries Fr Tommy and ignoring the other players, starts searching for a Hiram Goldblatt, sports writer for the "Times".

Ted Carroll approached a very moidered Fr. Tommy and told him about the sight seeing trip but Fr. Tommy had other things on his mind. " I'm supposed to meet some sports writer from the "New York Times" here in the lobby he wants to do an interview with me about the League final. The reception clerk tells me he knows nothing about him and hasn't even seen him. I think I will give him a miss and go back to bed for a few hours." Ted Carroll put a restraining hand on Fr. Tommy's arm and said quietly " You better think about this, Tommy. That guy might arrive and if he didn't find you here, he could write anything and they would be reading all about it back home before you even arrive." Ted Carroll was afraid to ask Fr. Tommy later had he any luck with the New York sports writer. The late Ted, was one of the characters associated with Kilkenny teams and was winner of three All Ireland medals with the county. There were big celebrations after winning the 1969 title against Cork. The victorious Kilkenny men were being feted in the Marble City, as they were driven on a lorry from the railway station to the town hall. There was a huge crowd. Ted Carroll was standing beside Billy Murphy on the lorry, and running along side of the bus was this character, who was doing an impersonation of Miceal OHehir 's commentary on the match. Ted Carroll turned to wing back Billy Murphy and said, " I tell you what, Billy, I'll get him to mention you in his commentary." Billy was the centre of another story which happened in New York. A bunch of the players were having morning breakfast in the "Van Dyke" before heading off for a bit of sight seeing. Billy Murphy arrived in late and sat on a counter stool. He asked for a cup of tea. The waitress planked a cup of hot water with a tea bag hanging out of it front of Billy. "Oh for God's sake, girl, I asked you for a cup of tay, not boiling water, will you let the tay draw?

Garrett Howard of Limerick

As I mentioned elsewhere in this book Garrett Howard still holds the unique distinction of being the only Limerick born player to have won 5 All Ireland senior medals, admittedly three of the medals were won with his native Limerick and the other two with Dublin. He was born in the parish of Patrickswell at the Croom end. As a local lad he went to work for the Parish Priest in Croom who had a sizeable farm. " I milked the cows and did a lot of the farm work" he told Con Healy, a neighbour of mine, who was writing a piece about the great Limerick star. " I remember well my first match with Croom. I wasn't expected to play as I was too young but I heard one of the selectors say - "We'll play young Howard- he is very fast. I suppose that's how I escaped the lunges of the strong able men- I was too quick for them." But Garrett's prowess with the caman was soon to be recognised and he went on to became a legend along side the other greats, the Mackeys, the Clohessys, Jackie Power, Mickey Cross, Jackie O'Connell, Timmy Ryan. Indeed there is a well- known poem which has the verse:" 'Twas hurling's greatest half- back line, That was never overpowered, In weather wet or weather fine, Cross, Clohessy and Howard" That line became known as the "Hindenburg Line" which related to the famous German World War 1 Line of Defence.   Garrett gave no great credit to a defender for beating a forward, simply because, he argued that the defender had the advantage of facing the ball at all times. He named Phil Cahill of Tipperary as being a very hard man to mark. " I always kept in front of him and on one occasion he kept moving outfield and I still kept in front of him. After a while he said " Garrett, aren't we out too far?" " The farther the better", I said " as far as you are concerned Phil." During Garrett's period with Dublin he played against Kilkenny and the great Lory Meagher. He claimed that you couldn't give Lory an inch. " I was asked to move over on him for the second half of a championship match. I knew that my only hope was to stick close to him. He didn't like that at all and after a while he said: " You're too close, keep out from me." " Lorenza," I said " you'll have very close company keeping for the next half hour." In 1934 Limerick played Galway in the All- Ireland semi final in Roscrea. Garrett was playing on Robbie Donohue, a fine handsome young fella, and a great favourite with the girls. He was fast and he got a half a foot ahead of Garrett for the first couple of balls. When they were both out on the touch line, Garrett anticipated a ball to come his way and said to Robbie:"Do you see that beauty there on the sideline admiring you?" "Where?" asked Robbie, turning around. Whatever about the blonde beauty, Garrett snapped up the ball and drove it over for a point. He had learned very well.

I met Garrett in the Burlington Hotel on the occasion when he was presented with the Bank of Ireland "Hall of Fame" award when he joined the other legend Mick Mackey, as the first two Limerick men to be selected as All Time All-Star Award winners. He recalled the glowing tribute paid to him by my late father, Sean Senior, on his Sunday night GAA programme for the part he played in Limerick's win over Dublin in the 1934 All-Ireland final replay. Garrett Howard never lost his love for hurling and would never miss a match on a Sunday. There is a lovely story told about Garrett. Some years ago he was heading for the local creamery sitting on the rider of his common cart which contained his milk churns. A passer-by remarked: "Isn't it a grand morning, Garrett- there is a stretch coming in the days." " Indeed then there is" replied Garrett, " it won't be long now until the sliothar is in the air again". A great hurler, a dedicated Gael and a lovely man.

Garrett Howard (second from left, front row) and the 1936 Limerick senior hurling team.

P.J. O'Dea of Clare

PJ is a familiar figure in Dublin around All Ireland final time. He never misses the big games. He is domiciled in Chicago, and is perhaps, one of the best known personalities in GAA and business life in the Windy City. PJ was an outstanding footballer and hurler and was a regular choice on Munster football teams in the early fifties. He figured successfully with big stars like Paddy "Bawn" Brosnan, "Weeshie" Murphy of Cork, John Cronin, Eamon Young, "Micksie" Palmer, Jim Brosnan and "Pakie" Brennan of Tipperary just to mention some. P J was a very skilful forward and had the great distinction of scoring in every match he played. He won many county football championship medals with Ennis Faughs, and was a lethal forward in hurling as well with Kilrush.

P J was invited to play in a New York hurling championship match at Gaelic Park and he was playing on a former Cork star, who was well into the autumn of his hurling career. All through the game, P J was getting a lot of stick from the Corkman, who kept pushing him and pulling P J's jersey when he attempted to play the ball. P J still managed to pick off some neat points and he had the satisfaction of scoring the all important winning goal. When the game ended P J turned to his Cork opponent and said " Well, Tom that's that, but I'll tell you something now, if they ever hang you for being a hurler, they'll be hanging one innocent man."

P J was playing in a junior hurling championship game in Tulla, County Clare, and his team Ennis Faughs were running away with the game, leading by 7 gls 2 pts to one point entering the closing stages. P J had made a big contribution to his team's wide margin. Very close to the call of full time, P J slipped two defenders, and hammered over another point to increase his team's tally, and as he was turning away, one of the other forwards said to him, "Good man, P J, that should make it safe."

Clare played Kerry in a Munster senior football championship match in Kilrush, a venue P J O'Dea knew to his finger tips. The Clare man had a special quality, he was fast on to a ball and faster still going away with it on a solo run. On one occasion during the game against the "Kingdom," P J grabbed possession out on the wing and made tracks for the Kerry goal. One of the Kerry midfielders shouted to a colleague "Catch him, Catch him " and the colleague turned around and said: " I wouldn't catch that fellow with a vice grip."

PJ has many claims to fame and not all connected with the playing fields. I know of no other individual who would have had the audacity to lock a noted, and indeed distinguished member of the Bar out of his hotel bedroom the night before P J turned out to play with Clare against Kerry in a National Football League game in Tralee. PJ takes up the story: " It was in November 1950 and I was accompanied by a friend, James Griffen of Kilrush. We went to the Limerick Greyhound Track before driving on to Tralee. I met Des Hanrahan, then a Limerick journalist and later Chairman of Bord na gCon. Thanks to the tips I got from Des, I won over £200, which was an awful lot of money in those days." " When we got to Tralee I was feeling very tired and went straight to bed, locking and bolting the door on account of the large sum of notes I had in my possession." About 2 a m in the morning P J was awakened by a lot of hammering on his bedroom door and calls to open it up. " I refused," said P J " I told who ever was doing the knocking to go away, even though he was pleading with me to give him out his pyjamas." After further pleas had been rejected by P J, the late night caller left knowing that he was not going to get any help from the occupant of the room. The next morning there was consternation in the hotel when P J entered the dining room for breakfast. The manager approached P J and told him, that the room he had slept in was the one booked by Judge Barra O'Briain, who was the Munster Circuit judge. P J had taken the wrong room, and he had made matters worse by refusing to give the angry Judge O'Briain out his own pyjamas, which was in the room with the rest of his clothes.

P J apologised profusely for his grave error, explaining his tiredness and his major coup at the dogs and the big money won, as the cause of the terrible mix-up in the rooms. Needless to say, after again apologising to the manager, P J quickly left the hotel after eating his breakfast. Coincidentally, I knew Judge Barra O'Briain well, who was a regular visitor to the menswear shop in which I served my time in O'Connell Street, Dublin. The shop was O Glasain, beside Kingstons. I worked in the tailoring department and I measured the well known judge for his suits, which were made of Irish tweed. He was a fluent Irish speaker and Irish was spoken by all the staff. I left to open my own sports shop in 1950, the year PJ had his brush with the Munster Circuit judiciary.

Tommy Barrett of Tipperary

Tommy is one of the longest -serving county secretaries in the GAA and as such has experienced all the trials and tribulations which have effected his native county through the years that he has been in office. Tommy has seen the great days when Tipperary ruled the hurling scene majestically and he has also tasted the bitter pangs of failure as well; the barren years when no championship trophies graced the Tipperary sideboard. Tipperary won three All- Ireland senior hurling titles in a row, 1949- '51, the second time for the county to pull off the coveted treble and they also added two National League titles to their list of championship honours in that spell. The League successes brought the added reward of trips to the U S A as League winners which many of their leading hurlers very much enjoyed. Teams travelled by liner to New York at that time and in 1957, after defeating New York in the St. Brendan Cup final at Polo Grounds, it was a very happy band of players who made the journey home. Bunked in together on the ship were legendary Paddy Leahy and "Irish Independent" Gaelic Games reporter John D Hickey. Travel by liner was pure luxury and the players revelled in it. "Irish Press" Gaelic Games reporter Mick Dunne was also making his first trip by liner and travelled with the party. Each cabin was supplied with a bottle of whiskey and an electric kettle if the occupants wanted to make a cup of tea, and a small bowl of sugar was also supplied. Paddy Leahy, who was always an early riser, being a farmer, pulled back the curtains in his cabin and the Atlantic sun streamed in. He immediately began boiling water, opened the bottle of whiskey, poured a good tincture into a glass and filled it with the hot water, and did like- wise for John D, who was now fully awake. Paddy stood looking out at the calm sea through the port hole while sipping his hot ' toddy ' remarking ruefully to John D: " Little do they know at home what we are suffering, for the Association." Leahy was of course, one of the shrewdest team selectors in the business and he was revered by the players. They saw both sides of his character, a wit of a man when savouring a win, but a tiger when teams weren't performing to his satisfaction. He was always the official singled out for after match comments by the press, but he also had to face the wrath of the Tipp supporters when reasons for defeats were demanded. It was on such an occasion that Paddy ran foul of one persistent follower after a losing game. Paddy was last to leave the dressing room along with County Secretary Tommy Barrett when they were approached by this irate supporter. He demanded to know why the proper changes had not been made, why a certain player was allowed to stay on when he was not playing well. Leahy tried to shake him off, seeing that the supporter wouldn't listen to his rational summing up of the game and the team performance.

Leahy nudged Tommy to stop, hoping that the persistent fan would depart the scene, but no luck. The fan kept hammering away at Leahy wanting to know the changes he intended to make for the next game until at last Leahy's patience was exhausted. He turned to the fan and said: " Listen, talk to me after the next match, we are going that way" pointing to where a row of cars were parked. That did the trick and the fan parted company with them. Leahy turned to Barrett and inquired "Do you know that fellow Tommy?", where is he from?" Barrett said he did not know the individual's name but he thought he was a teacher from North Tipperary. "Jasus, how did he get to be a teacher?"said Leahy. Tommy Barrett, Seamus O Riain and Paddy Leahy were in the bar in Gaelic Park, New York, in 1964 and an argument developed with John Kerry O'Donnell, who was as usual criticising the Central Council of the GAA for interfering with the way games were being conducted in the Big Apple. O'Donnell wasn't listening to any reasoning on the part of the visitors but was more interested in scoring points much to the delight of the onlookers in the bar, who were well used to him. O'Donnell's word was law and dare anyone cross him, he was that powerful a figure. But Paddy Leahy wasn't prepared to take some of the abuse being dished out and said in a loud voice: " You know John, you made big money out of the GAA, I have more time for the little club secretary at home in Tipperary, who cycles to his meeting every week or fortnight than I have for the likes of you." There was stunned silence in the bar as Leahy continued his tirade: " You made big money out of the GAA, John. We built the GAA in New York and America when Tipperary teams crossed from one coast to another in 1926 in cattle wagons to build the Association in San Francisco. I have more time for the little man who has to pay his way through life without having any big ideas above his station," said Paddy, turning back to talk to Tommy Barrett, who was wedged between himself and the other two. Seamus O Riain had been called away to meet a number of Tipperary men, who were domiciled in New York and he missed all the exchanges between Leahy and O'Donnell. The atmosphere was electric as customers in the bar waited with bated breath for O'Donnell to explode. But to show his adroitness in those situations, O'Donnell's face broke out in a big grin. " Give the man a whiskey, " O'Donnell said to his barman, who duly poured whiskey into Leahy's glass from the bottle. " Do you call that a drink, " said Leahy. "Do you call that a drink, would we offer you that measly drink back in the old country, when we are at home "? That stung John Kerry, who shouted to the barman "Fill up the bloody glass for the bastard."

Pictured at the Bank of Ireland, GAA All-Star Awards, from left Seamus O Riain, Tommy Barrett and also "Hall of Fame" winners from right Tommy Doyle and Garrett Howard.

For the remainder of the evening Leahy and John Kerry went on the proverbial bender and finished up with their arms around one another, the best of friends, not even a whisper of the hot air that had enveloped the bar a few hours previously. And that was how Seamus O Riain found them when he returned to pick up Paddy Leahy and Tommy Barrett hours later to bring them back to their hotel. When the teams had assembled at the airport for the journey home, they had a visitor in the person of John Kerry O'Donnell who was carrying three bottles of whiskey, which he duly presented to Paddy Leahy, all the heat of their previous night's engagement had since well and truly dissipated. The flight home for the Tipperary team and officials was not without a small scare. They ran into a storm which buffeted the plane about a lot, until the pilot, in his wisdom, altered his flight direction and skirted the raging storm. Some of the players did get a scare especially the younger players who had been making the journey for the first time. Paddy Leahy, who was feeling the effects of his previous night's booze up with his host, turned to Tommy Barrett and pointed to the locker above their heads, where now the three bottles of O'Donnell's whiskey reposed, and said: " Tommy, winch up for O'Donnell," as the safety belts were clicked into place. Tommy Barrett's action was soon spotted by several of the Tipperary players, Mickey Burns, Sean McLoughlin, Kieran Carey," Mackey" McKenna and John Doyle and glasses were filled until such time as John Kerry O'Donnell toasts had emptied all three bottles. The raging storm was soon forgotten, and the day after hangovers, were also quickly cured as the transatlantic flight headed for Shannon.

John "Kerry" O'Donnell

John "Kerry" was born in Gleann na nGealt, near Camp, Co.Kerry Born in 1899, he had emigrated as a very young man, the first of the family to leave home. He headed for Montreal in Canada, to relations. He became a lumberjack in the north of that country, where he made a few bucks and headed first for New York and then to Detroit, where he worked for a spell in the Dodge car factory. While working in Detroit he became interested in baseball. At night he attended school and learned bricklaying and plan-reading: a trade which was to help him greatly when he returned to New York in 1926. He quickly found work, a lot of hard work, and saved sufficient to pay his way home to Gleann na nGealt. He never lost his interest in Gaelic Games, and played in the West Kerry League with his more famous brother, Tim, who won All-Ireland medals with Kerry in 1929, 1930 and 1937, and would have won more, but for injuries, which kept him out of the 1931 and 1932 winning teams. John "Kerry" returned to New York and worked during the boom period. He got the nickname " Kerry" from his work mates in New York and the name stuck. He was earning big money until the Wall St. Crash and the Depression. He was out of work for three years, the most traumatic period of his life. He was really down on his uppers, and he remembered walking from 96th Street where he lived to 42nd Street and Fifth Avenue, just to see apples being sold. A lot of people went to Inisfail Park, not to watch games, but to find some friendly face from whom to borrow ten cents- things were that desperate. After the Crash, building work improved. John became involved with the Kerry club in the city and eventually he was able to buy his first saloon bar. Ten years later he had four or five going, and having played with the Kerry club for a spell, got involved in the managing side. Between 1932 and 1972 he steered them to win 22 New York football championship titles, a feat which hasn't been topped since, and more than likely, will never be surpassed . In 1940, John

Sean Og and John 'Kerry' O'Donnell at Kennedy Airport, New York, on the occasion of the first Cardinal Cushing Games tour to the States.

"Kerry" became President of the Gaelic Association of Greater New York, which controlled the New York championships in football and hurling. Fifteen years later he was again voted into the position, and was to hold office for five more years. In 1944, the then President Jim Cotter, asked John "Kerry" and Barney Prendergast, a Mayoman, to take over Gaelic Park. Two previous owners had gone bust and the Park was in danger of being taken over by another sporting interest, far removed from Gaelic Games. In order to keep the Park going he had to sell off his saloon bars, except for the Eight Ave. premises.

The popular profile painted of John "Kerry" was of a man who was constantly at loggerheads with the GAA parent body, intent on sabotaging all efforts of unity between the two. But John kept looking ahead, assessing the impact changes could have made had the status quo been changed in any way. He put it in another way to me many years ago. " I suppose it's like the ageing couple who had been at each other's throat from the honeymoon onwards. There arrived on the scene a parish priest whose concern about ailing marriages was a highly pastoral priority. In due course he visited the couple. Having discoursed at length on the Sacramental dignity of marriage with no apparent impact he proceeded to dwell on other aspects of the union. After pulling out all the stops the good priest appeared to have ignited a spark of reconciliation in the wife. But the husband wasn't giving an inch. As he was about to call it a day the visitor spotted the dog and cat lying back to back, in peaceful harmony under the table. Surely this is providential, says he to himself. Turning to the husband he said "Look at those two animals, deadly enemies in the wild, and there you see them in perfect harmony. Should that not be an example and a lesson to to you?." Back on the instant came the shattering reply "Ah, thats right, Father, but tie them together and see what happens.' John made his point. John and I were sitting together in his beloved Gaelic Park, down in the Bronx one morning where I was getting background to his life in New York. And again I asked him would differences between himself and the Central Council of the GAA ever be resolved. He told me" Let me put it this way. When my brother Tim and I were young we would help with the threshing, along with the other men. When the men were being fed in our kitchen during the threshing, they'd have bread and butter and a bowl of milk. My mother noticed that one young man was not drinking his milk, and she asked the reason why. "There's a mouse in it", he said sheepishly. My mother never said another word, but fished out the mouse, and threw it over the half door and went about her business tending to the other lads. When she went back to the young fellow, he was still looking at his bowl of milk. He hadn't touched a drop. "What's wrong with you" she asked. " You don't want your milk with a mouse in it and you don't want your milk with no mouse in it." Well, that's the way I am with the Central Council."

Cluichí Club, Coláistí agus Condae.

Spórt den Scoth

ar

TnaG

Art McGann of Dublin

A true- blue Dubliner who is never afraid to proclaim his allegiance to his native county. He still remembers with great pride, Dublin's halcyon years in the 70's when "Heffo", Lorcan and Donal, masterminded the winning of 3 All- Ireland Senior football titles and 2 National League crowns. "Arty" who played hurling and football with the famed St Vincent's club, recalled a Senior hurling league game between St Vincent's and arch rivals Eoghan Ruadh. Figuring with the "Vins" was Dan Hanratty, later to join the priesthood. I knew Dan well. I played with him when I joined the "Vins" in my minor days and later played against him when I transferred to Eoghan Ruadh. Dan was a very good left hander, a clever forward, speedy and a good score taker. He was also a gentle person who loved hurling. He was being marked by Eoghan Ruadh defender, Timmie Kavanagh, who was giving the unfortunate St Vincent's man a lot of stick when they clashed for a ball. Dan appealed to the referee on one occasion to watch the Ruadh defender, who he felt was concentrating more on the man than the ball, but the appeal was ignored. The St. Vincent's man was the victim of another ferocious challenge, with the referee close to the incident, and Dan, badly shaken by the challenge, shouted at the man in charge:"Ref, did you see that, I hope you saw it, there could be an action pending."

Dublin and Down met in the 1963 All-Ireland senior football semi final which Dublin won very convincingly and they went on to beat Galway in the final. The bulk of the Down team, which had made history by capturing the Sam Maguire Cup for the first time in 1960, played on that occasion. Dublin's midfield partnership of Des Foley and John Timmons, was one of the best pairings ever fielded by the Dubs. Figuring on the Down team in the positions were Jarlath Carey and Joe Lennon. Joe a very polished footballer, equally at home in defence or attack, who had won a second All-Ireland title in 1961. He was later to captain the team to a third success in 1968, and wrote a splendid text book "Fitness for Gaelic Football." Joe and his midfield partner Jarlath Carey had some great duels with the Dublin pairing throughout that '63 semi final. John Timmons had many fine attributes, not the least being his ability to take a high ball with one hand over the head of his challenging opponent. In the Down match the lionhearted Timmons performed that feat, soloed forward and kicked a mighty point from fifty yards, then turned and said to Joe Lennon:"Heh Joe, what page in your book is that in"?

Paddy Lawlor won 12 rugby caps for Ireland, representing his club, Clontarf and in 1952 he toured Argentina and Chile with an Irish squad (and later emigrated to Argentina). He was a product of O'Brien's Institution in Artane and St Joseeph's CBS, Marino, a nursery for the St Vincent's football and hurling club. Paddy wasn't long making his mark with the famed Vins, first as a minor and later senior before he eventually joined local rugby club Clontarf, with whom he won 13 interprovincial caps with Leinster. He always kept in touch with St Vincents and attended most of their major club matches. He met an old acquaintance in Art McGann one day and Art asked Paddy about the difference between playing rugby with Clontarf and football with St Vincent's. Said Paddy "Well, when we returned to our dressing room after a match there were infra red heaters, scalding hot water, and a masseur to tend to any minor injuries we may have picked up. In my playing days with St Vincents it was a little different. When we returned to the dressing room after a match, we had to wash out of a bucket of cold water and then had to endure a tongue lashing from trainer Tommy McCann."

Mickey Duffy of Monaghan

One of the best known and indeed best loved GAA administrative officials was Mickey Duffy of Castleblayney, chairman for many years of the Monaghan County Board and long serving Central Council delegate. He became a legend in his own time. He was fearless in the manner in which he administered the affairs of the county. Once he had ruled on a particular item there was no changing his mind- you had to put up or shut up. In virtually all County Boards there are certain characters who invariably like to make their presence felt. They stand up during Board meetings, claiming the chairman's indulgence "on a point of order" or by using another method "On a point of information " or "Through the chair." A Monaghan Board meeting was discussing the transfers of players from one club to another, always a contentious part of County Board life. More often than not, clubs object to good players leaving their own particular club for some rival club. The Board listens to objections to players moving from one club to another before a decision is taken on the matter. On one occasion after the counting of votes, Chairman Mickey Duffy declared a tie, with some spoilt votes, and then ruled that another vote be taken. At that stage a club member, noted for his constant interruptions, stood up and called for a clarification "On a point of information" and his question was directed to chairman Duffy. " Through the chair" he asked. "Can you tell me, when is a tie a tie?" To which Mickey replied " When its around my neck."

A slight problem arose before the start of a Monaghan Board Convention, the County Secretary took ill and was unable to perform his duties. Chairman Duffy asked one of the other officers to take over the chore of keeping notes of the meeting. The replacement official was new to the task and had to rely on the wisdom and experience of the chairman. There were a number of motions on the agenda, which took up a lot of time but the judicious handling of matters by Chairman Duffy kept matters moving briskly. There were the usual " on a point of order, Mr Chairman" interjections from the floor from time to time, but they got short shift, and protestations were firmly dealt with by the top table. One particular motion, a fairly contentious one was finally passed after the chairman had ruled that sufficient time had been devoted to the discussion. However the inevitable disruptive individual in the body of the hall wasn't going to allow matters pass that easily. Rising and delivering his chilling "On a point of order, Mr Chairman,I don't think the motion is 'aristocratic' (democratic). The acting secretary turned to the chairman and whispered, "how do you spell it" To which the chairman replied " Put it down, Jimmy, put it down, we'll spell it later."

Cardinal Cushing Games

I was chosen as the first journalist to accompany the Cardinal Cushing Games teams to America in 1965, the inaugural year of the series. New York and Boston were to be the venues for the games but shortly afterwards Hartford, Connecticut was added as a third venue, particularly because of the involvement of the Foley brothers, Big Pat and Jim, in GAA affairs in that city. Pat was chairman of the Cushing Games fund raising committee in Hartford, which, through its own activities, had raised in excess of $25,000 for the Cushing fund. Pat Foley had a busy schedule laid on for the Cushing party from Ireland when we reached Hartford, including a visit to Governor John Dempsey, born in Cahir, Co. Tipperary. Governor Dempsey was delighted to welcome the Irish party and after a brief speech, he presented each member of our party with a silver tie clip, bearing the State coat of arms. No provision, unfortunately, had been made to present the Governor with a suitable gift from our side and the situation wasn't helped when I was called upon to say a few words on behalf of the visiting party. As I moved forward, I was able to slip my Aer Lingus tie clip (green shamrock on the National colours) off. I said my few words expressing good wishes to the Governor for his hospitality and I ended up pinning on him my treasured Aer Lingus tie clip, which I had got from my school pal, Tom Kennedy, in the Aer Lingus Offices on Fifth Avenue in New York. As we were departing from the Governor's office, my elbow was grabbed by Joe Mullarkey, one of the Governor's office staff. Joe had Mayo connections. He pushed me gently into a side office and said: " You did fine, Sean, you did fine, but would you ever tell Aer Lingus to change the design of their tie clips." I looked at him quizzically, so he opened a drawer, and reposing within were about a dozen tie clips, similar to the one that I had just given Governor Dempsey: " It's not that the Governor doesn't like getting them," said Joe, "but we could do with a new design." We moved on to Boston that weekend and Christy Ring came into the picture. A week or two before we left, Christy phoned me to say that his firm "Irish Shell" would not release him for the trip. I contacted John Kerry O'Donnell, the organiser, of the Cushing Games and told him about Ring's problem. His reaction was predictable: " If Ring doesn't make the trip, we can call it off, he's the big attraction." I got back on to Ring and told him about O'Donnell's reaction. The Cork star, gave me his boss's telephone number at head office. I rang him the next day and explained the consequences if Christy Ring could not make the trip. I highlighted the charitable purpose of the whole venture, and stressed the importance of Ring's involvement. I made a good case and to my relief, he agreed to allow Ring travel.

When we reached Boston we headed for the Bradford Hotel (now demolished) where we were staying. Christy Ring asked could he stay in the coach until the rest of the players had been fixed up with their rooms. I thought it a strange request until Christy explained the reason why. He told me of a previous visit he had made to Boston to play in an exhibition game; he was whisked away by a couple of people to a dinner in his honour. Over 250 attended the dinner at 10 dollars a head. But Christy had not given permission for the dinner to be staged in his name. He was lauded by several speakers at that particular function, and given a watch which he claimed actually went backwards. He later found out that the group running the affair had pocketed the proceeds, and had only used his

Sean Og and Governor John Dempsey in Hartford, Connecticut.

Tall Tales & Banter

name as a means of filling the hall. He had taken a vow that never again would he be used unless it was strictly for charity. As the coach approached the Bradford Hotel, I made a brief announcement to the players and explained Christy's reason for staying hidden in the coach. In the lobby of the hotel the players were being allotted their rooms when two Irish lads were directed to me asking about Christy Ring. I told them that he would be joining us later that night. They became very agitated: " But we must see him, we have a function arranged in his honour," said one of them. I asked him had they Ring's permission to stage the function. They said they had written to him weeks before the trip, and not having heard to the contrary, they assumed that everything was in order. I assured them that Ring was not expected until much later. Two very worried gentleman left the Bradford and were going to have a lot of explaining to do to over 200 guests who had paid to see the Cork maestro. I must say they had my sympathies. When the visitors had departed, Christy slipped into his room. When I checked with him later he was certainly enjoying himself. He had ordered a huge meal, and was sitting back enjoying it, watching a baseball match on the television. I told him about the visit of his two admirers and the arrangements for the dinner in his honour. I asked him did he receive a letter inviting him to the dinner, and he replied,: " I get them all the time, you would never keep up with them." He dismissed my suggestion that he should attend the function which was taking place somewhere else in the city that night: " What did I tell you ?" he said " Didn't I tell you they would be around." But I also knew Christy wouldn't be, watch or no watch. Christy was of course , the big attraction the next day at the Charity match, when Cardinal Cushing, and his secretary, Monsignor George Kerr, presented all the players with a special trophy to mark the success of the games, which had enabled John Kerry O'Donnell to hand over a cheque for $35,000 to the Cardinal's Charity Fund for the poor of Peru.

A Cork School Teacher's Story

A young Cork school teacher asked his class to write an essay about the Gardai and about their work in the city. As he was to learn, not all of his pupils viewed the law and application of the law in the same light. Accepting that some members of the class held their own opinions about the guardians of the law he was surprised at the reaction of one of the boys, a known trouble maker. He wrote on his essay page "The Guards are Bastards." Shocked by this comment the young teacher got in touch with his good friend Srgt Paddy O'Driscoll, a former great Cork football star, who was well known for his work with the youth in the city.

Paddy was stationed in Union Quay Garda Station, the hub of Garda activity in Cork city. Paddy suggested to the teacher that he bring all the class into the station and he would show them around, explaining to them how the crime prevention system worked. There was great excitement the following day when the entire class arrived into the station and were taken in hand by Srgt Paddy. The boys watched with fascination listening to the radio calls going out to squad cars, messages coming in on the wire machines, law breakers being brought in by Gardai members. The boys were enthralled, after soft drinks and crisps had been distributed, it was time to call it a day. Back at school the next day the teacher sensed a complete change of attitude on the part of the class towards the Gardai so he asked them to write an essay about their visit the previous day, hoping that a new perspective would be reflected in their thoughts about the workings of the law. The class entered into the spirit of things with gusto as they scribbled away consigning thoughts to paper. The young teacher was pleased with the hive of industry. He had already noticed that the troublesome boy had completed his contribution, sitting back in his chair with arms folded. When the teacher collected all the essays later he immediately found the troublesome boy's copy, on which was scrawled " The Guards are cunnin' bastards."

Television Matches

In the early days of television I was sent to O'Toole Park on the Southside of Dublin to film a football tournament game between Dublin and Kildare. The appearance of a camera in those days was an open invitation to every child in the ground to assemble around the filming area. The camera position was on top of the dressing rooms, and while ideal for height and filming purposes, it was exposed to the elements Luckily the rain held off for that particular match. I had just climbed down from my lofty perch, having finished my assignment, when I was approached by a number of youngsters seeking an autograph. I scribbled my name on the back of an extended cigarette packet and other pieces of paper and began putting my gear away, when I heard a young voice saying to one of his pals: " Who did you get?" "Michael O'Hehir" was the reply. "That's not Michael O'Hehir," said the other voice ," that's your man Greene (Philip)" It was an awful blow to my ego.

Paddy Holden of Dublin

Paddy, from the Clanna Gael club, was easily one of the most wholehearted players produced by Dublin in the 60s. He was a player who could rouse a side and never spared himself in quest of a victory. His duels with Galway great, Mattie McDonagh, were a feature of the 1963 All-Ireland football final which Dublin won thanks to a Gerry Davey goal. Indeed, it could be said but for that second-half goal, Galway would have won four All-Irelands in a row. Paddy Holden nevertheless, fully deserved his All-Ireland medal for the service he gave to the county over a long period of time. In 1964 Dublin travelled to New York after beating Down in the National League (home final) but lost to New York by three points in the final. Dublin stayed in the Manhattan Hotel on 42nd Street, which was a very popular location for all visiting teams at the time. I stayed there with the Cushing Games players a year later. Each bedroom in the vast hotel, had a special door in the actual bedroom door, where the occupants could leave clothes to be laundered, or suits to be pressed. The clothes were collected late at night and were returned the following morning neatly pressed or cleaned, a service which didn't come cheap. Paddy Holden shared a room with big John Timmons and was first to occupy it, as big John was delayed coming up in the lift. There was a wardrobe in the bedroom and Paddy had carefully used up all the spaces for hanging his suit etc. When big John finally arrived he discovered that there was no room left for his clothes until Paddy pointed out the space in the door of the bedroom. John put away his suit, and most of his other wearing apparel in the space provided in the door. Both players went off with the rest of the team to do a bit of sight seeing and enjoy a meal. When Paddy and John arrived back later that evening, John went to the space in the bedroom door to get clothes for the next day, only to discover to his horror, that the clothes had disappeared. John was naturally very put out, his first trip to New York, and his clothes stolen. Paddy was trying desperately to keep a straight face and before he could stop him, John was into the lift and down to the foyer seeking the manager. After a few minutes the manager arrived into the bedroom with John, who showed him where he had placed his clothes earlier that evening. The manager wasn't impressed. He had to travel to the 20th floor to explain to the Dublin player that he had put his clothes into the laundry collecting receptacle in the door. He also advised John that he would have to pay for the laundered clothes when they were returned early the following morning. Paddy Holden hid in a nearby room until such time as John's fury had dissipated. John's clothes were returned, neatly cleaned and pressed, the following morning, with a sizeable bill attached, which he had to pay.

In 1965 Dublin met Kerry in the All-Ireland semi final, a Kerry team which included Mick O'Connell, Mick O'Dwyer, Donie O'Sullivan, Mick Morris, Niall Sheehy and Seamus Murphy. Dublin's midfielders, Des Foley and John Timmons had rare duels with Kerry's Mick O'Connell and Jim Lucey. It was a strong Kerry team and they held a definite edge in the forward division. Paddy Holden had his hands full against Pat Griffen but held his own in the battle for possession. With about two or three minutes remaining Kerry were six or seven points ahead and safely through to the final, which they subsequently lost to a rampant Galway team. The long whistle was imminent when Paddy Holden saw Mick O'Connell moving in his direction and the Valentia Island man trotted over to Paddy and gave him a comforting tap on the shoulder and said: "Well done, Paddy, but I think we have it now. It was a good sporting match. Paddy agreed and Mick went to move off when Paddy called him back "Heh Mick" the Kerry man looked back and said: " What is it? "Any chance of getting me two tickets for the final?" said Paddy. The Dublin man rated Mick O'Connell as one of the greatest midfielders he had the privilege of playing against. He also admired him for his exemplary sportsmanship: " I never saw Mick O'Connell commit a bad foul on any player. He played the game for the love of it." Paddy Holden has a photograph that he treasures. It was taken during a Grounds football tournament final between Dublin and Kerry. During the course of a tackle, Dublin's Christy Kane, grabbed Mick O'Connell's knicks, the Kerry man moved forward leaving his togs in Kane's fist. Mick O'Connell stood there wearing briefs, shouting at the referee to place the ball for Mick to kick the resultant free. The referee quickly signalled to the Kerry bench for a replacement knicks for O'Connell, who wasn't the least perturbed about his state of dress. When the matter was rectified the Kerry maestro kicked a mighty point from the free with no bother. Dublin won the game in a close finish.

Jack Ryan of Tipperary

J ack was a very skilful hurler and played in the 1968 All Ireland final against Wexford on the 40, flanked by "Babs" Keating and Jimmy Doyle. It was a period of great Tipperary teams who figured in seven finals between 1960 and 1968, their dominance in Munster broken only by Cork and Waterford. Local club rivalry in Tipperary was as keen as you would find anywhere else in the accepted hurling strongholds. Jack, who hurled with Monegall, was injured in a local championship game, and had to watch a semi-final clash with a rival club from the sideline. It was a year when the County Board decided on an open draw so the opposition facing Monegall wasn't too great. However, all was well as Monegall took complete control in the first half and they had built up a substantial first half lead, and looked in no danger playing into the wind in the second half. Both teams availed of the fine weather and opted to remain on the field at the interval Jack ambled across to where the Moneygall players were clustered but had to pass the opposing team on his journey. They were sitting in a circle with heads lowered around a team manager, who was laying down the law in no uncertain fashion. He held a hurley in his hand, and to add greater emphasis to a point he was making, he would whack the hurley against the ground. " Ye are no bloody good, yer all like a pack of old women, ye are letting Moneygall walk on ye and to make matters worse, not one of ye has even broken a bloody hurley!

Jack recalled a story about another great Tipperary character, Jackie Ryan from Upperchurch. In one of those rare upsets in Tipperary hurling, Upperchurch made it to the County final and there was great excitement in the build up to the game. However, it was not to be, Jackie Ryan's heroes were well and truly beaten and the manner of the defeat was the subject of much discussion for many days after, and all those who visited Jackie's pub found a ready answer when Jackie himself was asked to explain Upperchurch's defeat. "Well, it was like this" said Jackie " the problem was, they got this fellow out from Thurles to train the team when they got to the county final, and he told them to hurl the ball, and that wasn't their game at all and that's why they lost." Johnny Leahy, brother of the renowned Paddy, all former great All Ireland hurlers, would tell of matches around his time and remembered a man who would say to the players, "Don't mind the ball at all, just hurl away." One day they were playing a match and the ball was lost in long grass and they were hurling away for ten minutes before they knew the ball was lost.

Jim Hurley was one of Cork's greatest and best known hurlers and excelled not alone in defence but also in attack. He won four All Ireland senior medals with the Leesiders and was noted for his aggressive approach and no nonsense style. When his sons were growing up they too became proficient with the Blackrock club and many an inquest was held at dinner concerning the performances of the various sons in local matches. At times, Jim would criticise some aspects of one of the son's display, pointing out where he had erred in not releasing the ball, or for not laying it off to a better placed colleague. He was opposed in his views by other sons, and the arguments at the dinner table invariably became heated. Jim kept maintaining that they hadn't listened to instructions going out to play and that led to further arguments. Jim's wife did her utmost to stop the arguments that invariably started at the dinner table and frequently warned the warring factions unless they desisted there would be no dinner provided at all. But to no avail, until one day she declared, that she was leaving the house if one more word was said about the match at the dinner table, and they could talk and argue as much as they liked when the dinner was over. Jim, sitting at the top of the table was fuming, so he said "Right, there'll be no talk about the match, but" giving the table a whack with his fist " I know who is still the best hurler in this house."

Radio Sport

Forty five years have elapsed since I took over the Sunday night GAA results programme from my late father. I suppose I could also claim that I inherited his distinctive voice to some degree, as I am quickly identified through the spoken word when in company. It doesn't always help to be recognised in that respect as I found out one night. The phone to the radio Sports Department rang and I knew when I picked it up, that the caller was in a pub or club, judging from the background noises, clinking glasses and hubbub of voices. We get frequent calls for results of late matches, or games played earlier that day or perhaps someone who had missed the racing results, had an interest in some major race. Most sporting queries are directed to the Sports Department and the one I am going to relate on that particular night was no exception. " Would you ever settle a bet?" the caller asked: "What's the query?" I asked. "It's in two parts," the caller said. "I'll do my best, fire away." I replied. "Where did Manchester United win the European Cup; and what year? Ironically, I have always been a Manchester United fan, so naming the venue for that European Championship Cup win was not too difficult: "I can tell you the venue" I said. " The final was played in Wembley Stadium, but I am not too certain about the actual year. It could be either 1967 or 1968. If I was having a bet myself, I would say 1968, but if there is big money involved, you would have to try somewhere else." There was silence at the other end of the phone. "Hello," I said. " Are you still there?" The caller said: "Is that Sean Og?" I said it was. " How in f.....k would you know?" and slammed the phone down.

Johnny Leahy of Boherlahan

The legendary Johnny is accredited with the immortal wish to have " Cork bate and the hay saved", and many other anecdotes have been linked to his name. One such story concerns an occasion when the Tipperary hurlers were in a hotel for a meal after a big game. There were several tables in the dining room and the waitress brought soup to the men at every table except one, Johnny Leahy's in fact: " Why aren't you eating, Johnny?" one of the hurlers shouted across to his friend at the soupless table: " Yerra," answered Johnny, " we got a bye in the first round." Johnny was a brother of the equally famous Paddy and captained the 1916 and 1925 winning Tipperary All-Ireland teams. One of the last survivors of that team was Tom Duffy, who passed away some years ago. He was a great character and quick with the tongue. Whenever himself and Johnny Leahy would meet they always had a go at one another. Duffy was from Lorrha and always claimed in Leahy's company that forwards won matches not defenders, a comment that always riled the Boherlahan man. Somebody said to Leahy one day in Duffy's company, hadn't Duffy won an All Ireland: "He did" said Leahy, " but we always had to carry a few passengers."

Leahy, was a very powerful man, who stripped big. He suffered a nose injury in a match and his nose was a peculiar shape, permanently cocked upward. Tom Duffy was a great ploughman and always made a habit of examining a pitch before a match to see that it was in good order. He went to a match in Borrisokane and went through the same ritual of examining the pitch before taking his place on the sideline seats As luck would have it, his great rival Johnny Leahy sat in a row of seats behind him and shouted at him "Are you going to plough it, Tom?" just to get a rise out of him. And Tom roared back: "With your nose, Leahy, I would."

Paddy Leahy of Boherlahan

The Leahys were famous brothers, Paddy, Johnny and Mickey, who graced the hurling fields with distinction, all three winning All Ireland titles with the Premier County over a long period of time. Paddy, I knew very well. He was the prime team mentor, and the one you approached for match comments, prior to and after important matches involving Tipperary. He was a rogue, and when he pushed his cap or hat, worn in a jaunty angle, up a little higher on his forehead with his finger, before uttering his aftermatch comments, you could be sure the words were gems. He would praise Tipperary's conquerors very highly or conversely, play down his own team's successes. After Tipperary's defeat by Wexford in the 1960 All Ireland hurling final he was walking across the Croke Park pitch when he saw Nicky Rackard passing and immediately grabbed the big fellow's hand, and congratulated him on his performance, and on Wexford's success. As he was walking away, he turned around with a parting shot to Nicky: "And I'm going to demand a bloody saliva test for all you fellas." As he moved towards the Tipperary dressing rooms he was subjected to the usual words of commiseration:s "Hard luck, Paddy, we'll be back again" etc from friend and foe alike. But Paddy, in his own inimitable way brushed aside the words of consolation with a cheery note: "It's all for the good of the game, let it go around, it's all for the good of the game, the game needs new faces " in a kind of dissuasive fashion. But as he was joined by a couple of the Tipp selectors, making the sad trip back to the dressing rooms, he said quietly:, " Jesus help us, how are we to face going home." That comment epitomised the real heart of the man.

Paddy's wit was legendary. He always enjoyed social occasions and rarely turned down an invitation to a function where he was certain to meet old friends and enjoy a good chin wag. He enjoyed a good meal and was not adverse to having a glass or two of wine with the main course. He also enjoyed potatoes, brought up in a homestead where the spuds were boiled in a big pot and there was plenty to go around. He attended a major function in a leading Dublin hotel with members of a winning Tipperary team. The first two courses had been served and the main course was next to follow. The waitress placed a plate in front of him and another waitress put slices of roast beef on the plate. Another waitress moved in carrying vegetables and she put two small potatoes on his side plate, carrots and cauliflower's. Paddy picked up his knife and fork, cut the potatoes in halves and quickly eat them. He turned and called to one of the waitresses who had just served him and said: "Excuse me , mam, you can take up the spuds now, there're ready." Paddy Leahy was always the life and soul of any social gathering, not that he would look for such a role but he was the one that would be called upon to do a turn, whether it be a recitation or

tell a few stories. Big Jim Ryan of Loughmore, who played on the Tipperary footba
team on Bloody Sunday at Croke Park against Dublin, emigrated to America soon afte
He became involved in Irish affairs and the GAA, and was a very prominent figure
New York circles. He was also a very witty man and held many an audience enthrall
with stories of his boyhood. He was also a very fine singer and was frequently call
upon to sing some of the old ballads of the time. He returned to his native heath
the start of the Second World war and quickly became immersed in local football activiti
and he became a county selector. Years later a party of Americans, mostly Tippera
men, came home for a holiday. As Seamus O Riain explained: "Tipperary teams travelli
out to America were always made very welcome by expatriates when they reach
New York or in other locations. It was decided, as a show of gratitude, to put on a welcomi
function for the Tipperary visitors in a local hotel." The occasion was a huge succe
and later in an adjoining room the social part of the evening started. Big Jim Ryan, o
of the invitees and the redoubtable Paddy Leahy vied for attention, both being well know
raconteurs. Leahy, who prided himself on reciting poems stood up and delivered one
his party pieces, all about the hard working farmer; what the farmer meant to the count
and his value to the country etc, a well known poem that he had performed many time

The applause had barely died down for Leahy's splendid rendering of the "Farmer" wh
up jumped Big Jim Ryan, his coat off and his shirt wide open, and sweat running dow
his brow. The room quietened as he launched into "Biddy Mulligan, the Pride of the Coombe
a well known Dublin song. He sang it with gusto and his audience loved it. Big Jim al
got a rousing reception, and when it had died down, he turned around to Paddy Leahy ar
said: "Leahy, Biddy Mulligan could earn more money in one night than all you blood
farmers do in a year."

I said Paddy Leahy was a rogue and I meant it. When interviewed for his comments c
an upcoming important match he would go to great lengths emphasising the quality of th
opposition, and pointing out the strength of the individual players on the opposing side. H
would play down the successes of his own side. He was not only a selector, but the offici
who had to deliver the the final speech to Tipperary players taking the field for the big gam
I have been told by many Tipp players of Leahy's value for rousing a team going out c
the field and the importance of his words ringing in their ears as they lined up for the actio
Equally so after returning to the dressing rooms at the interval when, Paddy would again gi
them a dressing down, should they be in arrears. Before he would conclude his pep tal
the players would be straining at the leash, in order to get back into the action, to put his wor
into practice.

I had my own experience of the legendary character around 1967. I was conducti
interviews for a television programme covering the All-Ireland senior hurling final that ye
between Tipperary and Kilkenny and I travelled out to the Leahy household in Boherlah
to interview Paddy, one of the Tipp selectors. I wasn't by any means a lamb being led
the slaughter, as I had spoken to him on many an occasion after games and used the commen
for my match write-up in the "Evening Press" newspaper. When the camera unit arrive
at Paddy's house the star attraction was already dressed for the occasion. His hat was
usual, tilted at an angle, when I started my questions.

He had an impish grin on his face which should have warned me when I finally ask
him about Tipperary's prospects of beating the Leinster champions: "We haven't a hope

ell. Do you realise, Sean Og , whom we are dealing with on Sunday? We are playing the world champions, Kilkenny are the world champions, and make no mistake about it, it's an awesome task for this young inexperienced Tipperary team. I have to say this, Kilkenny must be out and out favourites to win this All Ireland final."(Paddy's reference to Kilkenny being world champions stemmed from the fact that Kilkenny as League champions, played New York in a tournament in New York).

Phil 'Fan' Larkin of Kilkenny

There is no disputing the fact that Kilkenny's Phil "Fan" Larkin will always be regarded as one of the best corner backs in the game. Tenacious, fearless and though small in stature,he never failed to turn in a uncompromising performance. Opposing forwards new well what to expect when "Fan" was around and when they left the field after a game which the Kilkenny defender was involved, they were a lot wiser. When I presented the Sunday Game" programme on television some years ago I invited "Fan" to appear as a guest analyst. He could read the game very well and was very astute in his summing up of same. aturally he was great favourite with Kilkenny followers who knew, whatever happened in match, the bould "Fan" would not let the side down. There are many stories told about e exploits of the Kilkenny defender, some of which cannot appear in print. "Fan's" club am James Stephens played The Fenians in a county senior hurling championship final in owlan Park. "Fan" was faced by one of the best forwards around at the time in Paddy Delaney, ho singled handed could win a game on his own. Delaney was big and very strong and as never afraid to take defences on. He was having a field day, as the scoreboard showed, d Delaney had contributed greatly to The Fenians winning total. After turning away having elted a second goal to the Stephens net, he met a shoulder from "Fan" who growled "I'll ive you up on the scoreboard" Unperturbed, Delaney replied "Well, "Fan, we have enough ores up there anyway." "Fan" always liked to let opposing forwards know that he was ound and in a League game against Tipperary he was marking Michael Doyle, a newcomer the Tipp colours. Michael was a son of illustrious John Doyle, who also became a legend his own time, a fearless defender with Tipperary All Ireland winning teams. The younger ember of the family was getting his first real taste of senior inter county fare and at the me time learning about the hazards of playing against "Fan" Larkin. After eluding the ilkenny defender in a chase for the ball, Doyle received a smack on the back of his leg. Turning e said to "Fan" "what's that for", to be told " Ask your father." "Fan travelled with a ilkenny team to Ballinasloe to play Galway in an important National Hurling League match. was a very exciting contest with little between the teams.Kilkenny were marginally ahead ith minutes remaining as Galway attacked in an effort to secure a winning score. A Galway rward came charging in near the end line, bearing down dangerously on the Kilkenny goal, hen he was met with a shoulder from "Fan" who put him over the end line. Danger averted. he Galway forward on his way back to his position, shouted at one of the umpires " Is there ng to go? is there long to go?" "Fan" supplied the answer "As far as you are concerned, ickey, 12 months."

'Fan' Larkin makes a despairing effort to block Sylvie Linnane of Galway.

Jack Conroy of Laois

I made a brief reference to great characters very much synonymous with the GAA earlier in this book and one of those was certainly Jack Conroy of Laois. Jack held many responsible positions at the highest level, and ruled meetings under his control with a firm hand. He never cared much about meeting procedures. Once he had made his mind up about a matter relating to a controversial nature, after a certain amount of discussion, he brought the issue to a close and gave his ruling. Protests were ruled out and he immediately got on to the next item. Jack had another great attribute, he often as not made quaint comments, which in time made him a legendary figure. He was Chairman of the Laois County Board at the time when a problem arose, after fixing a club championship match to act as curtain raiser to an intercounty match. A spokesman for one of the clubs asked the chairman, how he intended splitting the gate receipts, as the club match was a very important game and both clubs were entitled to a percentage of the gate. Many suggestions were made from the floor by the club delegates during the course of the discussion. Some felt that a fifty-fifty share should apply, others felt it should be 60 - 40 or even 70 - 30. Chairman Conroy listened to all the various suggestions as he pronounced that the discussion was getting them nowhere. So he rose from his chair and delivered his own verdict. " It's going to be 70 - 60 in favour of the County Board and that's that.!" A delegate complained about the composition of a Laois football team which had been sent to play Tipperary in a football challenge in Semple Stadium, Thurles, which Laois lost very surprisingly, as Tipperary at the time were not considered to be as formidable as they are today. Chairman Conroy, in his own inimitable way, pointed out that they had only 'the knuckles' of a team to begin with, and then ended the discussion by adding " Anyway, how could you play good football on a hurling pitch?"

Jack's wisdom and patience was really put to the test at a County Board meeting when a referee's report was being read which described a major row in a match which got out of control. Both clubs involved were asked to give their account of the incidents which had led up to the row. It took some time for the respective club spokesmen to give their opinions on the row until the Chairman called a halt to proceedings. He looked around the crowded hall and said " I have listened carefully to the evidence given by both clubs on this very important matter and I can only sum it up in two words: IMPOSSIBLE".

Jack filled many important roles at Laois Board level during a long and faithful service to his native county. When he was Chairman of the Minor Board he was very concerned over the poor performance of Laois minor teams and called for greater support from the clubs in the county. Some delegates offered their own reasons for the decline in the game and one delegate claimed that it was very difficult to get the young people out to train. Jack Conroy admitted there were difficulties and added: " Look lads, it's not the parents I blame, but the mothers and fathers." Jack was also a very prominent referee and took charge of many inter- county matches as well as local games in Laois. He was in charge of a game between two very keen rivals in the county and a row developed in one of the goal mouths. Despite the fact that a number of players got involved nobody got marching orders, much to the surprise of the clubs and indeed the spectators. Jack submitted his report to the County Board and while he mentioned the row he did not book any of the players. So he was asked to appear before the Board to explain his failure to name some of those who were involved. Jack made the following comment: " Mr Chairman, I spoke to my 'empire: who were closer to the action but I could get no 'corporation' from them." Jack Conro went on to become Chairman of the Leinster Council and proved a very worthy holder of the high office. He had his own distinct way of dispensing justice but few complained decisions went against them. Jack was a patient man, he would listen to both sides involve in a controversy and when he felt the arguments had reached a dead end he would act. Durin an appeal against a suspension imposed on a well- known player for allegedly striking, h county delegate was making a strong case for leniency. He pointed out the contribution th player had made towards the promotion of the game in the county. A few more county delegat joined in the discussion and they also pleaded for a less severe sentence on the well- know player. But another voice entered the discussion and he was taking the side of the play who was struck in the incident, and he made a strong case for less leniency and stiffer sentence Chairman Conroy eventually moved in and called a halt to the arguments and decided th: enough discussion had taken place. Jack was a very astute official and nobody could accus him of not allowing full freedom of speech. Jack looked down on the delegates and sai "Ye have all had your say on the matter, so I'll have my say. All I want to know is 'Wh Ha Who'".

Gerry Power of Kildare

Gerry played with Kildare football teams in the 80's. He was a fast clever forwar and was as good as any of today's crop of young attackers. But Gerry ha one drawback, he was very prone to injury, not an unknown ailment whic effected some other players around that period. But it was unfortunate for Gerry wh had plenty of ability but, often as not, was unable to complete a game that he had starte so promisingly but had failed to finish because of that injury factor. But, that was lif His father Paddy, was a former Fianna Fail Minister and the whole family inherited hi ready wit. The bould Gerry duly got married and a few days later one of his brother': who had been best man, was asked by an inquisitive neighbour how did the big event g off. "Great" he replied. "but I was terribly disappointed not to be brought on th honeymoon" "How so? asked the inquisitive one, who was a great Kildare supporte "Don't you know our Ger, he will probably have to retire injured and a sub will hav to be brought on."Kildare were playing Wexford in Dr Cullen Park at the end of th sixties. The Wexford goal keeper fielded the ball under the crossbar and was on his wa out to clear his lines when he was challenged by flying Kildare corner forward Carbury' Kevin Kelly. The 'keeper made his clearance but Kevin finished up in the back of th Wexford net from whence it took him a little time to extricate himself. On being aske by Pat Dunny, "what kept you? Kevin replied. "When I went in on that 'keeper the fu back put me into the back of the net with such a box in the ear that I had to ask th umpire for a pen knife to get myself out." Kildare had a very stylish full back aroun that time in Patsy Kelly, and his goalkeeper for many years was Allenwood's John Slattery a very droll character who had written and produced many scripts for Scor Novelty Act . Normally, a superb fielder of a high ball, Patsy was deceived by its flight. He calle to his 'keeper " Your ball, Johnny? Slattery, cool as ever, took one look at the inrushin orwards from a county not known to take prisoners, and was heard to remark, before lispatching the ball with great aplomb, "Could happen, but I have my doubts."'.

Travelling The Easy Way

In the two years in which I presented The "Sunday Game" on television, an hour long programme dealing with the major GAA matches of the day, the programme heads used helicopters to bring those working on the programme, and myself, to certain venues in rder to bring the film of the game back to the studio for later transmission. That mode of ransport enabled the VTR editors, who were at the match to get back quickly to base in Montrose, and start editing the film for the "Sunday Game" programme later that night. We sed the helicopter for one particular match, a Munster hurling final between Tipperary and Limerick at Semple Stadium, Thurles. Security is always a priority when a copter is pressed nto service. The Gardai have to be alerted and a guard has to be mounted while the machine s parked. The most adjacent parking spot for the "chopper" was the local church car park, nd I got permission from the Parish Priest to land and take off from the car park on that articular Sunday. On board with me were Liz Howard, an expert games analyst, programme ditor Maurice Reidy and VTR editor Julian Davies. The pilot, Colin, was an American, nd he was very anxious to see his first live hurling match. On the morning of the match ve arrived at our destination, and the good priest, making sure we were landing on the right pot, insisted on standing in the middle of our landing area, waving his umbrella frantically t us. It took a few minutes to indicate to him that we knew our landing area. Colin had ecided to leave the helicopter in the car park and join us at the match. He set us down mid great excitement. Thousands on their way to the match gathered to see us arriving: ne word had got around that our then President, Patrick Hillary, was attending the game. hopped out of the chopper, along with my colleagues, and noticed a Garda Sergeant heading my direction: " He can't park that there", said the sergeant, pointing towards the chopper: I'm sorry, Mr O Ceallachain, but he'll have to park that vehicle somewhere else." He was deadly earnest: "Where would you suggest, Sergeant?" I asked. Back came the reply: "I ould suggest the Greyhound Track across the way, it would be secure there." The dog track as adjacent enough, so Colin took off and duly parked the machine in the centre of the ack. A Tipperary man of my acquaintance slyly suggested afterwards, on hearing of my arlier experience, that parking the chopper in the safer confines of the Greyhound Track ft the local Gardai free to see the match in peace; they would have had to stand over the vehicle" had it remained in the church car park. But I think he was pulling my leg?

The Voice Factor

Having a recognisable voice has its compensations. I was travelling to Tullamore to cover a game for the "Sunday Sport" radio programme. Six miles from Kinnegad a red light started flashing on my dashboard and I stopped immediately. Steam was rising from under the bonnet. I discovered to my horror that the fan belt was in ribbons. I was in a right pickle: where was I going to get a replacement fan belt at noon on a Sunday and miles away from the nearest garage? I allowed the radiator to cool off and walked towards a distant house in the hope of finding a phone. On the way I saw a water pump in a disused yard. I decided to refill the radiator, and slowly drove the car into the yard. It was only then I noticed a caravan parked opposite the pump. I started drawing water while filling a bucket which had been hanging on the spout of the pump: " Can I help you?" cried a girl who was standing in the doorway of the caravan. I explained my problem quickly, apologising for my intrusion: " You're the radio man, aren't you, I'd know that voice anywhere," she said. It was flattering to be recognised but I was more concerned with my situation and getting back on the road. "Come out here, John," the young lady called into the caravan. John appeared:. "Listen, say a few words and see would he recognise the voice," she said. Again I had to explain about the fan belt. John just looked at me and said quietly: "You're Sean Og, and you never said a good word about Westmeath in your life." I started to explain why, when he grinned and added: "They didn't give you much to talk about, anyhow. Let's see what we can do about the fan belt." He walked down the yard to another caravan and arrived back with a box of tools and a couple of old fan belts. "I'll stick one of these on and it will take you to wherever you're going and back." John duly carried out the necessary repairs, and the fan belt worked like a charm. I was able to travel on to Tullamore for my radio assignment and return safely to Dublin afterwards. Despite all my efforts, my very obliging "mechanic" would take no money for the running repairs. The only promise I had to give was to say a few kind words about Westmeath the next time I watched them play. I carried out my promise. My very good friend, Paddy Flanagan, the Westmeath P.R.O., to this day cannot get over the high praise I lavished on his county team in a subsequent match report, because, as he said himself: "I thought they were bloody awful." But then, the same Paddy is an awful hard man to please.

Art Buckwald

A prayer for the wives of those husbands going on golf breaks.

"Almighty Father.... keep our husbands from looking at foreign women and comparing them to us. Save them from making fools of themselves in cafes and night clubs. Above all, do not forgive them their trespasses for they know exactly what they do.

Holy God

Golf is a Royal and Ancient game as all good golfers know,
and I will now relate to you, a tale of long ago.
A challenge match of ancient time you may perhaps recall,
was played between two famous saints, St. Peter and St. Paul.
And where I'm sure you're wondering could such a game be played,
in Cairo- near the Pyramids, perhaps - or old Port Said.
The best is only good enough for champions to meet.
And so Jerusalem's Old Course lay waiting in the heat.
No caddies could be seen around or little boys in rags,
Pacifico, a donkey, carried both the saintly bags.
St. Peter stood upon the tee, the cloudless sky was blue,
he drove the ball with easy grace not only straight but true.
And then St. Paul with muscles taut was swinging on the tee,
and hooked his ball to deepest rough beside an olive tree.
Now in the rough, a rabbit crouched, its mouth stood open wide,
the golf ball flying on its way bounced once and hopped inside.
A golden eagle in the sky was just the merest spec,
then swooping low, its talons fixed around the rabbit's neck.
It flew towards the distant green and circled slowly round,
then perched upon the flagstick, a few feet from the ground.
The bird released the rabbit and rabbitt dropped the ball,
which was of course the one so badly driven by St. Paul.
It trickled smoothly on the grass, a gentle steady roll,
and finally, like all good putts, it dropped onto the hole.
And now please, just imagine that you're back upon the tee,
for holes in one, were not exactly common you'll agree.
St. Peter stamped a sandalled foot and said "now look here, Paul,
"From now on cut out the bloody miracles and let's just play ball.

Philip Greene of RTE

In 1953 I was invited by Philip Greene, who was Head of Radio Sport in Radio Eireann at the time, to join Hermitage Golf club, a membership I have treasured ever since. Five years later Phil and I went on to win the prestigious Hermitage Open Four ball Match play championship. I very quickly learned the rules of golf playing with Phil. In our semi final match, we were one hole up playing the 17th green. One of our opponents, inadvertently indicated the line of putt for his partner by placing the flagpole on the surface of the green, which is contrary to the rules of golf. We played out the hole, which was halved in par 4's. As we were leaving the green, Philip, more in an educational gesture, explained to our opponents that they had broken a rule of golf by indicating the line of putt with the flagpole. They were surprised: "Are you claiming the hole, Phil?" asked one of our opponents. "No," said Phil. "I'm just letting you know about the incident in case you didn't know the rule." Our opponent's next remark stopped us in our tracks:. "Well, I'm sorry, Phil, I have to claim the hole from you for not applying the relevant rule yourself." I was stunned, but Phil was furious, and there was nothing we could do about it. The match was now all square going down the 18th, which was duly halved in a par four. It was on to the 19th which I won with a par four for the match. Phil and I went on to win the trophy beating two fine Hermitage members in the final, Kevin Byrne and Dr Jim Gormley. A little knowledge can be a dangerous thing in golf.

Dick Stokes of Limerick

I have been a friend of Dick Stokes for many years since my early days with the Eoghan Ruadh senior hurling team when Dick was playing with UCD in Dublin competitions He was on the winning Limerick team which captured the All-Ireland title in 1940 when they beat Kilkenny in the final. Dick would rank with the best in my assessment of the top hurlers in the game. He was physically strong, fast and was lethal when a scoring opportunity arose. He played on a College team which had many outstanding hurlers, who went on to win fame with their native counties. Eoghan Ruadh and College met frequently in League and championship and we had many a great battle with them. I recall mentioning in a previous book of mine a particular incident in a championship match between Eoghan and UCD, which acted as a curtain raiser to an important National Football League match. College were leading by a point entering the closing stages when I was fortunate to pick up a loose ball and hammer it over the bar for the equaliser. As I moved away, I got a tap on the shoulder, and Dick Stokes said: "Nice point, Sean" Dick was that type of player. Many years later we were to renew old acquaintances in the "Hurlers" Golfing Society of which he is President. Dick, who is a medical doctor of note, told a story at an outing in Dungarvan, about a lady doctor who was playing a practice round at a local golf course. She really enjoyed the game and she was accompanied by another associate member. Her friend drove off the tee at a particular hole and the lady doctor followed. However, on this particular occasion she hooked the ball badly, the ball sailed over trees and struck a male member who was playing on another fairway. The two ladies hurried immediately through a gap in the trees to find the poor man, doubled over, holding his groin, where he had been struck with the ball, and he was in obvious pain. The lady doctor quickly went over to the injured party offering her sincere apologies and explained that she was a doctor and would be able to offer him some help. As the man had both hands between his legs she assumed that the ball had struck him in the groin, and proceeded to massage the area gently. After a few minutes, she inquired if her efforts had given him some relief. The man readily agreed that it had, so the lady doctor started to move away, when the man held his hand out and inquired: "But, I won't lose the nail on my thumb, will I?"

Tough Going

There are parishes in certain parts of the country where local rivalry in matches over steps the canons of proper behaviour and many a myth or legend is thus created. Many years later, stories are told about an incident or incidents which may have happened in particular games and the same stories become embellished and pass into local folklore. Not all are true, of course, but they get better in the telling. In a local football game between two very keen rivals, one of the players was knocked unconscious after making a rash challenge for a loose ball. He had to get immediate attention so the ambulance was summoned only to be told that the local knights of Malta and St. John's Brigade ambulances were already at Knock for a pilgrimage.

It was agreed that no time be wasted getting the injured player to hospital, concussion was feared, so word was sent to the local taxi man, who had a station wagon, to come to the venue, which he duly did. The injured player was placed in the taxi and the driver was told to take the player to the local hospital. He was also instructed to tell the medical staff how the injury occurred.

But five minutes after the game had resumed the taxi was still waiting off the pitch. One of the club officials immediately went to the driver "Johnny, are you still here, what are you waiting for"? To which Johnny answered "Will I go now or wait for a load?

Aquaduct Race Meeting

In 1965 the Association of Gaelic Sports Journalists became involved in the Cardinal Cushing Games and I accompanied leading footballers and hurlers to New York for the purpose of raising money for the Cardinal's Mission to Peru, where poverty was rampant. During our enjoyable stay we were taken to the multi-million dollar Aquaduct Race Track. This beautifully laid out race course is controlled by the New York Racing Board, which stages racing there seven days a week during the season. Betting on the Tote exceeds two million dollars each day of racing. The quickest and most expedient way of getting to the track is by the "Aquaduct Special" which leaves hourly from Grand Central Station. We were among thousands heading for the track and were packed like sardines into the carriages. Offaly-born Frank Feighery was our tour guide and he was most helpful. Tom Maguire (Cavan) and I were fortunate to get a seat on the "Special", and we were seated opposite two typical New Yorkers. Both were Jewish, called Nat and Abe, and the conversation during the entire trip concerned the runners on the race card, which could be bought at the departure point. Abe had an unsmoked cigar butt in his mouth, and he was able to roll the cigar butt from one side of his mouth to the other, while he delivered judgement on the various racing fancies mentioned by Nat. Nat had some kind of facial affliction, a nervous twitch, and every word he uttered was accompanied by a twitch and a quick shrug of the shoulders. They really fascinated Tom and me. The conversation went like this:

Abe: "Whaddya fancy in the "foist.'"?

Nat: "I like the look of "Sunspot." The guys in the plant gave me a few bucks to put

Abe: on it."

Abe: "There's better pulling cabs around Central Park. I wouldn't back it with phoney money. (silence)

Nat: " I got a good tip for "Stormy Weather" in the second. He won well last week and is well worth a few bucks."

Abe: "Did ya see what he beat, did ya see what he beat, a bunch of ole cripples, that's what he beat, you can forget it." (again silence)

Nat: "What about "Blue Orchid in the thoid; you liked it last time out, but it shure didn't win.

Abe: " You dumb or somethin', I wouldn't let my taxman back that, not alone you. It has no class. Ya need class, but he's for the boids.(A long silence)

Nat: "We ain't doin' too well, Abe, are we.? We gotta back "Havana Chief" in the fourth, see the jock on him, Manuel Pedosa, he's good, he's real good."

Abe: "That son of a bitch, he's been throwing races all his life, whadda you think he's got that new Merc for, go on, ask me"?

Nat: "Don't tell me you won't back the "Black Demon" in the 5th, it's got class, it's got real class."

Abe: "Shure she's got class, plenty of class, but so has my moider but that don't mean she can stay a mile, and she's got breathin' problems as well."

Nat: " Who, your moider."?

Abe: " Dope, the horse of course, the horse." (Silence for a while)

Nat: "Well, my few bucks are going on "Flying Thunder" in the last. It has won its last four races."

Abe: " See what I mean, see what I mean, I keep telling ya, you know nothing about the ponies. Of course, it has won its last four races, but you tell me a horse that has won five on the trot, go on tell me. Man they really saw you comin'. You might as well stick your head out of the winda of this train and get it chopped off at the next tunnel. That's what I think of your "Flying Thunder"." (again silence for a while).

Nat: " Ya know something, Abe."?

Abe: "Naw, what's that."?

Nat: "We're wasting our time going to the track backing losers. I'm sorry I didn't drive the wife to Yonkers now to see her moider. I'm a dope."

Donal Carroll (Irish Independent)

I mention Donal in relation to a story which concerned him, and I was very keen to include it in this compilation of sporting memorabila. Donal was Gaelic Games correspondent for the "Irish Independent" when I was working in a similar capacity for the now defunct "Evening Press." We travelled a lot together. Both of us were non-drinkers so we rarely delayed after matches. Donal was a delightful passenger, quiet and unassuming but we did have our share of arguments about the merits of certain leading players we had seen in a game which we had just attended. There were times when the arguments shortened the journey with neither of us willing to concede. Donal, is now in retirement, and I am glad to say, we meet occasionally for lunch with a few other retired scribes and the 'craic' is great. Donal is a "Glen Miller" fan but is a more ardent fan of English band leader Syd Lawrence and his orchestra, who specialise in Glen Miller music arrangements.

Nothing pleased Donal more on his day off than to sit at home with ear cans on, listening to Syd Lawrence playing Glen Miller arrangements. I was delighted to meet up again with Donal at a lunch along with other former scribes, RTE colleague Mick Dunne, Paddy Downey (Irish Times) Peadar O'Brien (The Sun) Dave Guiney (Formerly Irish Press and " Indo") Ed Van Esbeck (Irish Times) Peter Byrne (Irish Times). It was one of our get togethers, which we indulge in during the year. I mentioned to Donal that I was compiling a book of humorous stories and I was thinking of including one about himself and his black cat. "You wouldn't put that story in your book" asked a slightly embarassed Donal, who had told me the story many years ago on our way home from a match. "Well, Donal," sez I: " that story appeared in one of Dave Guiney's books of short stories and if it was good enough for colleague Dave, I see no reason why I cannot include it in mine." Donal, who was used to having the final word had no answer to that. The story Donal told me was about a black cat which he and his delightful wife Miriam treasured. It all happened on a Monday morning and Donal was enjoying a day off relaxing peacefully and comfortably in bed. He had worked hard the previous day and left word with Miriam, that come hell or high water he was not to be disturbed.

Alas, the best laid plans - Donal's slumber was shattered when his wife Miriam came rushing into the room with the distressing and upsetting news that their household cat, had been involved in an accident with a car - and at that particular moment, was lying prostrate on the road outside the house. Without hesitation, Donal got up and dressed hurriedly and went out to the road - and there was the pitiful and gory sight of the black cat, badly mutilated and covered in blood. Some neighbors were also on the scene and the suggestion was proffered that the poor animal should be brought to the veterinary surgeon.

Donal didn't hesitate. He scoured the "Yellow Pages" and quickly located a vet and was told to bring the cat immediately, with every possible care and speed to the surgery. Donal hurried back to the scene of the accident and lifted the cat gently from the road and placed it on a blanket provided by Miriam. He wrapped the blanket very tenderly around the blood soaked cat and placed it in the front seat of his car.

The journey to the surgery was taken with great care and Donal kept an anxious eye to ensure that his pet cat was not suffering unduly from the motions of the journey. He reached the surgery and again, very carefully lifted the little bundle and walked into the surgery waiting room- only to be greeted by a long line of other animal owners. Donal who is noted for his extreme patience, sat there waiting his turn, with the cat in his arms and blood everywhere.

Eventually the cat was taken by the veterinary surgeon who shortly reappeared- and Donal knew immediately the news was grim. The cat had been thoroughly cleaned and and just as thoroughly examined. Every aspect of possible treatment had been discussed with his staff and the decision was unanimous. Quietly and with obvious concern for Donal, he broke the news that the cat would have to be put down. The damage had been too serious, the injuries too intense and the only logical solution would be to put the badly mutilated cat to sleep. Once Donal had agreed, the vet pointed out one other matter. The cost of the examination, the efforts to save the cat and of course, the final depressing act of putting down the cat and the subsequent disposal would have to be paid. Donal duly wrote out the cheque and still noticeably marked with blood, departed for home to break the sad news to Miriam and the family. That too was a trying experience but once that was over and with his day off from the "Irish Independent" now in total ruins, a weary and dejected Donal Carroll took himself off to bed to finish off his rest.

And there he was, slowly beginning to relax just a little again, when he heard a rustling at the open window- he turned and looked up. And there.... there was the Carrolls' own black cat, sleek, well-fed, alert, bright, preening himself for immediate attention. I can only conclude that it may have been one of those rare days in his life that Donal Carroll ever lost that magnificent patience of his.

Percy McCooey of Monaghan

Percy was a fine goalkeeper who played for Monaghan in the 50's and earned a big reputation as one of the best in the game. In fact, Percy was in goal for Monaghan against Cavan in the 1952 Ulster final which I refereed. Like all good goalies Percy could see danger threatening and was constantly on the alert, shouting instructions to his defenders to watch the lose forward or the one who normally constituted the greatest danger to his citadel. During a particular match with his club Donaghmoyne, Percy's brother Mervyn was at full back and getting the run-around from a young full forward. After picking the ball out of the net on three occasions Percy's patience was wearing a bit thin as Mervyn was being led a merry dance by the young full forward, who had chalked up his third goal. " Mervyn, will you take him, take him, " declared Percy to his brother. A few minutes later the young full forward came dancing in on a solo run and was on the point of scoring another goal, when Mervyn met him head on and flattened him with a charge. Mervyn turned to Percy and simply said "He's took."

More Television Days

I figured in many programmes for the RTE TV Sports Department. Most of the actual filming was carried out by freelance or contract cameramen, Joe McCarthy (Cork), Eamon O'Connor (Limerick), John O'Keeffe, Breffni Byrne, Ken Murphy, Paddy Barron, the Deasy brothers, together with RTE staff cameramen Sean Burke and Sean Kelleher. The Cork based Joe McCarthy was a joy to work with if only for the meticulous way he approached his filming assignments. We were engaged to film a Leinster football championship match in Dr Cullen Park, Carlow. The Park in question is completely modernised now and filming arrangements and facilities differ greatly from those early days of television. When inquiries were made with the Carlow officials concerning the facilities, we were assured that we could film the game from an excellent vantage point, which turned out to be a concrete structure on the dressing room corner of the pitch. Unfortunately, it was too far removed from the centre of the pitch for our purposes, but Joe solved the problem quickly enough. His motto had always been, "Nothing ventured, nothing gained." Joe espied an ice-cream vendor selling his products from a small van, which had a flat roof. He talked the vendor into driving the van to the halfway part of the embankment, and paid him a generous tip for the use of the facilities. When I arrived back from the dressing-rooms, having checked out the teams, Joe had already assembled his filming equipment on top of the van roof. I climbed up beside him and we were ready and waiting when the big game started. We could do little about the off air sound effects during the course of my commentary on film, with cries of "Get your ice cream, get your TV ice cream." The vendor had sold all his stock by half-time, and he was quite happy. He replenished his stock for the second half and was happier still. Joe and I were able to continue our filming assignment and we were were quite happy too.

Munster Finals

It was a typical Munster hurling final between Cork and Tipperary. The tension was great, the atmosphere was electric as two well matched teams battled for hurling glory. The first half had been fought out at break neck speed. with Tipperary holding a slender lead at the interval. Cork's prime star Christy Ring had yet to make an impact as he had been closely watched by Tipp's Tommy Doyle who was having one of his blinders. Cork trainer Jim Barry waved at Ring to move to the other wing sensing that the Cork wizard might perform better away from the close marking tactics of Doyle. But Doyle also read the situation and proceeded to follow the Cork maestro to the other wing, so stalemate. The match was definitely not going Cork's way.

One Cork attack after another was beaten off by the rocklike Tipperary defence with Tommy Doyle providing the inspiration. Ring had yet to score from play, his contribution was mainly from frees but it was from direct play that the Glen Rovers man was dangerous as Tipp only knew too well and that supply had been well and truly sealed off by the no nonsense Doyle. As the final stages were reached Tipperary were hanging on desperately to a two points lead and looked well set to record a gratifying win over their great rivals. The Cork supporters kept up their vocal support knowing that only a last second goal would save the day. Cork drove up field, Ring for once eluded the shackles of his Tipp marker and slipped into space. Paddy Barry got possession and quickly handpassed to the unmarked Ring who quickly sped goalwards.

Shrugging off a fierce tackle, Ring turned and in that movement shot low and hard to the Tipperary net. All hell broke lose . Cork supporters were on their feet as pent up emotions were released. As the referee whistled up full time with Cork the winners by one point, an avid Cork supporter shouted " Toscanini for the music, Katie Barry for the crubeens but by Jaysus it's Ringey boy for the goals."

A Munster Hurling final with all its trappings is an occasion to be savoured and especially if Cork and Tipperary are providing the opposition. Cork is a very sport orientated county. Naturally the game of hurling is like a religion to the Corkman, and commands the widest support of any of the codes followed in the Rebel County. One of the great Munster hurling finals involving Cork was the famous 1940 replay between themselves and Limerick played at Semple Stadium, Thurles, which Cork won. It was the great Limerick team of the Mackeys, Dick Stokes, Jackie Power, Timmie Ryan etc. Cork, the winners, were to go on to win four All Irelands in a row, with the legendary Christy Ring, Jack Lynch,"Mica" Brennan, Willie Murphy, Con Murphy, Alan Lotty , Jim Young and Con Cottrill. The Munster final replay meeting between the great rivals brought a huge crowd to Thurles. Included among the vast throng was a party of officers attached to the American Airways Services at Foynes, and they were allotted a special section on the sideline. They were watching hurling for the first time. They were deeply immersed in the game and appeared to be enjoying the cut and thrust of the exciting exchanges immensely. When Cork scored they clapped, when Limerick scored they clapped again. Brilliant passages of play- and there were plenty that day- were applauded with great enthusiasm and impartiality. But it was more than an over excited Leesider just behind them could take. Eventually he could stick it no longer. He tapped one of the Americans on the shoulder and said " Excuse me mister, but which side are you on?" "Say" replied the American visitor: " I'm on neither side in particular, don't you know, I just like to see good play. "Holy God," rejoined the Corkman: " Ye must be bloody atheists!"

Jim Hogan of Limerick

J im Hogan followed a line of great goalkeepers to wear the Limerick jersey. He won an All- Ireland senior hurling medal with the county in 1973 against Kilkenny. Regular goalie Seamus Horgan was injured for the semi final that year when London provided the opposition and Jim was recalled to fill the gap. Seamus Horgan returned for the All-Ireland final. Jim Hogan had been Limerick's regular goalie for many years and he ranked with the best. In the early 50's he lived in Cork and joined the famed Sarsfields club, with whom he won a Cork senior title in 1957. He had many great memories of Christy Ring who was the leading figure with Glen Rovers during that period: "Ring was really in a class of his own. You would never know when he would strike. He would lie in waiting for a loose ball and once he gained possession, he was off like a hare and a score inevitably resulted," said Jim. When Jim Hogan returned to Limerick he teamed up with Claughaun. Quite a number of the successful Limerick All-Ireland minor winning team of 1958 and the beaten Munster minor team of 1959 had been promoted to the senior county side. Jim Hogan was in goal and John Joe Bresnan, 6'4" tall, a gangly young lad was chosen at midfield. It was the time when the six forwards and two midfielders from each side lined up for the throw in at the start of a match. John Joe Bresnan knew he would be marking Christy Ring so he asked Jim Hogan how best could he handle Ring. Jim's advice was: "You have the legs on him, so get out in front of him and get to the ball first, he prefers to operate around the square." The weather around April was very unkind. Minutes before the game the field was lashed by hail stones and there were more showers during the match. J.J. Bresnan watched as he waited for his opponent Christy Ring to arrive from the throw-in. The Cork maestro, wearing his usual cap, ran towards Bresnan and looked up at the towering Limerick defender: "Are you new, boy"? asked Christy. JJ nodded and muttered under his breath " I won't be long letting you know whether I am or I amn't." Jim Hogan's earlier advice to the tall Limerick defender proved timely as Bresnan had a blinder on the great Cork star, who had slowed up a lot but was still capable of beating defences. Despite frequent showers of hail the game proved very enjoyable. Bresnan continued to impress and allowed the Cork supremo very little scope. Entering the closing stages Limerick held a two points lead. Cork beat off another Limerick raid, a long delivery from midfield dropped between Bresnan and Ring. Something whizzed past Jim Hogan's ear in the Limerick goal. The net shook and he was showered with rain drops.

Hogan looked behind him and picked up the ball nestling in the back of the net, and he also picked up Ring's cap which was beside the ball. He could only conclude that Bresnan's pull for the ball had caught Ringey's cap, while Ringey's pull had connected with the ball. Said Jim Hogan : "I never saw the ball when it hit the net as I watched Ring wheel away. John Bresnan had held him scoreless for 58 minutes but in one flash Ring had availed of his scoring chance, and he took it. That was Ringey" admitted an admiring Hogan. Cork won the game by a single point.

Patrickswell and Mungret qualified for the final of a local church tournament. They were great rivals, being neighbours and a big attendance turned up one Sunday evening to watch the game. The   Patrickswell goalie was very good, he had several outings on the county team. He was a bit keyed up facing keen rivals Mungret especially since the Mungret full forward was well known to him as a man who liked to make his presence felt. The full forward was noted for his aggressive approach and always made a point of charging in on a goalkeeper under a dropping ball. The "Well" goalie was quite aware of that practice. He was surprised to see the Mungret full forward actually playing because it had been hinted that in view of his mother's illness, she was in the local hospital, he was going to cry off. But the Mungret full forward was togged out and obviously raring to go. The Patrickswell goalie decided to have a quiet word of sympathy with the Mungret player, so during the puck around before the start, he slipped up to him and told him how sorry he was to hear of his mother's ill health. The opposing full forward fixed him with a steely glare: "If you don't go back to your goal, you'll be in the bed beside her tonight."

Donal O'Flynn of Castletownroche

Cork-born Donal O'Flynn is best remembered for his sterling defensive displays for Galway during a seven year period in which the county made their own piece of history by capturing the Railway Cup hurling crown for the first time in 1947. I partnered Dan Kennedy of Kilkenny at midfield on the Leinster team beaten by a point by Connacht that year in the semi final. Donal figured at corner back on the Connacht side in the final and teamed up with other great stalwarts, Jim Brophy, M J Flaherty, Bernie Power and Peter Forde. which held a highly vaunted Christy Ring led Munster attack to a meagre tally of 1-1, a solitary score in each half. Donal, born in Castletownroche, was a Vocational school teacher and while in Dublin played with the Kevins club. He got his first teaching job in Spiddle in Galway, moved on to Rosmuc before returning to Cork, to Kanturk for five years. He later taught in Mitchelstown for five years. During his teaching stint in Galway he played with Liam Mellows in hurling and Miceal Breathnach in football.

He became the proud holder of a West Galway junior football championship medal in 1946. Donal played with Mellows at a time when hurling in the county was certainly no kid gloves affair, especially when championship time came around. He was well built and was chosen at centre half back. He remembered his first stint in the club colours in a vital championship tie against Castlegar. He watched a high ball dropping down between himself and the Castlegar centre forward. Donal stretched his hand to grab the ball at the same time as the centre forward was pulling on it. The ball flew wide and Donal was left nursing a badly bruised hand. A team defender had a look at it and said: " Ta do lamh ceart go leor, ach in ainm De na cur suas aris e, a mhic, ta caman id do lamh, tarraing faoin liathroid." Donal never made the same mistake again.

He figured on Galway teams in the mid 40's in defensiv roles and had a great regard for Jim Brophy, one of the best defenders to have worn a Galway jersey. Cork's Christy Ring was a lethal force around that period and Donal recalled a National League game against Cork in Ballinasloe. The same Cork team had chalked up four All Ireland victories in a row and they were warm favourites to collect the points on that occasion, which they did. Cork included noted sprint champion Fr Joe Kelly in their attack, along with the incomparable Ring. The Galway team trotted onto the pitch and fellow defender Richard Quinn asked Donal was he marking Ring or Joe Kelly, to which Donal replied : " To be honest with you, I don't know, I never looked at the Cork lineout in the local paper." "Well," said Quinn, "if I'm marking the runner, I won't long bringing him down to my pace."

The game was only a few minutes old when a ball dropped between Dick Quinn and Joe Kelly. Quinn swiped at the ball and caught Kelly across the ribs which certainly slowed the Cork man down.

Dick Quinn hadn't reckoned on the presence of Jack Lynch, who, following the dropping ball, accidently, caught the Galway man with a shoulder to the chest and laid him out. That left one Galway man deprived of his pace along with his Cork marker. As the teams left the field at the interval, Dick Quinn remarked to Donal O'Flynn: " Didn't I tell you Flynn, that I would bring the runner back to my pace. Didn't I bring him back to my pace.? Donal said quietly : " Did you ever hear that quotation from Shakespeare, Dick? "These growing feathers plucked from Caesar's wings will make them fly the ordinary height of men."

Naturally Donal had his own battle with Christy Ring. "You could never really close him down. He would suddenly disappear from your sight, and the next minute he would be scoring a point from the opposite wing. Once he got a ball in his hand you could write it down for a score." Donal admired Jim Brophy greatly for his tenacious style of hurling and maintained that Brophy rarely gave the Cork wizard room or space to perform his magic. " I remember on one occasion Jim Brophy calling to Christy, "Go on, Christy, lie down and you'll get a great ovation from the crowd."

The advent of television changed the whole image of the national games. The eye of the camera brought the match action into sitting rooms and viewers, who may not have been identified with the national pastimes, began to take a keener interest. More importantly, those who were sick or infirm had the benifit of the televised matches and that factor was also a help in spreading interest. It must be said the camera brought another dimension to outdoor sport events, inasmuch, that controversial incidents were highlighted and that led to calls for greater controls and punishment for unsporting acts. The presence of the camera was also an inhibiting factor forcing certain players to change their ways and desist from an over robust approach.

There was a story making the rounds in Galway which Donal was keen to tell and it had a bearing on the televising of matches. In the late 50's Dublin and Galway footballers were invited to London to participate in the Wembley Tournament sponsored by the London County Board. There was always a great rivalry between the two counties and that remains to this day. The Timmons brothers, John and Joe, were prominent members of the 1958 All Ireland final win over Derry and John went on to collect a second medal when Dublin beat Galway in the 1963 final. It was natural for Galway and Dublin to get an invitation to the Wembley games. Galway had a big colony working in London and Dublin were not far behind. Prior to the game, both dressing rooms were visited by a London Board official and a BBC sports producer. The BBC man explained that they were televising the game live into one of their regional programmes.

The programme had a good Irish audience and televising the game live from Wembley was by way of being a pilot programme. He was visiting the dressing room seeking the assistance of both teams to ensure that the game would contain no unseemly incidents that might spoil the viewers enjoyment of the occasion. The BBC man was a bit apologetic about having to make the request but he was assured by both team officials that all would be well and that the game would be played strictly according to the rules. Now Dublin-Galway clashes, whether they be, challenge matches, league or championship outings have always been fiercely contested, and perhaps at times, the canons of good behaviour might have been breached but normally, they have been very exciting affairs. The Wembley meeting of the counties was no exception, the exchanges were in the main very competitive but sporting and to all intents and purposes provided excellent T V fare. All was going well, but five minutes from the end as Galway hung on tenaciously to a one point advantage, Dublin launched a major offensive on the Galway rear lines. Burly John Timmons gained possession thirty yards out from the Galway goal and was hell bent on securing the levelling score or a winning goal. Sean Meade, the Galway centre back had other ideas. He met Timmon's charge head on, straight into the chest of one John Timmons. Timmons and ball were scattered to the four winds. Watching proceedings from a distance back was Joe Timmons, John's brother. He let out a bellow and charged upfield, his eyes fixed on the prostrate figure of brother John and then focusing on the culprit Sean Meade. There was steam rising from Joe, it was said, as he passed mid field. Pateen Donnellan saved the day. As Joe passed him, Pateen grabbed Joe's arm and said: "Joe, the cameras, the cameras,"

Joe was stopped in his track. He looked at Pateen, eyes still blazing, and Pateen put an arm around him and said quietly: " the cameras are on you, Joe, the cameras are watching, don't do anything rash." Joe, noting that brother John was back on his feet, turned and said: "Tell Meade, I'll see him, the next match." A crisis averted. Joe did not carry out his threat either as both teams joined up to enjoy the aftermatch jollification's.

Dr. Pat O'Neill of Dublin

Pat was born in Rhodesia (now Zimbabwe) and had a very distinguished football career before taking over the role of coach with Dublin footballers and leading them to All Ireland glory in 1995. During a very fruitful playing career he won an All-Ireland club championship medal with U C D, five Leinster senior championship medals, 2 All-Ireland senior football medals 1976 and '77. He won two National football league medals in 1976 and '78, won a Bank of Ireland All Star at wing back in 1977. As Dublin selector his charges captured the National League title in 1992-93. He also won a Railway Cup medal playing with the Combined Universities. Pat O'Neill was a fearless wing back and was never known to go around an opponent, preferring to brush him aside in an none too gentle fashion.

He recalled a sequel to a story already related by former Dublin county chairman., Jimmy Grey, elsewhere in this book. It concerned a disastrous charity match played in "Gaelic Park", New York between Dublin and Kerry after their 1978 All Ireland final clash. Pat O'Neill is in no doubt the game should not have been played because of the state of the ground and the weather conditions. Both teams registered their protests about the ground conditions but all to no avail. To make matters worse, very few turned up to watch the match, which many thought, would be called off because of the conditions. The rain poured down and hadn't stopped for virtually 24 hours. The Gaelic Park" pitch was in a terrible conditions, with large pools of surface water everywhere. It was dangerous to play on and fears were genuinely expressed for the players safety. It was no wonder that tempers became frayed during the course of the match. There were a lot

Pat O'Neill in his Dublin playing days.

of niggly incidents involving players from both sides, in a free riddled match. After a spell it was difficult to recognise the players, now wearing sodden muddied jerseys and as a result passes went astray to players on opposing sides. It was pure farce. Midway through the second half Pat O'Neill was floored by a blow as he got possession of the ball, which put him flat on his back in a deep pool. Being O'Neill, he jumped to his feet and hauled off and struck the nearest opponent, a Kerry player, who suffered a nose injury. While he was being attended to O'Neill walked off the pitch before being sent off by the then referee Seamus Aldridge (Kildare) (When asked years later was he ever sent off in a match, Pat would say no, but did admit to walking off!) The Dublin man stood on the sideline in the pouring rain by no means in the best of humour, nursing the clout that he had received. He was approached by an individual who had run along the sideline, and who had a distinctive Kerry accent with a New York twang: " Would you ever go to the Kerry dressing room, there is a player needing attention for a nose injury, he is swallowing a lot of blood.? Pat looked at him and replied:" Get the local doctor in the ground to attend to him. I came out here to play football not to practice medicine."

The Kerry man gave him a sharp look and whipped back with:" Well, be Jasus, you're doing a bad job on both of them." Standing behind the railing at the spot where Pat O'Neill and the Kerry man were discussing doctor problems was a bunch of Dublin supporters, who had travelled out with the teams, led by Anto Whelan, who after hearing the Kerry man asking Pat for medical attention for the player, shouted:"But he has already seen a doctor."

When the Dublin team returned from New York, Dr. Pat O'Neill, had to resume his medical duties at Dr Steevens Hospital immediately. News of the incidents which had happened in the match in "Gaelic Park" had appeared in the Irish papers. Dr Pat was asked about the trip and assured all his patients, that it went well. Pat, being a well known "Dub" on the playing field, was well known to all the patients and staff at the hospital. He had just finished surgery when he was handed a copy of the "Evening Herald" which had a photograph of Dr. Pat, and two other Dublin players, under a bold caption which crossed the front page, "Dubs in U S A Brawl." Pat was mortified and for the remainder of the week he had to suffer slagging from all the porters in the hospital. But to all the patients, mainly from the Ballyfermot area, he was a real live folk hero.

The previous year, 1977, Dublin as All Ireland winners, travelled with the Bank of Ireland All Stars to the States for the usual exhibition matches. The "Dubs" played the All Stars at the Hanson Stadium, Chicago, on the astro-turf, which is artificial grass. Luckily, handballer Pat Kirby, who was well used to playing on that surface, warned the team mentors to ensure that the players had proper protection. The astro-turf can cause very severe burning of the skin, on hands or legs, should a player take a fall. The stadium is used for High School American football. The Dublin versus the All Stars game was very competitive and there were minor abrasions of one kind or the other because of the astro-turf factor. Ten minutes from the end of the match, Jimmy Keaveney suffered a bad nose injury and had to retire. When the game ended Pat O'Neill attended to Jimmy and told him that he had a broken nose which needed hospital treatment. Jimmy's reply to that suggestion was: " I'm going to no bleedin' hospital, can't you fix it, "Nailer". Dr. Pat "Nailer"O'Neill said he could, if Jimmy would be prepared to put up with the pain of the nose being put back into place. Jimmy, didn't fancy a stay in the hospital so he agreed to have the job done by Pat. The footballing doctor put Jimmy sitting on a bench in the dressing room. He asked a couple of the other players to press Jimmy's shoulders back against the wall of the room. Dr. Pat pressed Jimmy's head against the wall and told him to keep perfectly still. In order to have more control over what he was doing Dr. Pat had to sit astride Jimmy's lap. Having completed his preparations, cleaning up Jimmy bloodied nose, he was now ready for the final part of the operation.

Dr. Pat, using both hands, gave Jimmy's nose a quick wrench. There was an unmerciful roar from Jimmy, Dr. Pat got a knee from Jimmy into the testicles, he fell back onto the floor in agony while Jimmy stood over him shouting: "You bastard, "Nailer" you fecking bastard, you never told me that it was going to hurt that much." The poor unfortunate 'Doc' was not taking much notice of his patient, he was trying to ease the pain on his embarrassing 'injury' inflicted on him by his patient. The rest of the players fell around the room laughing their heads off, as they watched a very relieved Jimmy touch his replaced nose tenderly, still scowling at a not bemused Dr. Pat. Good relationships between Doctor and patient were quickly restored. Jimmy, of course,used the nose injury to cry off further participation in matches - at least, till they got to Los Angeles.

He was satisfied that the nose injury would give him much more freedom to enjoy

Jimmy Keaveney ... weighing up his options.

the trip and the social engagements which went with it. He became a little bit worried to hear his name being mentioned as a runner for the Los Angeles match. He mentioned it quietly to Dr Pat, hoping that he might not be called into action. But Dr. Pat told him that sufficient time had passed for the nose to heal and he saw no reason why he shouldn't play. The matter was quickly settled when manager Kevin Heffernan told him that he was playing and was chosen at full forward.The Los Angeles match between Dublin and the All Stars was remarkable for two reasons.

The temperature was over 100 degrees and it was played in the confined Franciscan High School Stadium, Sherman Oaks. A visitor to the Dublin dressing room, incidentally, was Fr. Fintan, a Capuchin from Church St, Dublin, who was a brother of the late great Dublin hurler, Fran Whelan. The High School stadium had a high roof over the stand and the shadow of the roof covered one side of the pitch, which Jimmy was quick to spot. He played on the shaded side during the match, at half time of which, Dublin were ten points in arrears. But a good half time dressing down from manager Heffernan had the desired effect, and Dublin won the game by a point at the end. Naturally, Jimmy Keaveney's roving tactics on the shaded side of the pitch helped as well, as it left a gap up front which Hickey, McCarthy, O'Toole and "Doyler" exploited.

Dr. Pat's services were needed again when the team returned to New York and the patient was wing back Paddy Reilly. He was the life and soul of the party on the trip. He was a great joker and invariably exploited situations which cropped up involving his playing companions. Reilly, and some of his pals, were enjoying themselves in an Irish bar and during a bit of horse play, Paddy cut his finger on a jagged edge of a beer cooler.

Paddy went to Dr. Pat's bedroom the following morning and showed him the finger, which indeed had a bad tear. " I told him he would have to get a tetanus injection and a shot of penicillin for fear of any infection setting in and being the team doctor, I had all the necessary medicines required for the job with me." said Pat. Some of the players had accompanied Paddy to Dr. Pat's room. They were by no means helpful with some of their comments about the possible effects of the injections. Paddy, the life and soul of the previous night was by this time, a very very nervous patient. Dr. Pat told him to lie on the bed, he opened his medicine case and proceeded to take out hypodermic needles which he placed on a clean white towel.

His movements were carefully watched by the patient, looking at an array of , what appeared to Paddy, as huge hypodermic needles. The comments from the onlookers didn't help, "Jasus, Pat, you are not going to use those huge needles on him." "He'll never survive those needles." Dr. Pat noticed Paddy's reaction in the bedroom mirror as the colour began draining from the patient's face. Dr. Pat asked Paddy to let his trousers down and turned him over exposing a bare bottom. Dr. Pat gave him a jab of the needle, an operation Paddy couldn't see, lying in the prone position.

Dr. Pat was in no hurry, he walked away on the pretext that he had something further to do. Paddy Reilly could still see the array of hypodermic needles and plucked up courage to say " For Jasus sake," "Nailer" will you give me the injection and get it over with.?" Dr. Pat said quietly, " What are talking about, I gave you the injections a couple of minutes ago." The other players fell around the room laughing and Paddy Reilly fell off the bed in sheer relief.